Workshop on Speech and Language Processing for Assistive Technologies 2010

(SLPAT)

Held at NAACL HLT 2010

Los Angeles, California, USA
5 June 2010

ISBN: 978-1-61738-682-4

Printed from e-media with permission by:

Curran Associates, Inc.
57 Morehouse Lane
Red Hook, NY 12571

Some format issues inherent in the e-media version may also appear in this print version.

Printed by Curran Associates, Inc. (2010)

For permission requests, please contact the Association for Computational Linguistics at the address below.

Association for Computational Linguistics
209 N. Eighth Street
Stroudsburg, Pennsylvania 18360

Phone: 1-570-476-8006
Fax: 1-570-476-0860

acl@aclweb.org

Additional copies of this publication are available from:

Curran Associates, Inc.
57 Morehouse Lane
Red Hook, NY 12571 USA
Phone: 845-758-0400
Fax: 845-758-2634
Email: curran@proceedings.com
Web: www.proceedings.com

Introduction

We are pleased to bring you these Proceedings of the First Workshop on Speech and Language Processing for Assistive Technologies (SLPAT), held in Los Angeles, California, USA on June 5, 2010. We received 16 paper submissions, of which 8 were chosen for oral presentation and another 4 for poster presentation – all 12 papers are included in this volume. In addition, four demo proposals were accepted, and short abstracts of these demos are also included here.

This workshop was intended to bring together individuals from the Augmentative and Alternative Communication (AAC), Assistive Technologies (AT), Natural Language Processing (NLP) and Speech research communities, along with representatives from the AAC user community and companies working in this domain, to share research findings, and to discuss present and future challenges and the potential for collaboration and progress. While AAC is a particularly apt application area for speech and NLP technologies, we purposefully made the scope of the workshop broad enough to include assistive technologies as a whole, even those falling outside of AAC. While we encouraged work that validates methods with human experimental trials, we also accepted work on basic-level innovations, inspired by AT/AAC related problems. Thus we have aimed at broad inclusivity, which is also manifest in the diversity of our Program Committee.

We are very excited to have three invited speakers. Rick Hohn and Jan Staehely will speak on their experiences and perspectives as users of AAC technology. Also, Greg Lesher will give an invited talk entitled "Exploiting Web Content for Augmentative Communication". We would like to thank all three for taking the time to participate and provide their collective insight to the workshop.

We would also like to thank the members of the Program Committee for completing their reviews promptly, and for providing useful feedback for deciding on the program and preparing the final versions of the papers. Thanks also to Priscilla Rasmussen, David Traum and Richard Sproat for assistance with logistics. Finally, thanks to the authors of the papers, for submitting such interesting and diverse work, and to the presenters of demos and commercial exhibitions.

Melanie Fried-Oken, Kathy McCoy and Brian Roark
Co-organizers of the workshop

Organizers:

Melanie Fried-Oken, Oregon Health & Science University
Kathleen F. McCoy, University of Delaware
Brian Roark, Oregon Health & Science University

Program Committee:

Norman Alm, University of Dundee
Jean-Yves Antoine, Université François-Rabelais
John Arnott, University of Dundee
Bruce Baker, Semantic Compaction Systems
Melanie Baljko, York University, Canada
Jan Bedrosian, Western Michigan University
Jeff Bilmes, University of Washington
Tim Bunnell, University of Delaware
Ann Copestake, University of Cambridge
Alistair D.N. Edwards, University of York
Michael Elhadad, Ben-Gurion University
Leo Ferres, Universidad de Concepción, Chile, & Carleton University, Canada
Jeff Higginbotham, University of Buffalo
Graeme Hirst, University of Toronto
Linda Hoag, Kansas State University
Matt Huenerfauth, CUNY
Alexander Kain, Oregon Health & Science University
Heidi Koester, Koester Performance Research
Richard E. Ladner, University of Washington
Greg Lesher, Dynavox Technologies, Inc.
Yael Netzer, Ben-Gurion University
Alan Newell, University of Dundee
Rupal Patel, Northeastern University
Helen Petrie, University of York
Ehud Reiter, University of Aberdeen
Howard Shane, Children's Hospital Boston
Fraser Shein, Bloorview Kids Rehab, Canada
Kumiko Tanaka-Ishii, University of Tokyo
Annalu Waller, University of Dundee
Tonio Wandmacher, Commissariat á l'énergie atomique, France
David Wilkins, Language and Linguistics Consulting, Australia

Table of Contents

Workshop Program

Saturday, June 5, 2010

Morning Talks

8:45–8:50 Opening Remarks

8:50–9:15 *Using NLG and Sensors to Support Personal Narrative for Children with Complex Communication Needs*
Rolf Black, Joseph Reddington, Ehud Reiter, Nava Tintarev and Annalu Waller

9:15–9:40 *Automatic generation of conversational utterances and narrative for Augmentative and Alternative Communication: a prototype system*
Martin Dempster, Norman Alm and Ehud Reiter

9:40–10:30 Invited Speakers: *AAC from a user's perspective*
Rick Hohn and Jan Staehely

10:30–11:00 **Break**

11:00–11:25 *Implications of Pragmatic and Cognitive Theories on the Design of Utterance-Based AAC Systems*
Kathleen F. McCoy, Jan Bedrosian and Linda Hoag

11:25–11:50 *Scanning methods and language modeling for binary switch typing*
Brian Roark, Jacques de Villiers, Christopher Gibbons and Melanie Fried-Oken

11:50–2:10 Lunch and Poster/Demo/Exhibit Session

Posters

A Platform for Automated Acoustic Analysis for Assistive Technology
Suzanne Boyce, Harriet Fell, Joel MacAuslan and Lorin Wilde

An Approach for Anonymous Spelling for Voter Write-Ins Using Speech Interaction
Shanee Dawkins and Juan Gilbert

Using Reinforcement Learning to Create Communication Channel Management Strategies for Diverse Users
Rebecca Lunsford and Peter A. Heeman

A Multimodal Vocabulary for Augmentative and Alternative Communication from Sound/Image Label Datasets
Xiaojuan Ma, Christiane Fellbaum and Perry Cook

Saturday, June 5, 2010 (continued)

Demo Session: *Abstracts*

"How was School today...?" A Prototype System that Uses Environmental Sensors and NLG to Support Personal Narrative for Children with Complex Communication Needs
Rolf Black, Joseph Reddington, Ehud Reiter, Nava Tintarev and Annalu Waller

Interactive SIGHT Demo: Textual Summaries of Simple Bar Charts
Seniz Demir, David Oliver, Edward Schwartz, Stephanie Elzer, Sandra Carberry and Kathleen F. McCoy

Project Jumbo: Transcription as an Assistive Technology for Instant Messaging
Ira R. Forman and Allen K. Wilson

COMUNICA - A Voice Question Answering System for Portuguese
Rodrigo Wilkens, Aline Villavicencio, Leandro Wives, Daniel Muller, Fabio da Silva and Stanley Loh

Afternoon Talks

2:10–2:35 *State-Transition Interpolation and MAP Adaptation for HMM-based Dysarthric Speech Recognition*
Harsh Vardhan Sharma and Mark Hasegawa-Johnson

2:35–3:00 *Towards a noisy-channel model of dysarthria in speech recognition*
Frank Rudzicz

3:00–3:30 **Break**

3:30–3:55 *Collecting a Motion-Capture Corpus of American Sign Language for Data-Driven Generation Research*
Pengfei Lu and Matt Huenerfauth

3:55–4:20 *Automated Skimming System in Response to Questions for NonVisual Readers*
Debra Yarrington and Kathleen F. McCoy

4:20–5:20 Invited Talk: *Exploiting Web Content for Augmentative Communication*
Greg Lesher

5:20–5:30 Closing Remarks

5:30– Open Discussion on Future Directions

Using NLG and Sensors to Support Personal Narrative for Children with Complex Communication Needs

Rolf Black
School of Computing
University of Dundee
rolfblack@
computing.dundee.ac.uk

Joe Reddington, Ehud Reiter, Nava Tintarev
Department of Computing Science
University of Aberdeen
{j.reddington, e.reiter n.tintarev}@abdn.ac.uk

Annalu Waller
School of Computing
University of Dundee
awaller@
computing.dundee.ac.uk

Abstract

We are building a tool that helps children with Complex Communication Needs[1] (CCN) to create stories about their day at school. The tool uses Natural Language Generation (NLG) technology to create a draft story based on sensor data of the child's activities, which the child can edit. This work is still in its early stages, but we believe it has great potential to support interactive personal narrative which is not well supported by current Augmentative and Alternative Communication (AAC) tools.

1 Introduction

Many tools have been developed to help children and adults who cannot speak (or who have limited speech) communicate better. However, most of these tools have focused on supporting communication for practical goals, such as *"I am thirsty."* But human communication is also used for social goals; we develop friendships and other inter-personal relationships via social interaction and communication. The bulk of conversation is characterized by free narrative (Cheepen 1988). One of the most important types of conversational narrative is personal narrative: someone telling a story about what happened to him or her.

People with limited or no functional speech do tell stories, but these tend to be in monologue form, or in a sequence of pre-stored utterances on voice output communication aids (Waller 2006). Individuals who use Augmentative and Alternative Communication (AAC) tools tend to be passive, responding to questions with single words or short sentences (e.g. Soto, Hartmann et al. 2006) and if able to initiate and maintain extended conversations tend to relate experience word for word each time they tell a story, even though much of conversation is reused (Clarke and Clarke 1977). This is time consuming and physically exhausting – typical rates range from 8 to 10 words per minute up to 12 to 15 per minute when techniques such as word prediction are used (Higginbotham, Shane et al. 2007), with the result that people seldom engage in storytelling. Despite the importance of narrative, little work has been done on specific tools to help language-impaired individuals engage in personal storytelling. In this paper, we describe our work in progress on building a tool that uses Natural Language Generation (NLG) technology to help children tell stories about their day at school, describing both the work we have done to date, and the challenges that we face in further developing this concept.

2 Background

2.1 AAC

Technology underpins much of Augmentative and Alternative Communication (AAC), a field that attempts to augment natural speech and provides alternative ways to communicate for people with limited or no speech. At the simplest level, people with Complex Communication Needs (CCN) can cause a pre-stored message to be spoken by activating a single switch. At the most sophisticated level, literate users can generate novel text using input methods ranging from a single switch to a full keyboard.

Despite advances in AAC, there are still many individuals for whom communication remains problematic. Although some individuals with CCN become effective communicators, most do not – they tend to be passive communicators, responding mainly to questions or prompts at a one or two word level. Conversational

[1] The term Complex Communication Needs (CCN) describes individuals who, due to motor, language, cognitive, and/or sensory perceptual impairments (e.g., as a result of cerebral palsy), do not develop speech and language skills as expected. This heterogeneous group typically experiences restricted access to the environment, limited interactions with their communication partners, and few opportunities for communication (Light and Drager 2007).

Proceedings of the NAACL HLT 2010 Workshop on Speech and Language Processing for Assistive Technologies, pages 1–9,
Los Angeles, California, June 2010.

skills such as initiation, elaboration and storytelling are seldom observed (Waller 2006).

One reason for the reduced levels of communicative ability is the cognitive demands of AAC interfaces. Current AAC technology provides the user with a purely physical link to speech output. The user is required to have sufficient cognitive abilities and physical stamina to translate what they want to say into the sequence of operations needed to produce the desired output. Mnemonic codes and dynamic displays (Beukelman and Mirenda 2005) provide some help in the retrieval process, but users still have to master complex retrieval and production strategies.

A second reason for the impoverished quality of conversation is the focus of AAC devices on transactional communication; conversation which expresses needs wants and information transfer, for example, *"I am thirsty"*, *"I use a straw for drinking"*. Instead, interactive conversation is characterized by free narrative and phatic conversation, for example, *"Guess what happened this morning..."*, *"Hello"*, and *"How are you?"* Without easy access to extended interactive communication, it is difficult to develop the skills needed to initiate new topics and engage in storytelling.

2.2 Importance of Narrative

Conversational narratives (oral stories told during interactive conversations) are crucial to social engagement. Narratives provide a means for people to relate and share experiences, develop organizational skills, work through problems, develop self image, express personality, give form and meaning to life, and allow people to be interesting entertainers (Waller 2006).

Narrative skills develop experientially with children being able to engage in storytelling even before they are verbal (Bruner 1975). Early personal experience stories consist of a high point, for example, *"Mummy fall!"* with adults scaffolding the full story, eliciting the 'who', 'what', 'when' and 'where'. However, not all experiences make good stories. An experience becomes a story if the storyteller has an emotional connection to the event (Labov, 1972), or if the event is unusual (Quasthoff & Nikolaus, 1982).

Parents of typically developing children encourage development of narrative skills by eliciting stories from their children (Peterson and McCabe 1983), but the development of narrative skills is problematic for people with CCN. We recall a study where disabled children were told different stories more often than typically developing peers who were read the same story night after night (Light, Binger et al. 1994). In doing so, the disabled children did not have the chance to learn the sequence of stories, or the structure commonly used in narrative such as beginning, middle and end. As such, initially children should use the same story template consistently until they are ready to progress to another one.

It is difficult to provide access to event information which may become a story, and few AAC systems provide support for interactive story narration. However NLG gives us a possibility to change the underlying paradigm of AAC. Instead of placing the entire cognitive load on the user, AAC devices can be designed to support the retrieval of story events and the scaffolding of story narration for individuals with CCN.

2.3 NLG, Data-to-text

NLG systems generate texts in English (or other human languages) from non-linguistic data (Reiter and Dale 2000). Our vision is to use an NLG system to generate a draft story, which the child can edit. The non-linguistic input to our story-generator is sensor data about the child's activities, including location data (where the child was) and interaction data (what people and objects the child interacted with). We also want to allow teachers and school staff to enter information about the child's activities (such as voice messages).

A number of data-to-text systems (Reiter 2007) have been developed in recent years, which generate English summaries of sensor and other numerical data. The most popular application area has been weather forecasting (generating textual weather forecasts from the results of a numerical atmosphere simulation model), and indeed several weather forecast generators have been fielded and used operationally (Goldberg, Driedger et al. 1994; Reiter, Sripada et al. 2005). A number of data-to-text systems have also been developed in the medical community, such as BabyTalk (Gatt, Portet et al. 2009), which generates summaries of clinical data from a neonatal intensive care unit, and the commercial Narrative Engine (Harris 2008) which summarizes data acquired during a doctor/patient encounter.

Most previous research in data-to-text has focused on summarizing technical data for expert users, with the goal of effectively communicating key information. In our work, in contrast, the focus is on summarizing data about everyday events, with the goal of having something interesting to talk about. There has been considerable work in the computational creativity community on generating interesting stories (Péréz and Sharples 2004), but it has focused on fictional written stories, where the computer system can say whatever it wishes, without the constraint of describing real events.

Most previous work in NLG has focused on computer systems which generate texts without human input. However, in our case we want children to be able to annotate (evaluate) and edit stories, as far as their abilities permit. There has been some research on human post-editing of NLG texts (Sripada, Reiter et al. 2005), but this has focused on editing at the text level.

Since editing at the text level is very laborious for AAC users, we need a higher-level interface that lets children edit content and structure without needing to type words. We also want children to be able to control how a story is narrated, perhaps in response to a listener's questions or body language. For example children may wish to add comments such as *"It was awesome!"*, or tell events out of sequence.

In short, we need to develop interfaces and interaction techniques that allow our users to control the NLG system. Unfortunately there has been very little previous work on this topic, indeed almost nothing is known about Human-Computer Interaction aspects of NLG systems. Developing a better understanding of these aspects is one of the main research challenges we face from an NLG perspective.

3 Current and ongoing work

3.1 "How was School today…?"

We developed an initial version of *"How was School today…?"* in 2009; see Reiter et al (2009) for more details about this system.

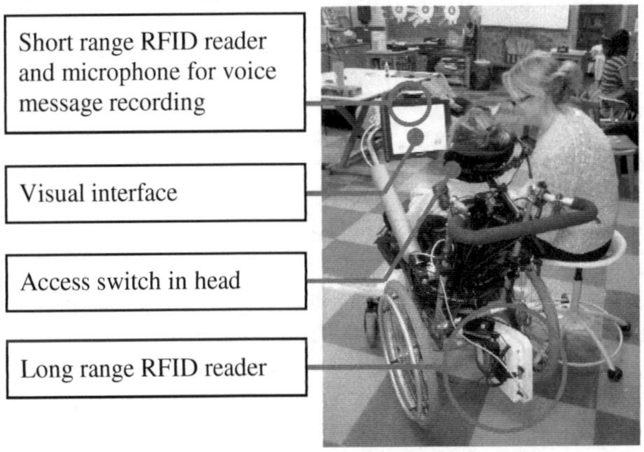

Fig. 1: *Participating pupil with support worker: The prototype system is mounted on the wheelchair, and the pupil has access to the system via head switch controlled row/column scanning.*

This system used Radio Frequency Identification (RFID), an emerging application in AAC to identify or give access to relevant vocabulary (Bart, Riny et al. 2008; DeRuyter and Fried-Oken 2010). Sensors were used to track both location (by putting tags on doors, which were automatically sensed by a long-range RFID reader) and interaction (by asking staff to manually swipe RFID cards in a short-range reader when the child interacted with a person or object). Staff could also record spoken messages about interesting events during the day (see Fig. 1).

The software analyzed this data to remove sensor noise, and then compared it to a timetable which specified where children were supposed to be, what they were supposed to be doing and which teacher was supposed to be taking the class throughout the day. This allowed the software to both fill in missing information, and to identify divergences from the schedule. The result of this process was a series of events (which corresponded to classes, for example, maths class), each of which had a set of associated messages (interactions during the event, divergence from schedule, etc.).

After the data analysis was completed, an NLG system identified the events most interesting (to the child), using a heuristic that took into consideration both how inherent interesting an event was (for example, lunch was regarded as an inherently interesting event that children were likely to want to talk about) and also whether an event was unusual or not. The latter is based on the observation that most personal narratives focus on unexpected or unusual events. Unusual events were identified by the presence of recorded voice messages and by divergence from the timetable, e.g. a different teacher present or a different location. The system selected the five most 'interesting' events and displayed them to the child in a simple visual editing interface. In this interface the child could delete events he/she did not wish to talk about, and also annotate events with simple opinions (evaluations), such as *I liked it*, using the evaluation buttons on the interface, generating appropriate utterances according to the last narrated event or message.(see Fig. 2).

When editing was finished, the NLG system generated texts describing the events and messages, which the child communicated using a simple narration interface (which was similar to the editing interface). Emphasis was placed on providing quick access to messages to minimize the length of pauses between utterances due to the physical accessing difficulties of the users. The narrative model is based on the Labov social narrative model (Labov 1972) which emphasizes the highpoint and evaluation. The dialogue model from beginning through to highpoint to the end with the user being able to add evaluations at any point of the narration. Stories are initially chronological order but interactively under the control of the user. This control of narration differs significantly from current AAC interventions where narrative tends to be output in a monologue format.

From an NLG perspective, the system was fairly straightforward. The most challenging microplanning tasks were choosing connectives, time phrases, lexical variety in embellishments, and pronouns based on discourse context. Connectives and time phrases were necessary since children could narrate events in different orders (for example, *"I went to maths. Then I went to lunch"* versus *"I went to lunch. Before lunch, I went to maths"*). Document structuring was simple because we assumed that the children would choose their own order in which to narrate events. In fact some children are not able to do this; such children would need to be supported by a more sophisticated document planner that had a model of appropriate text structures in this domain.

We asked two children to use the system for one week for a qualitative formative evaluation. Researchers supplied ongoing support during this, primarily trial observing how the children used the system, and discussing it with teachers, therapists and parents. Generally it worked well for one child, Julie[2], who had severe motor impairment (no independent means of mobility and interacted with a computer using a head switch with row/column scanning, see Fig. 1). Her expressive abilities were limited but her comprehension skills were comparable to her non-disabled peers with some developmental delay. The other child, Jessica, had more cognitive impairment, and found the interface too difficult.

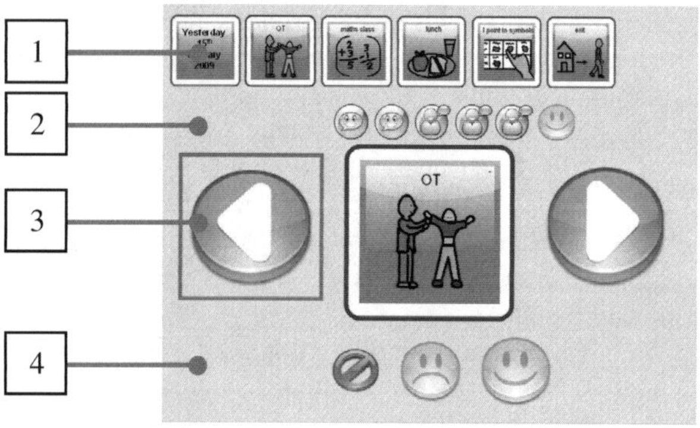

Fig. 2: Example screenshot from interface
1: Navigation: Day and date of story, maximum of five story events, exit; 2: Event messages, numbers vary for each event. Here: 2 computer-generated messages, 3 recorded messages, 1 user added evaluation; 3: Sequential message navigation: previous, repeat, next; 4: Evaluation: delete event, negative evaluation, positive evaluation;

In a second evaluation, a third child, Eric, joined and all three children used the system over two weeks each. In this evaluation, we asked teachers and other staff to use the system without on-site support from the researchers. This highlighted many practical usability issues, such as delays caused by starting the system in the morning, and problems caused by limited battery life. We eliminated the long-range RFID sensor because of its difficult setup; instead we asked staff to swipe door cards when children entered rooms. However, this strategy was not successful, as it was difficult for staff to remember to swipe both interactions and location changes.

The participants took the system home for use with their parents who gave positive feedback but also reported issues with system usability (e.g. lack of access to stories from previous days) or suitability (too complicated interface for Jessica).

Eric's timetable was different from Julie and Jessica's, because he visited college one morning a day, and we could not collect data during this period. Since some of the most exciting events in a school day happen outside the school building (sports and school trips as well as college), in the long term we do need to see if we can collect data outside as well as inside the school.

3.2 HWST example

Julie used the system on her DynaVox™ Vmax™ Voice Output Communication Aid (VOCA) via head switch using row/column scanning. The above transcript shows an extract of a conversation Julie had with her Speech and Language Therapist (SLT) on day three about her experiences during day two. The researcher (RA) had been present all day for technical support. The conversation extract starts with Julie reporting about her morning break.

In this example Julie is able to quickly reply to context related questions from her communication partner using the evaluations (*"So what happened?" – "It was fun!"*). Compared to conversations usually observed between aided and unaided partners Julie is able to control the conversation when starting a new topic after talking about the morning break, inviting her communication partner to prompt for more detailed information. Julie provides this with her next generated phrase. When she is asked about the event she replies with an evaluation the system has generated in relation to its previously generated message *"A visitor was there."*. We note that the system is able to refer to the correct gender of the visitor.

1	Julie	{next} [I had break.]
2	Julie	{next} [Lesley was there.]
3	SLT	Lesley was there?
4	Julie	((Opens mouth in agreement, then turns back to screen))
5	SLT	Ok mhmh. So what happened?
6	Julie	{positive evaluation} [It was fun.]
7	SLT	Oh good! ((laughs)) I'm glad to hear it!
8	RA	We like Lesley.
9	SLT	((nods in direction of RA))
10	Julie	((smiles))
11	Julie:	{next} [Then I went to Junior Primary instead of Reading Class.]

[2] The names of the children mentioned in this paper are changed to ensure anonymity.

12 SLT: Right, you went to Junior Primary? I wonder why that was?
13 Julie: {next} [A visitor was there.]
14 SLT: Oh, a visitor, right. Wonder what the visitor was doing?
15 Julie: {next} ["The dental hygienist came to give a talk."]
16 SLT: Oh, dental hygienist.
17 Julie: {previous} [A visitor was there.]
18 SLT: That was the visitor, okay. That's why you went to junior primary, uhm, what did you think of the talk?
19 Julie: {positive evaluation} [She was nice.]
20 SLT: She was nice, that was good! ((laughs))

Notation:
- Switch selected button by Julie: {curly brackets}
- Natural speech: standard text.
- Computer generated language accessed using one button: [standard text in square brackets].
- Recorded messages accessed using one button: ["quoted standard text in square brackets"].
- Paralinguistic behaviors: ((standard text in double brackets)).

3.3 "How was School Today" – in the Wild

We have now started a new project to further develop our work, called *"How was School today…?" – in the Wild* (*'in the wild'* indicates that the focus is on how the technology works in a real school environment). The basic goal is to improve the system sufficiently so that it can be tried out over a period of several months, with children with varying levels and types of impairments; we will also work with several schools in the initial phase, although for practical reasons the evaluations may be at just one school.

During this project we will do some work on the issues described in Section 4; in particular we will try to make the system usable by children with different impairments and ability levels (Section 4.1). This means having a very simple interface for children with considerable cognitive impairments (such as Jessica); but also giving children with more cognitive abilities the opportunity to exert more control over the story (during both editing and narration), for example by supporting a richer range of annotations, and by making it easier to describe events and messages in any order.

Another intermediate goal is to improve the integration of voice messages entered by staff with the computer-generated messages. This could be done by some combination of training staff to enter messages in a specific way (referring to the child in the first person); asking staff to annotate the messages so the computer knows something about their content; and/or using speech recognition to analyze the voice messages. In general there is a lot of interesting information that can only come from staff, and we need to think about the best way to help staff enter information in a way that is easy for them and useful for our system.

Now that a complete system is built, we are also able to thoroughly and formally evaluate the system. Multiple baseline single case study methodology will be used (Schlosser 2003) to evaluate the use and impact of our system. We intend to have up to four children (with varying ability levels) use the system for a period of 3 months. This will give us a chance to observe the impact of the system on the users and their environment such as the children's interaction with the system and how staff at the school envisage using this new tool. The observations will be supported by semi-structured interviews with the children, their classroom teacher, their speech and language therapist and a parent.

We will look at the children's conversations (with and without using our system) about interesting, staged events with different partners, analyzing them conversational characteristics such as narrative initiation, structure, length and evaluation. Analysis methods will include the Revised Edinburgh Functional Communication Profile (REFCP) (Wirz, Skinner et al. 1990).

However, much of our focus will be on addressing the practical issues that make it difficult to use our current research prototype over a period of months. We have identified many such issues, both from our previous evaluations (Section 3.1) and also from a questionnaire that was distributed to school staff during an in-service day.

Location tracking – There are problems with both of the techniques we have tried to date (automatically reading RFID tags on doors, and asking staff to swipe location information). In this project we intend to try tracking the location of a child using Wi-Fi location tracking, which seems to be rapidly gaining popularity in the commercial world (Liu, Sen et al. 2008).

Data entry, 2D bar codes – We need to allow staff to easily enter and update information about the children (for example, their timetables) and sensor tags (e.g., if a new tag is given to a visitor). For the latter, we want to investigate 2D bar codes, which could allow encoding of alphanumeric input data without reference to a central database.

Portability, battery life – The current system runs on a tablet PC (8"-12" touch screen, generic or VOCA hardware). During the evaluation, late powering up, rundown batteries or simply forgetting a component caused significant data loss and usability issues. A future prototype should favor an 'always-on' system, such as a mobile phone, allowing for easy portability and extended battery life.

Story generation – The prototype system was only able to create a story towards the end of a day and gave only access to stories generated on that day. However, often the user desired to tell stories that had occurred on previous days, or to, say, tell a story at lunch that occurred in the morning. When data was insufficient for the system to create a story, the only output was an error message *"Can't generate story right now."* This frustrated users, so future systems should be able to deliver a story with incomplete data.

Voice messages – as mentioned above, we want to handle these in a more sophisticated way. From a more practical perspective, we also want to make it easier for staff to listen to and change previously recorded messages. We also want to allow parents to record messages about events at home.

4 Long-term vision and issues

4.1 Supporting children with different levels and types of impairment

A key issue in AAC is of course the diversity of AAC users. Children with CCN differ enormously in terms of cognitive ability, motor ability, and social ability. This was clear even in our initial evaluation where we worked just with two children, and discovered that our interface worked well for Julie but not Jessica.

Julie has little functional speech and severe physical impairments, and accesses her VOCA using a head switch through the slow process of scanning the interface. Her VOCA interface consists of a grid of 15 to 30 buttons per page, with more than 20 pages of vocabulary. However, her cognitive skills were sufficient for her to master the interface on the second day. She used the system quite successfully, as shown in the example in Section 3.2.

Jessica also has severe physical impairments but does not use technology to support her communication (she has functional speech). She has cognitive impairments, which (amongst other things) affect her ability to remember and place events correctly in time. She had more difficulty mastering the interface than Julie. We simplified the interface for her (no editing, minimal control of narration), and then she displayed pragmatics known from typical language development in children, by telling her story with no room for interaction of her communication partner.

We also need to keep in mind that abilities are not static, but are likely to progress with age (see also Section 4.2) and (hopefully) with the assistance of communication aids. For example, the WriteTalk project showed how pupils were both able to initiate and control communication more effectively with Talk:About™ and how their formal writing skills improved over time (Waller et al., 1999).

In summary, some children may need a very simple interface because of cognitive impairments, but this should grow with them. For example, the best narration tool for Jessica at her current stage of development is probably a single button that advances sequentially through the computer-generated story. The challenge is to provide an interface that Jessica can initially use via repeatedly pressing an 'Advance' button, but which gives her the possibility of exerting more control as her skills and abilities develop.

Other children (such as Julie) may have motor difficulties that restrict the way in which they can interact with computer systems, and thus may require simple controls although they have reasonable cognitive skills. Restricted motor skills make certain tasks, such as entering an arbitrary word, quite difficult and time consuming; hence the interface must avoid such tasks, and instead endeavor to give the child as much control as possible with a minimum amount of data entry. Once these users master a basic story telling structure, it may help them develop their conversation skills if they use a wide variety of conversation patterns. For this purpose, it may be worthwhile for the system to randomly vary the structure and language used in the narratives.

Still other children, for example on the autistic spectrum, may have good cognitive and motor abilities, but not have the experience of expressive communication necessary to develop interactive skills. These children are more likely to benefit from a system that supports the pragmatics of language in general and personal narrative in particular. For example, children on the high functioning end of autism may be comfortable with rather advanced software, which can help them adapt their storytelling according to the intended listener. Indeed, giving these children more complex controls, if done correctly, can make the software fun and challenging in a positive way.

In the long term, as we broaden the range of children we work with, there may be overlaps between our work and research on tools to help typically developing children create stories, such as Robertson and Good (2005), and also between our work and research on tools to help adults with CCN tell personal narratives, such as Dempster (2008). Ideally it would be very nice to combine these efforts and create a story telling tool that could be used across the age and impairment spectrum.

4.2 Narrative across the lifespan

We would like our tool to be able to support children over time, as their abilities grow and as their experiences accumulate. From the perspective of changing abilities, the challenge is to offer children an interface which is not only appropriate for their current stage of development (Sect 4.1), but also allows and indeed encourages them to exert more control over story content, language, and narration as their abilities grow.

We would also like our tool to become a repository of a child's personal stories. The ability to relate relevant stories can influence the quality of life, as well as social development and successful transitions. The life stories of people who use AAC are often held by parents and siblings (e.g., stories relating to health care (Hemsley, Balandin et al. 2007)), and there is the inevitable concern that these stories and others are lost as parents age and siblings move away.

Technology has the potential both to support the acquisition of conversational skills for people who use AAC and to provide a repository for life stories. In the context of our work, it is essential that we provide ways of enabling children to develop their narrative skills so that they are more able to manage their own story repository. In terms of development, young children will narrate recent stories regardless of conversational context. By enabling the child to develop story structure by scaffolding interaction and enabling children to easily annotate stories, the child will begin to anticipate and control conversation.

Conversational narratives have traditionally not been supported by AAC tools partly due to the fact that they are so nebulous; they emerge during interactive conversation (to date, events have to be manually input into a system and it is difficult to predict what events will become a story); 'new' stories are repeated often (to date it is difficult to save conversation online); as stories age they are repeated in context (retrieval is often contextual e.g. topic based) and they grow longer having more embellishments added to them. The technology we are developing provides an opportunity for children to access information about personal events over time, which they can communicate and narrate during a conversation. They can also evaluate (annotate) their stories, thereby embellishing and lengthening the stories. However this will only be possible if the children can easily access previously experienced, generated and saved stories.

We can provide fast access to recent stories while anticipating the use of older stories such as for example those which closely match the current conversation topic. In a research prototype called PROSE (Waller and Newell 1997), stories had to be physically tagged; there is now the potential to automate topic matching by recognizing topic words spoken by a listener and parsing stored information for appropriate stories. Over a lifetime, some stories may fall into disuse, while others will be weighted more strongly depending on frequency of use and relevance.

4.3 True dialogue in narration

The ultimate goal of our research is to enable children to tell stories in the context of a social dialogue; for example, we want children to be able to chat to their parents and other interested parties about what they did during the day.

Our current system incorporates a simple model of a conversation, where children are restricted at any point to choosing from a small number of options. The child chooses an event to talk about, and then goes through the sequence of messages associated with that event. The child has the freedom to switch to a different event, hence controlling the conversation, and to add annotations/evaluations (for example *"it was fun!"*).

This is adequate in many cases, but in the long term we would like to support more complex conversations; for example interrupting a discussion about today's events to talk about what happened yesterday, or to discuss a particular teacher instead of an event. We would also like children to easily be able to add conversational phrases, such as *"Guess what happened today at school"*.

Because our children have motor and cognitive impairments, we cannot present them with a large number of options for conversational moves. Ideally, the system would detect what the conversational partner wishes to talk about, and from this present the child with a small number of appropriate choices. For example, if the conversational partner asks the child what happened over the past week, our system would detect this and then give the child the option of talking about any individual weekday or the week in general.

One way of detecting what the conversational partner intends is to use speech recognition and Natural Language Processing (NLP) technology to analyze what he or she says. Speech and NLP technology tend to work best when it is possible to train the system to the user's voice, and also (in essence) train the user to understand what the speech/NLP system can and cannot do. This should be possible in our context, at least for people (such as parents) with whom the child regularly interacts.

Another possibility is to create a graphical user interface for the conversational partner, perhaps on the same device that the child uses, which the partner could use to indicate what he/she wants to talk about. This is probably technically easier, but does move away from the goal of having as natural a dialogue as possible.

4.4 Pragmatics of interacting with others

Currently, *"How was School today…?"* supports storytelling between language-impaired children and adults who are the children's parents, carers, teachers, and therapists. But of course for normally developing children, many of their most important social interactions are with other children.

An interesting example here is the STANDUP system, which was developed to help children who use

AAC create and tell novel punning riddles. The study results suggested that children saved the jokes so that they could retell them to friends and family (Waller, Black et al. 2009). Whilst the evidence is anecdotal, there did also appear to be a marked increase in joke telling by participants, both amongst their peers and with adults in the home environment. Hence STANDUP succeeded in supporting interaction with other children as well as with adults.

One of the key challenges in interacting with other children, and indeed with adults who are not formally involved in the care or teaching of the child, is to adapt the story to the interests of the recipients. In other words, a child's parents and teachers will not insist on stories that are interesting to them, but other conversational partners will. These conversational partners may also need additional information. For example *"Jane came to take me to the OT room"* makes more sense if the recipient knows that Jane is the occupational therapist; parents and teachers already know this, but other people may need to be told this. Also if the conversational partner was present at an event, this should be acknowledged and indeed used in the story. For example, *"Did you really enjoy maths? I thought it was boring!"*

In short, telling stories to peers and adults who do not know the child well requires adapting the story to the interests, knowledge, and involvement of the partner; this is part of learning pragmatics. This is not something we are looking at currently, but it is something that we hope to look at in the future.

4.5 Security and privacy issues

We need to ensure that data about the children is private and secure. Taken to its logical conclusion, our project would result in an intimate record of the child's life at school, home and beyond. It is important that both the raw data and the generated content are under the control of the child and his/her guardians, with the child exercising as much control as possible. This is especially important since children with learning difficulties are very vulnerable; there is potential for great harm if data about a child's activities got into the hands of a malicious outsider.

In a study on the software tool TalksBac, which supports personal narrative (Waller, Dennis et al. 1997), privacy issues were coded along with stories. This allowed the NLG process to decide the appropriateness of telling a story to a specific communication partner. Children in general do not care who they tell their stories to. Only when older children learn to distinguish which story is appropriate for a conversation partner. This process could be embedded into the prediction algorithm that presents stories for narration. Currently prediction on AAC devices only support character, word or phrase selection.

Another concern is information that is embarrassing or otherwise puts the child in a negative light; for example, imagine a staff member entered the voice message *"I refused to eat my lunch today"*. We believe that the child should be free to delete such messages; she should never be forced to include material in a story that she does not want to include.

A related issue is whether we should allow stories generated for one child to use information acquired about another child. In principle this is very valuable, for example it allows messages such as *"Jane didn't eat her lunch today"*. But is this acceptable from the perspective of ensuring the privacy of data about Jane's activities? On the other hand, this is exactly the sort of thing that a normally developed child would say about a classmate.

5 Conclusion

In addition to having difficulty in communicating desires and needs, language-impaired children also find it hard to participate in social linguistic interaction that would help create and build up friendships and other interpersonal relationships. We believe that we can help these children participate in such interactions by giving them a tool that helps them tell a story about their day at school, by using an NLG system that has access to sensor and other data about the child's activities. We are still at an early stage in this work, but our initial prototype system has shown great potential to improve the quality of life of children with limited speech. Our current work plans to explore this potential further while evaluating the efficacy of the system for four children with varying ability levels.

Acknowledgements

We would like to express our thanks to the children, their parents and staff and the special school where this project had its base. Without their valuable contributions and feedback this research would not have been possible. We would also like to thank DynaVox Systems Ltd for supplying the communication devices to run our system on.

This research was supported by the UK Engineering and Physical Sciences Research Council under grants EP/F067151/1, EP/F066880/1, EP/E011764/1, EP/H022376/1, and EP/H022570/1.

References

Agrawal, R. and Ramakrishnan, S. (2000) Privacy-preserving data mining. ACM International Conference on Management of Data, pp. 439--450,

Bart, H., V. Riny, et al. (2008). LinguaBytes. Proceedings of the 7th international conference on Interaction design and children. Chicago, Illinois, ACM: 17-20.

Beukelman, D. R. and P. Mirenda (2005). Augmentative and Alternative Communication: Management of Severe Communication Disorders in Children and Adults. Baltimore, Paul H. Brookes Publishing Co.

Bruner, J. (1975). "From communication to language: A psychological perspective." Cognition **3**: 255-289.

Cheepen, C. (1988). The predictability of informal conversation. Oxford, Printer Publishers Ltd.

Clarke, H. H. and E. V. Clarke (1977). Psychology and Language. New York, Harcourt Brace Jovanovich.

Dempster, M. (2008). Using natural language generation to encourage effective communication in nonspeaking people. Proceedings of Young Researchers Consortium, ICCHP'08.

DeRuyter and Fried-Oken. (2010). "Context-sensitive messaging with RFID technology." Retrieved 2010, April 10, from http://aac-rerc.psu.edu/index.php/projecttypes/list

Gatt, A., F. Portet, et al. (2009). "From Data to Text in the Neonatal Intensive Care Unit: Using NLG Technology for Decision Support and Information Management." AI Communications **22**: 153-186.

Goldberg, E., N. Driedger, et al. (1994). "Using natural-language processing to produce weather forecasts." IEEE Expert **9**(2): 45-53.

Harris, M. (2008). Building a Large-Scale Commer-cial NLG System for an EMR. Proc of INLG-2008.

Hemsley, B., S. Balandin, et al. (2007). "Family caregivers discuss roles and needs in supporting adults with cerebral palsy and complex communication needs in the hospital setting." Journal of Developmental and Physical Disabilities **19**(2): 115-124.

Higginbotham, D. J., H. Shane, et al. (2007). "Access to AAC: Present, past, and future." Augmentative & Alternative Communication **23**(3): 243-257.

Labov, W. (1972). Language in the inner city: Studies in the Black English Vernacular. Philadelphia, University of Pennsylvania Press.

Light, J., C. Binger, et al. (1994). "Story Reading interactions between preschoolers who use AAC and their mothers." Augmentative and Alternative Communication **10**: 255-268.

Light, J. and K. Drager (2007). "AAC Technologies for Young Children with Complex Communication Needs: State of the Science and Future Research Directions." Augmentative and Alternative Communication **23**(3): pp. 204 – 216.

Liu, X., A. Sen, et al. (2008). A Software Client for Wi-Fi Based Real-Time Location Tracking of Patients. Medical Imaging and Informatics. Berlin/Heidelberg, Springer. **4987/2008:** 141-150.

Péréz, R. P. y. and M. Sharples (2004). "Three Computer-Based Models of StoryTelling: BRUTUS, MINSTREL, and MEXICA." Knowledge-Based Systems **17**: 15-29.

Peterson, C. and A. McCabe (1983). Developmental psycholinguistics: Three ways of looking at a child's narrative. New York, Plenum.

Reiter, E. (2007). An Architecture for Data-to-Text Systems. ENLG-2007.

Reiter, E. and R. Dale (2000). Building Natural-Language Generation Systems., Cambridge University Press.

Reiter, E., S. Sripada, et al. (2005). "Choosing Words in Computer-Generated Weather Forecasts." Artificial Intelligence **167**: 137-169.

Reiter, E., R. Turner, et al. (2009). Using NLG to Help Language-Impaired Users Tell Stories and Participate in Social Dialogues. ENLG2009. Athens, Greece, Association for Computational Linguistics.

Robertson, J. and J. Good (2005). "Story creation in virtual game worlds." Communications of the ACM **48**: 61-65.

Schlosser, R. W. (2003). The Efficacy of Augmentative and Alternative Communication. San Diego, Elsevier Science.

Soto, G., E. Hartmann, et al. (2006). "Exploring the Elements of Narrative that Emerge in the Interactions between an 8-Year-Old Child who uses an AAC Device and her Teacher." Augmentative and Alternative Communication **22**(4): pp. 231 - 241.

Sripada, S., E. Reiter, et al. (2005). Evaluating an NLG System using Post-Edit Data: Lessons Learned. Proceedings of ENLG-2005, 10th European Workshop on Natural Language Generation, Aberdeen, Scotland.

Waller, A. (2006). "Communication Access to Conversational Narrative." Topics in Language Disorders **26**(3): 221-239.

Waller, A., R. Black, et al. (2009). "Evaluating the STANDUP Pun Generating Software with Children with Cerebral Palsy." ACM Trans. Access. Comput. **1**(3): 27.

Waller, A., F. Dennis, et al. (1997). "Evaluating the use of TalksBac, a predictive communication device for non-fluent aphasic adults." International Journal of Language and Communication Disorders **33**: 45-70.

Waller, A. and A. F. Newell (1997). "Towards a narrative based communication system." European Journal of Disorders of Communication **32**: 289-306.

Automatic generation of conversational utterances and narrative for Augmentative and Alternative Communication: a prototype system

Martin Dempster & Norman Alm
School of Computing
University of Dundee
Dundee, Scotland, DD1 4HN, UK
m.k.dempster@dundee.ac.uk
nalm@computing.dundee.ac.uk

Ehud Reiter
Computer Science Department
University of Aberdeen
Aberdeen, Scotland, AB24 3UE, UK
e.reiter@abdn.ac.uk

Abstract

We detail the design, development and evaluation of Augmentative and Alternative Communication (AAC) software which encourages rapid conversational interaction. The system uses Natural Language Generation (NLG) technology to automatically generate conversational utterances from a domain knowledge base modelled from content suggested by a small AAC user group. Findings from this work are presented along with a discussion about how NLG might be successfully applied to conversational AAC systems in the future.

1 Introduction

Augmentative and Alternative Communication (AAC) systems assist non-speaking people communicate. Reasons for lack of speech are varied and can be complex, but they are typically related to some profound cognitive and/or motor impairment.

Most AAC systems are computer based, utilize synthesized speech output and employ a *phrase-construction* approach to input. This approach requires the user to construct the majority of their utterances live during conversation. Undoubtedly this facilitated communication is hugely important to those without natural speech. However, this process is often unacceptably slow and can lead to problematic and stilted interactions, mostly due to the rapid nature of unimpeded face-to-face communication.

Previous work has shown that it is possible to hold mutually rewarding conversations using wholly pre-stored material, known as the *phrase-storage* approach. Utterances are authored ahead of time and can be selected and output immediately leading to quicker communication rates. However, this approach suffers from several drawbacks which may have affected its more general adoption.

Furthermore, Natural Language Processing (NLP) technology has proven to be a fruitful line of inquiry within the field. It has offered a powerful means to improve system productivity and usability. We are currently investigating how Natural Language Generation (NLG) might be applied in a useful way within an AAC device geared towards fast-paced and rewarding social interactions. It is hoped that the linguistic control and automaticity offered by NLG may go some way towards addressing the previous criticisms of pre-stored material regarding its inflexibility and cost in effort.

2 Background

2.1 Limitations of current AAC

High-tech AAC systems typically augment communication for non-speaking people by allowing live message construction through some orthographic means. Completed messages are generally sent to a speech synthesis engine for output during communication with others. Many people who require AAC have associated physical disabilities which reduce the speed achievable using input methods such as keyboards, pointing devices or touch-screens. The rate achievable using most commercial AAC systems is highly dependent on the nature of the user's disabilities but a generally accepted figure is in the region of 2-15 words per minute (Higginbotham, Shane et al. 2007), at least an order of magnitude slower than most natural speakers.

This relatively slow rate of input is a crucial factor in some of the issues that arise in AAC-facilitated communication. Because of the effort and time required to create utterances, the user may not be able to construct messages quickly enough to take active roles in fast

Proceedings of the NAACL HLT 2010 Workshop on Speech and Language Processing for Assistive Technologies, pages 10–18,
Los Angeles, California, June 2010.

paced conversations. As a result users may become passive while also typically using a smaller communicative repertoire than natural speakers (Light 1988).

Narrative, an important type of interpersonal communication, is not well handled in most communication aids (Waller 1992). Delayed response and slow rate of aided-communication are correlated with higher incidence of breakdown in communication and lesser perceptions of the AAC user (Todman and Rzepecka 2003; McCarthy and Light 2005). This is primarily due to conflict between the relatively long time necessary to formulate an utterance and the fast paced nature of conversation.

These problems are particularly critical in social contexts. AAC users typically have small social circles and are dependent on contact with families and carers. They often lack self-esteem and have negative self-image. As a result, developing new relationships and experiencing new things can be difficult, despite being a major priority in their lives (Datillo, Estrella et al. 2007).

Some work has suggested that the use of pre-stored conversational material based on conversation models could help increase communication rate and conversation quality. Alm (1988) showed that it is possible to successfully model short 'chat' conversations involving greetings, personal enquiries and small-talk. Furthermore, the TALK system allowed a user to pre-store a large volume of material on specific topics so that whole utterances could be selected and output. The system also made heavy use of *quick-fire* phrases, classes of regularly used utterance which could be accessed quickly, and showed that communication using solely pre-stored material was viable (Todman and Alm 2003).

Despite encouraging results and the development of a commercial product, the *phrase-storage* approach to social communication has not gained wide popularity. The reasons for this are complex, but include: the relative inflexibility of pre-stored material; the costs associated with authoring the material and keeping the material up-to-date; and the vastly different nature of the approach and different training requirements necessary to achieve success.

2.2 The role of NLP in AAC

NLP technology has provided many benefits to AAC system designers. Possibly the first technology to be included in many commercial systems to date was word prediction and completion. There have also been many research prototypes exploring the applicability of more emerging technologies such as named entity recognition from synthesized speech (Wisenburn and Higginbotham 2008), the generation of well-formed utterances from telegraphic input (McCoy, Pennington et al. 1998) and the automatic identification of contextual vocabulary from the web (Higginbotham, Bisantz et al. 2008). Netzer and Elhadad (2006) used NLG to allow the semantic authoring of utterances.

However, NLG, in the sense of data-to-text (Reiter and Dale 2000), has had limited application within AAC thus far, although Reiter et al. (2009) showed it is possible to generate stories from sensor data which allow a child using AAC to tell others about their day at school.

2.3 System Rationale

This project is exploring the use of NLG to produce conversational utterances in AAC systems designed for social interaction. At the outset it was hoped that using NLG might address some of the difficulties observed in pre-storage systems. For instance, the generation component could theoretically produce a range of utterances and speech act types automatically from the same underlying data and adapt these somewhat to the interactional context. Using NLG would also have the benefit of offering control over the well-formedness of the output, an important consideration given the difficulty some AAC users have in achieving literacy (Sandberg and Hjelmquist 1997). The fact that the system has an inherent awareness of the semantic content of the linguistic output, rather than simply being stored as canned text, is also a potential benefit. In other words, NLG might offer a level of automaticity and flexibility that traditional pre-storage systems cannot offer, as well as potentially reducing the level of pre-authoring required from the user.

3 System Development

3.1 User-centered methodology

To try to assess how useful NLG could be in this context we adopted a user-centered approach to the design of the system. A group of 3 AAC users has been recruited, all of whom currently use some form of high-tech AAC. Literacy amongst the group is varied. Two of the individuals use the alphabetic keyboard-based Lightwriter communication device currently, and have normal cognitive and visual-perceptive skills. All of the users have cerebral palsy and dysarthria, and have been involved in previous software evaluations.

Weekly or twice weekly sessions were held with each user for several months while the software was being produced. Sessions consisted of various activities:

discussion about the user's ideas for the software and technology; the identification of topics and collation of input data to the system; demonstrations of the new features or changes since the last session; system training; and *dry-run* test conversations between the investigators and the users.

3.2 System Architecture

A growing line of inquiry in the NLG community is the generation of language from ontologies (Mellish and Sun 2005). An ontology is a logical and hierarchical model of the different concepts and the nature of relationships between concepts in a particular domain. These concepts and relationships can be mapped onto linguistic constructs to allow for the production of natural language descriptions (Karakatsiotis, Galanis et al. 2008) of parts of the ontology.

In the case of our system, we are trying to model conversational topics that would be of interest in social conversation between users of the system and their co-conversationalists. The current categories of topic we are experimenting with include travelling, listening to music, watching films and attending concerts. Many categories are based on a simple event model which defines the basic characteristics common to all events, such as a time of occurrence (see Fig.1). We have also included concepts such as Person and Place which are associated with events to form a logical model of a particular event type.

A separate file is created unique to each user which is linked to the original model. This is filled with *individuals* consisting of data from the user. In other words, rather than defining the concept of an event as we did with the original ontology, here we are creating a description of an actual event and any other details, such as people or places, associated with it. We have defined our ontology in OWL, a standard language for the definition of ontologies, and each piece of knowledge is effectively stored as a RDF Triple consisting of a subject, predicate and object.

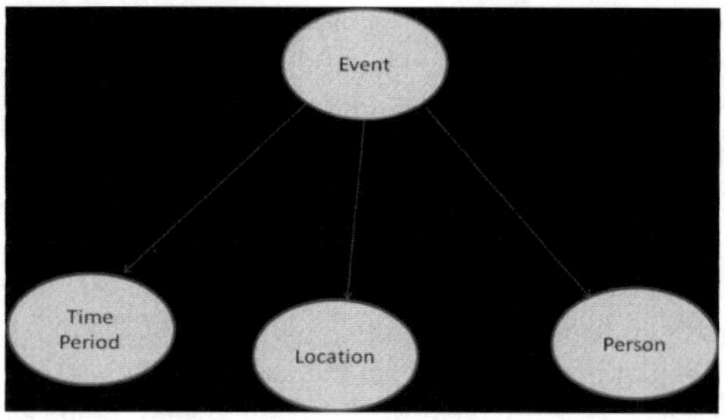

Figure 1: The abstract event model

The user's knowledge base is turned into useful conversational utterances through a template-driven utterance generation system (e.g. Van Deemter, Krahmer et al. 2005). A large set of templates has been authored, using the SimpleNLG programming interface, which turn data from the onotlogy into natural language utterances. The templates are created as *concrete syntax trees* containing unspecified 'slots' and parameters (See Fig.2). These syntax trees map out the syntactic structure of the template), and are linked to a particular class in the ontology so that only appropriate templates are applied to each *individual*. Slots are used to add contextually relevant clauses to our utterances. For example, a template might contain a *'time'* slot, the contents of which are derived from the time of the event in question. For instance, the slot might be filled with "next Tuesday evening", "a month ago" or "this morning" depending on the context. Example parameters include the *tense* with which the utterance should be generated, and whether a pronoun or full noun phrase should be used to refer to the subject of the utterance.

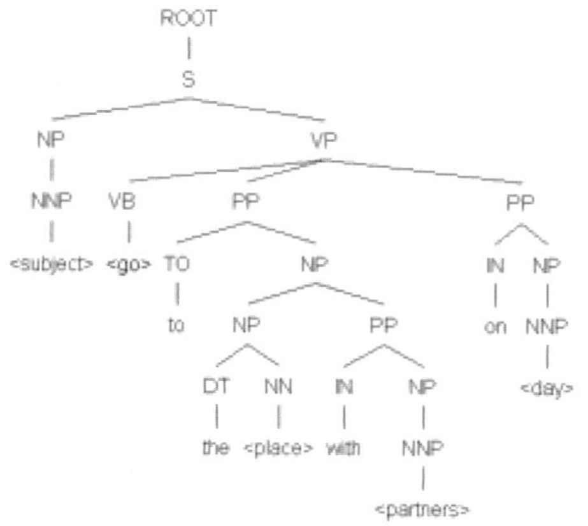

Figure 2: An example syntax tree with empty slots

In addition to the language produced from the model and knowledge base we have included the ability to add canned text phrases to each individual.

This is necessary because there may be things that you wish to be able say about a topic which it is not feasible to model. Because we have a fairly diverse set of topics it is simply not possible to model all aspects of these topics in a reasonable time. There is effectively a trade-off between complexity of the model and how maintainable and representative it is. A more complex model will lead to more expressive generated language, but will cost a great deal more to design and maintain. In the case of our system, a 'lowest common denominator' domain model combined with additional canned text has proven to be a relatively straightforward and inexpensive design.

The system has also been designed to learn over time the sequences of utterances a user selects and suggest next moves based on past behavior. The system does this by maintaining a *directional weighted graph* which records sequences of utterances as they are used. The graph works by recording each individual utterance as a node in the graph and creating relationships between these nodes as they occur. The more often two utterances appear in sequence the higher the value given to the edge between the two corresponding nodes.

3.3 Conversation model and interface issues

Perhaps the most challenging aspect of taking the system from initial concept to working prototype has been finding the most effective way of interfacing the technology. We have found that due to the complexity of the underlying technology, reaching the stage where generated utterances are both useful and accessible to the user during conversation has required careful consideration and the trialing of several approaches with the user group.

It was envisaged that the generative power of NLG would be its most powerful benefit. The system could realize the same piece of data as numerous speech act types and, within a speech type, in several different phrasings. This offered the ability to counteract the inflexibility and uniformity of pre-stored utterances somewhat. However, we have had mixed success in achieving this goal as it has proven difficult to find an effective way to interface this enhanced choice and variety to the user. If there is a large volume of generated utterances available to choose from we must provide an efficient means by which the material is presented or organized so that the desired utterance can be located quickly. If a large choice results in a delayed selection and thus conversational turn, we may then lose any rate and speed of response benefits which would negate the need to use pre-stored and generated material at all.

To address this problem, we attempted to design a conversational model which controlled the generation of utterances so that only the utterances deemed most likely were presented to the user, thus reducing the cognitive load required to search through a large set. This was done using a basic system where the templates were tagged according to where it might be most likely to be used in a conversation on a topic. For instance, a template might produce a pre-sequence, an introduction, elaboration or concluding remark, or it may produce a interrogative. With the addition of historical sequential moves from our directional graph we could begin to present subsets of utterances to the user according to where they were in topic development.

Another approach trialed was inspired by the Gricean maxim of quantity. Each template contains meta-data about the information it expresses. For each generated utterance selected, we can 'rule out' further generation of the same information. This is based on the assumption that speakers will generally avoid repetition. We have found that this technique provides a useful way of supporting discourse coherence within conversations.

Finally, using the logical model of topics we have created, it is possible to support and model stepwise topic progression. We can suggest, based on the model and the user knowledge base, other topics linked to the one currently selected. For example, if we were talking about an upcoming holiday to London with a friend called Bob we may want to the change topical perspective to related aspects of the trip. We might want to talk about London as a place, Bob as a friend, and other trips we have taken with Bob or to London. Because these concepts are all distinct within the model, they each have their own set of associated templates and result in sets of candidate utterances with differing perspectives. Navigating to related topics in this manner should be quicker since related topics do not have to be located manually. Although the users are still being trained in this approach to topic change, early evaluations are promising. It enables a 'one-click' transition to related topics, allowing the user to elaborate on certain aspects of a previous topic and respond quickly to questions from their conversational partners.

Building on the last two mechanisms, we can also generate bridging phrases which allow for more cohesive changes in topic. This allows for a more eloquent transition to a new topic and also aids the discourse coherence.

All of these approaches in fact belie, to some degree, the complexity of conversation. By its very nature, conversation is unpredictable, and the purpose and meaning of sequential moves are highly dependent on their context (Clark 1996). However, any form of context identification, such as speech recognition (Wisenburn and Higginbotham 2008), is likely to present a major technical challenge in any production AAC system at the current time. The above are simply at attempt to model, using the NLP/AI techniques available, aspects of communication process, to show the potential benefits when using NLG-produced utterances rather than simple canned text utterances.

Application of some of the above techniques resulted in a highly fluid interface in which the utterances displayed changed rapidly according to the conversation model. This presented a major challenge to users learning the system, with all displaying a strong preference for a static interface where the same utterances could be found in the same location each time they were desired.

	UTTERANCE	USER SELECTION
A:	**Hi Robert**	**[GREET]**
B:	Oh, Hi. Nice to see you.	
A:	**And you.**	**[GREET]**
A:	**How's it going?**	**[INTRO]**
B:	Fine. And you?	
A:	**Not too bad.**	**[INTRO]**
B:	So you been keeping busy?	
A:	**Yeah**	**[YES]**
A:	**I certainly have!**	**[YES]**
A:	**I was out at a concert on Thursday night. (G)**	**[GIGS] [Select 'Martin Taylor']**
B:	Great. Who did you go to see?	
A:	**Have you heard of Martin Taylor? (G)**	**[ARTIST] [Select 'Martin Taylor']**
B:	No.....I don't think so.	
A:	**He is a Jazz guitarist. (G)**	**[Select 'Martin Taylor']**
B:	Oh, great. I like jazz music.	
A:	**Me too.**	**[AGREE]**
B:	So how was the concert?	
A:	**It was really good. (G)**	**[GIGS] [Select 'Martin Taylor']**
A:	**John and David came with me. (G)**	
A:	**We all enjoyed it. (C)**	
A:	**We had a bit of an interesting journey home because it was snowing heavily, but we made it back safe. (C)**	
B:	Well that's good news. Where was the concert?	
A:	**It was at the Tron Theatre in Glasgow. (G)**	**[GIGS] [Select 'Martin Taylor']**
	I've been to Glasgow a few times lately. [G]	**[Select 'Glasgow']**
A:	**Anyway, I best be getting on.**	**[WRAP UP]**
A:	**It was great talking to you.**	**[WRAP UP]**
B:	Yes, likewise.	
B:	See you soon.	
A:	**OK. Cheerio.**	**[FINISH]**
B:	Bye	

Table 1: An example conversation produced using the system. Speaker A is the user and speaker B is an unaided speaker. The right-hand column shows the interface selections necessary prior to selecting the utterance from a set of possibilities. The marker G represents a generated utterance, C represents canned text. The remainder are *quick-fire* utterances.

We believe this does not suggest that use of such conversational models and semantic processing is not feasible, but simply that in the scope of the current work it has not been possible to fully evaluate their potential. Thus we have chosen to generate candidate phrases in a static manner without the predictive aspects described above. These changes have allowed for quicker achievement of proficiency and have lowered the cognitive effort required to navigate the interface.

In the latest version of the software, we have defined a set of templates for each topic which when realized in series produce a coherent narrative. They can still be selected individually by the user for output, so they retain ultimate control of what is said, but the utterances are presented in a natural order. This means that the user can easily make use of the utterances as a narrative or can choose according to the particular situation and context. Any interrogative templates are displayed in a different part of the interface. We have set up a two column display so that interrogatives and other statements are clearly delineated.

This approach has had very promising results as we have found that users no longer have to search through a list of suggestions which changes after each conversational turn. They can also use the structured nature of the generated utterances to confidently introduce the different topics in conversation. We are finding some evidence of increased self-selection at the end of their current turn as the user is easily able to continue their narrative automatically without having to worry about the location of their next turn in the interface. There is some other evidence of this structured application of NLG to narrative as being a promising area (Reiter, Turner et al. 2009).

We also believe that the passivity and lack of initiation observed in AAC users could be positively addressed if AAC systems can better support a more varied communicative repertoire and suitable training is administered to show users how to confidently use these different constructs (e.g. Todman 2000). Early training sessions with our user group have again proved positive with increased use of the trained features and interaction styles.

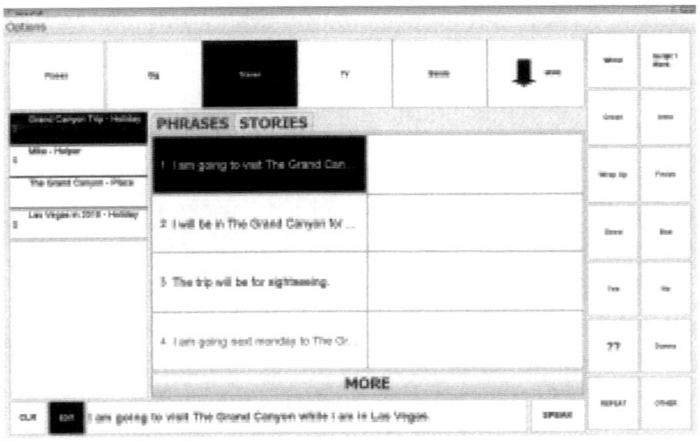

Figure 3 - System interface

3.4 Authoring user content

Currently we have not managed to produce a tool that the user can use to update their knowledge base themselves. The ontology editing tool used in the program, Protégé, is a free academic software package designed for knowledge engineers and thus has a high degree of internal complexity and takes time to learn. It is also not a particularly accessible piece of software.

We have worked with the users to build up their knowledge bases over a series of meetings by allowing them to suggest individuals to add while entering the details for them into the system. The process of defining new individual is very quick, usually requiring the input of just a few words and selection of the associated individuals. However, one of the main criticisms on the part of the users is that for the system to be useful in the long term, it must be kept up to date, as old material will quickly become less relevant and useful in less frequent situations. For this reason it is critical to the success of any NLG-driven communication system that the data input is as simple and seamless as possible.

We have shown in our system that it is possible to get some limited data automatically from online sources, rather than having to input it manually. Many web services are being made available which enable programmers to access data from online services in their applications. For instance, both Amazon and YouTube have their own APIs which allow 3rd party applications to request content information from these services.

The notion of the semantic web is also related to this. There is a large effort underway to define how we might structure and link information on the web in such a way that more of it can be processed automatically by computers and made available in interchangeable formats.

Shared data and semantic web technologies such as these operate on the same premise as our proposed communication system in that they map out the basic vocabulary required to describe a domain, and allow people describe aspects of the domain in these terms.

We have used an API provided by social music website Last.fm to show that it is possible to create relevant conversational utterances without any authoring requirement whatsoever. By supplying the users Last.fm username, we can use a web service supplied by the site to query the user's recent activity, for instance the songs they have listened to, songs rated highly or events which they have signed up to attend. Because the output from these services comes as structured XML document we can simply map it's schema onto our own vocabulary and feed the appropriate data to our templates to produce utterances.

If web services are to be used we must have an equivalent local vocabulary to which we can map the data returned from any queries we send the service. However, in the case of semantic web sources, for example the FOAF (friend-of-a-friend) vocabulary (Brickley) describing online social networks, the process is simpler as we can simply use the pre-existing vocabulary standard ourselves rather than having to develop our own. Despite the semantic web being in its infancy, the notion of shared data is growing in popularity and many popular websites and organizations are providing access to their information in a structured way.

One problem with using these types of data acquisition methods for our purposes is that the data is largely generic and any personal opinion or evaluative information personal to the user is limited. In some cases we may be able to query the data source for a rating awarded to a particular piece of content, for instance the star rating system on YouTube, but it is not clear how expressive the produced language will be since the process is likely to be a simple mapping from the rating to a suitable adjective. As in our system, the potential usefulness of the generated language is likely to be increased if it is possible for the user to annotate the topics with their own canned text expressions and evaluations. This will enable the system to express more of the individual's personality and opinions.

We believe this is an area of great interest for AAC. There is growing evidence of the importance of the internet in the lives of disabled people, particularly its role as a communication medium for people with communication impairments (Cohen 1999). By harnessing the large volumes of data created when using modern hardware and software systems and transforming it into useful utterances, we can begin to address one of the main criticisms of whole utterance approaches to AAC since there would be no authoring requirement on the part of the users. This is certainly by no means a simple process and this approach will require further investigation, but as semantic web technologies reach maturity and gain wider adoption it should be clearer what the potential of the technology is.

4 Formal Evaluation Methodology

In our evaluations so far, we have concentrated on training the users in its operation, updating conversational material and implementing changes based on the user feedback. We have recently begun testing the system in real conversational encounters and the results have been promising. We have found it is possible to hold pleasing conversations lasting up to 20 minutes with unfamiliar partners, with the aided communicator achieving a rate of upwards of 40 wpm.

There also seems to be higher incidences of initiations on the part of the user, with them making good use of both the scripted NLG material, the quick fire phrases and their own pre-stored material. The topic progression feature is currently being underused but subjects are responding well to training sessions on how to incorporate this to reduce their response time and expand on topics to extend the amount they are able to say.

Formal evaluations are now being undertaken. An AB multiple-baseline study design is being conducted in which each aided communicator has a series of conversations with 12 unknown and unaided conversation partners. In the A condition, the aided participants use their existing AAC system, while in the B condition they use our prototype system. Each conversation will be limited to approximately 10 minutes, and the sessions will be split across a three non-consecutive days to avoid user fatigue.

There will be at least 3 conversations in both the A and B conditions, and the intervention point will be randomized across the remaining 6 conversations to allow for valid inferences to be made despite the small *n* value (Todman and Dugard 2001). This also reduces the bias introduced by any training effects and avoids the need to use a response-guided intervention after baseline performance has been established. The difficulty and expense of recruiting large numbers of subjects in AAC studies is a known problem (Higginbotham 1995) and therefore any findings from quantitative analysis performed cannot be generalized across the AAC population. However, we expect to be able to achieve a p value using the randomization design of <0.05 so the results should at least be internally robust and give a good indication of whether further investigation is warranted.

The conversations will be audio-recorded and analyzed for a number of metrics. Primarily we are interested in measuring the rate at which people are able to communicate using the new system as this seems to be one of the clearest indicators of success when evaluating a new AAC intervention. We expect to the effect size observed across the conditions to be large.

We are also particularly interested whether it is possible to use automatically generated material while maintaining or enhancing the enjoyment and quality of the encounter for all participants. It is still unclear how acceptable generated material will be to the user so we will measure the relative frequency of generated and canned-text utterances.

In previous studies it has also been shown that the use of a whole-utterance approach can change the dynamics of communication, such as relative speech act distribution and number and type of initiation, so we are interested to see how the availability generated material might impact this and what role it might play. A coding schema based on Wang (2007) will be used to categorize the utterances used.

We are also asking the aided and unaided conversation partners to complete questionnaires regarding various subjective ratings of the interactions and, in the case of the unaided speakers, impressions of the aided communicator. The questions will be based on a re-evaluation of those suggested by Todman (2000) and answers will be requested on a 7-point rating scale. Previous work has shown that quicker, flowing interactions with less breakdowns or delays can lead to more rewarding interactions for both participants. We expect to observe these effects in our system but it's as yet unclear what impact the automatically generated phrases will have, if any, on perceptions of the user.

Although the relatively small number of participants means it is unlikely that we will be able to make robust inferences from this data, we hope that results will be indicative of the naturalness and acceptability of automatically generated utterances.

5 Discussion & Future Plans

One of the primary reasons that AAC systems featuring NLP technology prove useful is that they go some way to leveling the playing field for many users. They have the potential to support the user in ways which reduce the effort required to communicate yet may improve the quality of the communication. There are many NLP technologies, such as NLG, that deserve further attention within the field of AAC to determine what they can offer.

Although our system has shown some encouraging preliminary results there are still many unanswered questions with regards to the role NLG can play. For example, it is not clear how appealing NLG utterances are to use. Given that the user has not authored the form of the utterances themselves there is an argument that using them may feel unnatural. After the formal evaluations we should be able provide analysis indicating whether NLG phrases are being used and in which situations they are proving most useful.

One of the most challenging aspects of designing the system was the HCI challenge of incorporating some of these technologies. While it is obvious to the user that phrases are being generated automatically, and that these phrases are generated when a topic is selected, it is still important to note that the technologies have been intentionally kept largely transparent to the user. When using a communication system, the most important thing is the ability to say what you want to say, but is not yet clear whether the technical nature of the software may be an alienating factor since the user currently has no access to the template construction or domain modeling aspects of the system.

At the current time, the domain modeling and template construction processes are quite complex and expensive. Tools are becoming available, from the NLG community, which go some way to addressing the difficulty of interfacing these types of technology to non-experts (Bilidas, Theologou et al. 2007; Power, Stevens et al. 2009) but these are largely unsolved problems.

Domain modeling itself is problematic in that one persons notion of what defines a particular concept is often different to someone else's. For instance, one person's idea of sport might encompass the sporting activities they take part in, while another person's idea of sport is that which they follow or watch on the television. This has clear implications for the general usability of the system. Using semantic web vocabularies may address this somewhat since they are likely to be more specific to a particular purpose and be more mature and interoperable than the *'home-brew'* domain models we have used for the prototype.

Using whole-utterance approaches to communication clearly requires the adoption of a different mindset. Rather than being able to construct a novel message the user has to *'make do'* with whatever is available in the system. Despite the advantages observed while using such systems, they have still not become generally popular. It is likely that any NLG whole utterance system would similarly not gain immediate acceptance because it is vastly different to other systems and approaches to communication available. To some degree we are asking the user of our NLG system to think in an object orientated manner since they must understand the underlying model and the way the concepts are structured to make the most of the system. Again it is not yet clear how natural this process is and how much training is required to become an expert user of such a system.

However perhaps the major strength of these types of system is the way in which they help scaffold interaction so the AAC user can be much more active in conversation and use an increased repertoire. The design of the software is such that it encourages the use of types of phrases often underused by AAC users, for example, initiations, elaborating moves, questions and the different classes of quick-fire remarks. One interesting question is whether the use of NLG might make it easier to encourage the user to use new types of conversational move. Since no full text-authoring is required the user does not even have feel confident authoring the utterance, it is simply provided and can be used or experimented with. Scaffolding interactions in this way may be one of the most interesting avenues for NLP and AI technologies with AAC in the future.

The architecture of the prototype, although effective, lacks efficiency and may be difficult to reuse. A great deal of work is being done by NLG researchers investigating how NLG architectures might be made more modular and reusable. This is an ongoing problem but it seems sensible to consider how a pipeline architecture (Reiter and Dale 2000) might work in practice for this type of system.

At the moment, the system requires a reasonable level of literacy because the interface is mainly text based. However, semiotic systems are preferred because of the literacy problems observed in many AAC users. It is not clear how NLG may impact on semiotic message construction but systems such as Compansion (McCoy, Pennington et al. 1998) show there may useful applications in this area too.

6 Conclusion

Despite having only been able to perform informal evaluations so far, we believe we have seen some encouraging signals that NLG may have potential as an augmentative communication technology to assist in generating conversational utterances. We believe that the rapid access to well-formed, contextually generated material offered in our system could lead to significant benefits for the AAC user and their interlocutors.

There are further exciting possibilities with regards to the technology, particularly the ability to harvest personal data from the internet and other computer usage so that it can be transformed into useful phrases for inclusion in communication aids. We hope to have a richer set of data and results in the coming months after the system training and formal evaluations have been completed.

7 References

Alm, N. A. (1988). Towards a Conversation Aid for Severely Phisically Disabled Non-Speaking People. Applied Computing Department. Dundee, University Of Dundee. **Doctor Philosophy:** 197.

Bilidas, D., M. Theologou, et al. (2007). Enriching OWL Ontologies with Linguistic and User-related Annotations: the ELEON system. 19th IEEE International Conference on Tools with Artificial Intelligence, IEEE.

Brickley, D. (25.2.10). "FOAF Vocabulary Specification ", from http://xmlns.com/foaf/0.1/

Clark, H. H. (1996). Using Language, Cambridge University Press.

Cohen, K. J. (1999). Using the Internet to Empower Augmented Communicators. CSUN'99.

Datillo, J., G. Estrella, et al. (2007). ""I have chosen to live life abundantly": Perceptions of leisure by adults who use Augmentative and Alternative Communication." Augmentative & Alternative Communication **24**(1): 16-28.

Higginbotham, D. J. (1995). "Use of nondisabled subjects in AAC Research : Confessions of a research infidel." Augmentative and Alternative Communication **11**(1): 2-5.

Higginbotham, D. J., A. M. Bisantz, et al. (2008). "The Effect of Context Priming and Task Type on Augmentative Communication Performance." Augmentative & Alternative Communication.

Higginbotham, D. J., H. Shane, et al. (2007). "Access to AAC: Present, past, and future." Augmentative & Alternative Communication **23**(3): 243-257.

Karakatsiotis, G., D. Galanis, et al. (2008). NaturalOWL: Generating Texts from OWL Ontologies in Protege and in Second Life. 18th European Conference on Artificial Intelligence.

Light, J. (1988). "Interaction Involving Individuals using Augmentative and Alternative Communication Systems: State of the Art and Future Directions." Augmentative and Alternative Communication **4**(2): 66-82.

McCarthy, J. and J. Light (2005). "Attitudes towards individuals who use Augmentative and Alternative Communication: Research Review." Augmentative and Alternative Communication **21**(1): 41-55.

McCoy, K. F., C. A. Pennington, et al. (1998). "Compansion: From research prototype to practical integration." Natural Language Engineering **4**(1): 73-95.

Mellish, C. and X. Sun (2005). The Semantic Web as a Linguistic Resource: Opportunities for Natural Language Generation. International Conference on theory, practical and application of Artificial Intelligence. M. Bramer, F. Coenen and T. Allen. Cambridge, UK, Springer: 77.

Netzer, Y. and M. Elhadad (2006). Using Semantic Authoring for Blissymbols Communication Boards. HLT-2006.

Power, R., R. Stevens, et al. (2009). Editing OWL through generated CNL. Workshop on Controlled Natural Language (CNL'09). Marettimo Island, Italy.

Reiter, E. and R. Dale (2000). Building Natural Language Generation Systems. Cambridge Cambridge University Press.

Reiter, E., R. Turner, et al. (2009). Using NLG to help language-impaired users tell stories and participate in social dialogues. Proceedings of the 12th European Workshop on Natural Language Generation. Athens, Greece, ACL.

Sandberg, A. D. and E. Hjelmquist (1997). " Language and literacy in nonvocal children with cerebral palsy." Reading and Writing **9**(2): 107-133.

Todman, J. (2000). "Rate and quality of conversations using a text-storage AAC system: Single-case training study." Augmentative and Alternative Communication **16**: 164-179.

Todman, J. and N. A. Alm (2003). "Modelling conversational pragmatics in communication aids." Journal of Pragmatics(35): 523-538.

Todman, J. and P. Dugard (2001). Single-case and small-n experimental designs: A practical guide to randomisation tests. Mahwah, NJ, Lawrence Erlbaum Associates.

Todman, J. and H. Rzepecka (2003). "Effect of pre-utterance pause length on perceptions of communicative competence in AAC-aided social conversations." Augmentative and Alternative Communication **19**(4): 222-234.

Van Deemter, K., E. Krahmer, et al. (2005). "Plan-based vs. Template-based NLG: A false opposition?" Computational Linguistics **31**(1).

Waller, A. (1992). Providing Narratives in an Augmentative Communication System. Applied Computing. Dundee, University Of Dundee. **Doctor of Philosophy:** 163.

Wang, Y. (2007). A model of conversational structure for augmentative and alternative communication (AAC) systems. University of Dundee, Unpublished PhD Thesis. **PhD**.

Wisenburn, B. and D. J. Higginbotham (2008). "An AAC Application Using Speaking Partner Speech Recognition to Automatically Produce Contextually Relevant Utterances: Objective Results." Augmentative and Alternative Communication **24**(2): 100-109.

Implications of Pragmatic and Cognitive Theories on the Design of Utterance-Based AAC Systems

Kathleen F. McCoy
Dept. of Computer and Information Sciences
University of Delaware
Newark, DE 19716, USA
mccoy@cis.udel.edu

Jan Bedrosian
Dept. of Speech Pathology and Audiology
Western Michigan University
Kalamazoo, MI 49008, USA
jan.bedrosian@wmich.edu

Linda Hoag
Dept. of Communication Sciences and Disorders
Kansas State University
Manhattan, KS 66506, USA
lhoag@ksu.edu

Abstract

Utterance-based AAC systems have the potential to significantly speed communication rate for someone who relies on a speech generating device for communication. At the same time, such systems pose interesting challenges including anticipating text needs, remembering what text is stored, and accessing desired text when needed. Moreover, using such systems has profound pragmatic implications as a prestored message may or may not capture exactly what the user wishes to say in a particular discourse situation. In this paper we describe a prototype of an utterance-based AAC system whose design choices are driven by findings from theoretically driven studies concerning pragmatic choices with which the user of such a system is faced. These findings are coupled with cognitive theories to make choices for system design.

1 Introduction

There are more than 3.5 million Americans with disabilities who cannot effectively use speech to communicate (Beukelman & Mirenda, 2005). There are many conditions that can result in such severe speech impairments including cerebral palsy, autism spectrum disorders, multiple sclerosis, amyotrophic lateral sclerosis (ALS), brain-stem stroke, Parkinson's disease, and traumatic brain injury (TBI). Any one of these conditions can have a negative effect on the quality of life of these people. The field of Augmentative and Alternative Communication (AAC) has, especially over the last ten years, dramatically enhanced access to communication for these individuals through the use of high-tech systems. These electronic systems allow the entering of text that is then converted to natural-sounding synthetic speech. While the population using AAC systems is quite diverse with regard to their linguistic and cognitive skills, here we focus on AAC systems for cognitively high-functioning literate adults with motor impairments.

Even with a focus on this population, the communication rates of people who use AAC systems differ greatly based on their motor abilities and available interface choices (Trnka et al., 2009). Nevertheless, overall communication rates are slow to the extent that they are acknowledged as one of the most problematic areas of AAC interactions. Rates of 10-15 words per minute have been identified as upper limits for letter-by-letter selection on a keyboard (e.g., Wobbrock & Myers, 2006)—a significant contrast to 130-200 words per minute for spoken communication. These slow rates and long pauses continue to be a major barrier to the social, educational, and vocational success, particularly when communicating with unfamiliar partners who have little or no experience in conversing with someone who uses AAC.

One method that holds a great deal of promise for enhancing communication rate is the use of systems that offer a selection of prestored messages. With these systems, a phrase or full sentence/utterance can be selected at once. In such systems, sometimes called utterance-based AAC systems, people compose whole utterances in advance and store them for later use. These systems appear to be best suited for situations where relatively predictable conversational routines take place. Examples include short, transactional exchanges in stores, restaurants, or other public places where services are provided.

Although it might appear that utterance-based technology could solve the problem of slow com-

Proceedings of the NAACL HLT 2010 Workshop on Speech and Language Processing for Assistive Technologies, pages 19–27,
Los Angeles, California, June 2010.

munication, at least in these predictable exchanges, the individual who uses these prestored messages must deal with additional challenges to use the prestored messages that have been stored in their system. Users must be able to: 1) remember that they have messages prestored that are appropriate for a given situation; 2) remember where these messages are stored; and 3) access the desired prestored messages with few keystrokes. In addition, it must be recognized that the prestored messages are not always going to exactly fit the communicative situation in which the user finds him/herself (e.g., a prestored message may not have enough information for the needs of the partner).This results in a fourth challenge to the user—to decide if it is better to use the message as stored, or either edit or construct a new one. Each challenge, or trade-off choice, directly affects communication rate.

An adequate solution to these challenges has proven elusive over the years, despite a long tradition of research in utterance-based technologies (e.g., Todman, 2000; Todman & Alm, 1997; Todman et al., 2008; Vanderheyden et al., 1996). What has been lacking is a design process that employs a theoretical framework (or perspective) dealing with conversation conventions, empirical evidence to identify priorities, and systematic testing to determine whether the design enables the communicator to achieve the goals of an interaction.

A hierarchy of conversational rule violations based on a series of experimental studies has a great deal of potential to positively influence the design of future utterance-based technologies. In this paper we first describe a set of such studies and the resulting hierarchy. We then discuss the implications of this hierarchy on the design of an utterance-based AAC system, while integrating considerations from cognition and Natural Language Processing. Finally, we present our partially implemented prototype system and describe plans for evaluating this technology.

2 Theoretical Background

To shed light on the design of future utterance-based technologies, studied conversational trade-off choices that a person faces when using an utterance-based system in goal-directed public situations with service providers who are unfamiliar with AAC, and how the particular choices made affect the attitudes and conversational behaviors of these providers (Bedrosian et al., 2003; Hoag et al., 2007; Hoag et al., 2004, 2008; McCoy, et al., 2007). We were interested in determining which message choices resulted in the most favorable attitudes and conversational responses leading to the success of the AAC customer's goal in these transactional exchanges.

Notice that no matter how well a user anticipates text need, it is inevitable that some prestored messages are not going to exactly fit the pragmatic context in which the user finds him or herself. Four public situations (i.e., bookstore, movie theater, small convenience store, hair salon) where such mismatches could occur were studied in a series of investigations. Possible pragmatic mismatches were characterized in terms of rule violations according to Grice (1975) who articulated a set of classic conversational maxims that implicitly guide people in exchanging information. Using videotaped interactions across experiments, these violations were scripted in messages that involved trade-off choices between prestored message use and real time message construction. Specifically, the trade-offs examined in these investigations were between speed of message delivery and a message with either: 1) repetitive information with repetitive words or phrases; 2) excessive information, with more information than was needed by the listener but where the information was still topically relevant; 3) inadequate information, lacking some of the information needed by the listener, or 4) partly relevant information, where some of the content was not topically relevant. An example of such a trade-off involved the message choice of a quickly delivered (i.e., 4 seconds) prestored message with excessive information or one that was delivered slowly (i.e., 90 seconds) to allow editing of the excessive information.

In essence, these experiments simulated situations where the user was faced with a choice: whether to quickly deliver a prestored message that was not exactly what was desired because of the pragmatic mismatch, or whether to take the time to edit the message so that it was exactly what was needed. The experiments looked at goal oriented situations with unfamiliar partners. This is an extremely important set of circumstances where the attitudes and actions of the communication partner can greatly affect whether or not the user can independently meet his or her goals.

The experimental hypothesis was that there existed a hierarchy of conversational maxims involving the maxims of speed, relevance, repetition, and Informativeness, such that adherence to some of these maxims would result in more positive evaluations by public service providers than others. With regard to the results of the experiments, similar hierarchies of conversational rule violations were found across experiments, such that some violations, regardless of degree or particular public setting, were indeed consistently responded to more or less favorably than others. Consistently at the bottom of the hierarchy (i.e., responded to least favorably in all experimental situations, and with less success in meeting the target customer's goal) were quickly delivered messages with only partly relevant information. The finding places a high priority on selecting entirely relevant messages. As such, it suggests the development of a system architecture that makes it easy and fast to retrieve entirely relevant messages and difficult to retrieve messages that are only partly relevant to the current exchange.

On the other hand, consistently at the top of the hierarchy were quickly delivered messages with repetitive information. These messages were responded to the most favorably and with much success in meeting the target customer's goal. The limited negative impact of the messages with repetition indicated that modification of system design to remedy this message flaw would yield less benefit for the user.

The other trade-off choices, the fast inadequate message, the slow adequate message, and the fast excessive message, occupied the middle of the hierarchy across the experiments, although their positions with regard to each other were not exactly the same. Thus, the implications of these findings for system design are a little less clear, but suggest that users given options to edit or easily construct messages with respect to Informativeness.

In sum, these findings have several important implications for future utterance-based technologies. A system design must provide a mechanisms to maximize the availability of situationally relevant prestored messages. Additionally, utterance-based technologies must be integrated seamlessly into an AAC system design that allows these prestored messages to be easily edited for their excessive or inadequate information. Finally, this design must also support the on-line construction of new messages, while still easily accessing prestored messages when appropriate.

3 Prototype Development

The research findings cited above, particularly those regarding the critical role of relevance in conversation, led to the underlying structure of the prototype we are in the process of developing. Specifically, we are interested in a prototype that will support relevant conversation in familiar routine exchanges with relatively predictable content, such as those that occur in public settings, as it is these types of exchanges that provide the best situations in which to use prestored text. Schank and Abelson (1977) suggested that people develop mental scripts in such familiar situations (e.g., going to a restaurant), and that these scripts (representing typical sequences of events) are accessed by people in order to act appropriately in these situations, and understand/interpret what is being said. Each script consists of a series of scenes (subevents) that previous experience has led one to expect to occur. According to the cognitive theory, when faced with a new situation (e.g., going to a new restaurant), a person can pull up his/her mental script and step through the scenes in order to participate appropriately.

We propose an underlying organizational structure for prestored utterances that leverages this mental script notion from cognitive science, as it nicely supports the Bedrosian, Hoag, McCoy, and Bedrosian findings about relevance. A slightly different notion of scripts has been used in previous research in utterance-based technologies (e.g., Dye et al., 1998; Alm et al., 2000). The notion referred to here is inspired by the early work of Vanderheyden (1995). In particular, in our prototype system the prestored utterances are organized (grouped and ordered) according to scenes within a script. For example, a "going-to-a-restaurant" script may have scenes associated with entering, ordering drinks, ordering entree, paying, etc. Associated with each of these scenes are the prestored utterances appropriate for use during that scene (e.g., utterances pertaining to entering might include, "Hello." "Fine, thank you.", "Non-smoking.").

Not only would this organization ensure the relevance of utterances to the current situation, but it would also significantly aid the user in remembering where these messages are stored so that they can be accessed. Essentially the user could direct the system to step through messages appropriate for each scene of a given script as he/she is actually experiencing the scene. The utterance-based system would have a "now point" which corresponds to the scene in which the user is currently located in the script. Utterances useful for the conversation during that scene are easily available using very few keystrokes. Moreover, because the script mirrors the way a user thinks about a typical situation and how it flows from one scene to the next, the interface could lead the user to utterances appropriate for the next scenes to be encountered. Thus, users do not need to remember exactly which utterances are stored; they need only to activate the appropriate scene in the script to be shown relevant messages that can be selected, as well as other scenes that may follow.

At the same time, this underlying structure can also provide time-saving benefits to the user with respect to entering text. This is in part because of its hierarchical organization [see Figure 1, influenced by Vanderheyden (1995)]. At the top of any given hierarchy, are the most general scripts which can be used in a multitude of new situations (e.g., a new type of restaurant that the user has never gone to). As shown in the figure, the most general script here involves a "going-to-a-restaurant" script with scenes containing "general purpose text". For instance, in the ordering scene, slot fillers appropriate for many different kinds of restaurants are shown. Below this script, are scripts that pertain to more specific types of restaurants (only two are explicitly shown in the figure). In these scripts, notice some scenes and text are inherited verbatim from above, but text may also be added to or modified as appropriate for the situation and according to the preferences of the user. By inherited we mean that one or more scenes, with the corresponding messages, from the most general script would automatically be made available in the more specific instances. Unavailable in other prestored text systems, this feature is a significant benefit to users, because they only have to enter the information one time at the highest level of the hierarchy, and yet they will have access to it again in other scripts further down in the hierarchy.

Another advantage of the inheritance is that it results in a consistent organization of messages across scripts. When accessing any script within the restaurant hierarchy, for example, not only can users expect to find the entering scene that was inherited from the "parent" script, they can also expect to find the prestored utterances "Hello" and "Fine, thank you" near the beginning of that scene. This illustrates a memory enhancement feature of this system that is not available in other prestored text systems – consistency in placement of messages from one particular script to another. Overall, this underlying organizational structure, which we will refer to as a deep structure, represents a significant change in the way that utterance-based systems in AAC have been designed. With respect to appearance, or surface structure, some current systems may have, for example, a restaurant "page" consisting of a grid of small rectangular boxes forming rows and columns across the computer screen. Although each box would contain a prestored message appropriate for use in a restaurant, there is no deep structure specifying how the messages on that page should be organized (grouped and ordered) nor how the messages might be related (the notion of consistency) to those stored on other pages. The only organizing principle is that these messages are "things I can say in a restaurant." If the messages are not ordered (either by row or column) in a way that steps the user through a scripted sequence of events for a given situation, the user must search through a set of messages, some of which are unlikely to occur at that stage in the interaction. This search process, which is likely to include irrelevant messages, may slow down the selection process and negatively impact the rate of communication. Even if health providers or manufacturers programmed messages in these boxes to follow such a sequence, this would still remain a surface structure "fix." The strength of our prototype is the deep structure—the machinery—such that the consistent location of the messages can be easily remembered and accessed in a few keystrokes to enhance communication rate. Additionally, the hierarchical advantage of the deep structure provides the user with a choice of scripts (depending on the specificity of the situation), and saves the user time and energy in entering text, making the user more independent in meeting individual communication needs.

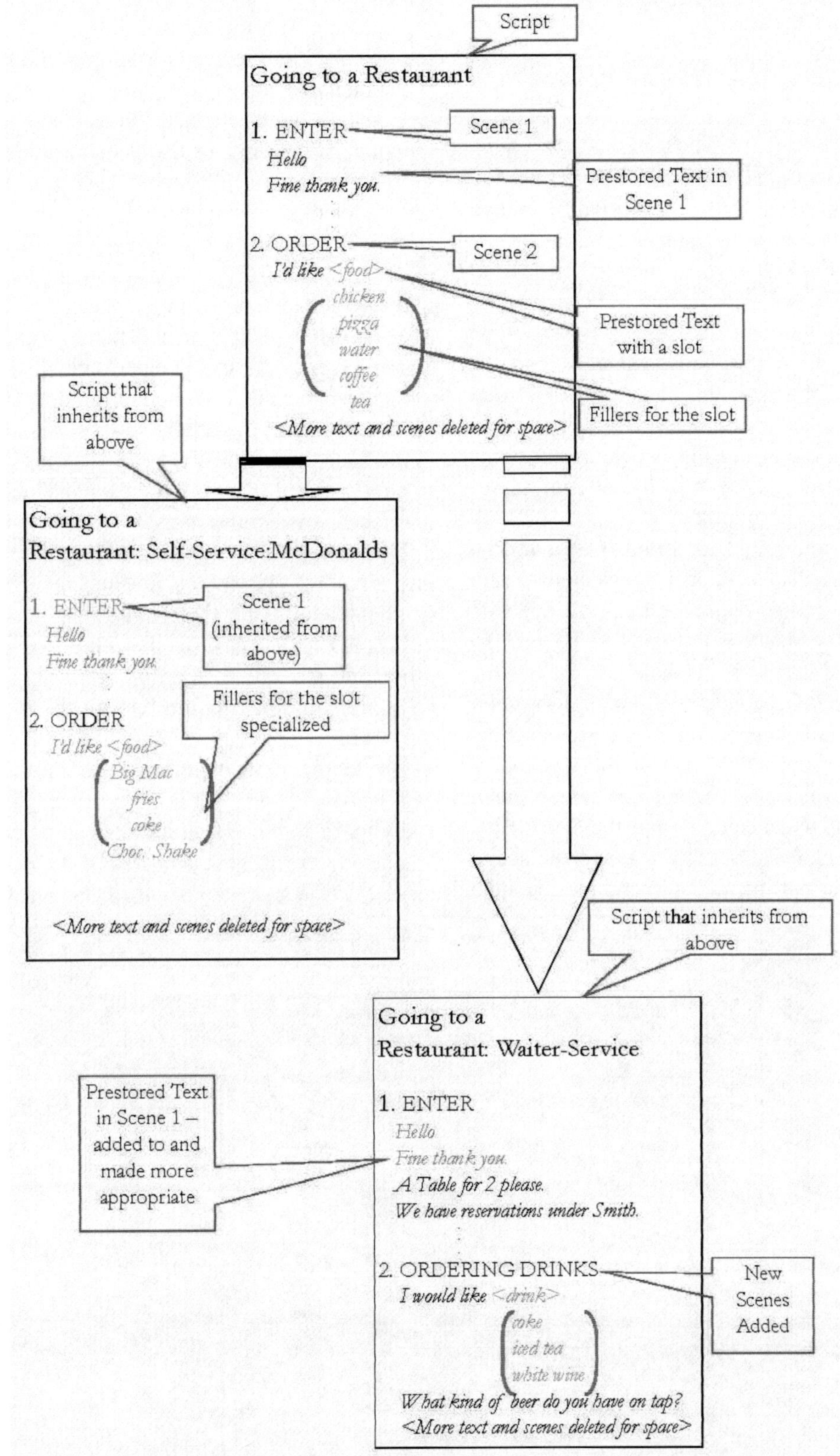

Figure 1: Hierarchical Script Representation

4 Communicating with the system

In this section we discuss the user interface and what the user does in order to actually communicate using the system which has been our focus to date. Future work will investigate issues in entering prestored text into scripts and adapting the scripts to the individual user. In a situation where the user anticipates using prestored text, he or she will be taken to a window menu where the desired script (and scene) can be selected. The user may then navigate to the script that best fits the actions in which he or she is about to engage. Upon selecting the script, the user will be taken to a screen such as that displayed in Figure 2.

The large window at the top is the display window. This is where the words of the utterances selected by the user to be spoken will be displayed. There is a clear button to clear the display window (on the left of the display) and a speak button (the arrow on the right-hand-side of the display) that causes the display window contents to be sent to the speech synthesizer to be spoken.

The next area of the display helps users keep their place and navigate within the chosen script. First is the scene map which is a numerical representation of the scenes in the current script. From this, for instance, users can see that the script they have selected contains seven scenes, and the scene they are currently performing is scene number one which corresponds to the "enter" scene. The number of the current scene is colored differently than the rest. Below the scene map is a line of tabs, under which are boxes containing prestored text that can be selected by the user. In this case, the text for the first five scenes of the script are displayed (or partially displayed). These scenes are named "enter", "drinks", "appetizer", "soup/salad", and "entrée". Under each of these scene-name tabs is the list of possible prestored utterances associated with the scene. For example, there are three pieces of text displayed that would be appropriate for the "enter" scene. As is the case with the scene-map, the current scene (tab and utterances) is colored differently from the others so that it is more salient to the user.

Under the boxes are four tabs which bring up overlays with some general prestored text that might be needed at any time during the script. Asking for some assistance, talking with the waiter, small talk with the table mate, and quickfires are just some examples of the kinds of pages that might be accessible. Finally, at the bottom of the page are some navigation buttons for navigating in the device. Here we see buttons that allow the user to go to the device home page, move the script backward and forward, and go to a page containing a keyboard so a novel utterance can be composed.

The system is set up in a way that allows users to select text that they might need while perform-

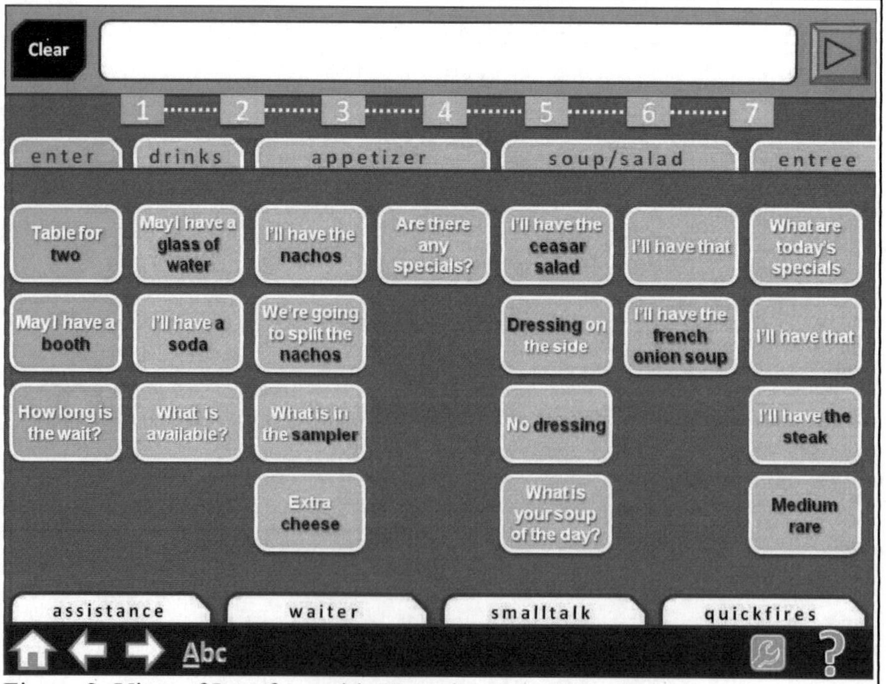

Figure 2: View of Interface with "Entering Scene" Active

ing an action as they step through a scene. Thus, it is assumed that the user would select text in left-to-right order with the left-most scene being the active scene (i.e., the scene the user is currently performing). The user may select one of the boxes in the active scene, and the text would be automatically put up into the display window at the top. The speak button (arrow in the upper-right corner) is used to actually say the desired text. The user could select and speak any number of utterances in the active scene without any significant changes in the display. If the actions the user is performing have progressed to the next scene, then the user may navigate to the appropriate text in two different ways. First, the user could click on the scene map or displayed tabs to have the context shift to the new scene. Once selected that scene tab and associated text boxes will be shown on the left-hand-side of the device. Second, if the utterance that the user wishes to say is currently visible on the screen, the user may simply select that utterance. In this case, in addition to putting the utterance in the display window making it ready to be spoken, the screen will automatically scroll over to display the scene from which the utterance was chosen on the far left (revealing subsequent scenes to the right of it on the screen). Figure 3 displays an example of this kind of movement, resulting from the user selecting the "I'll have the nachos" text from the appetizer scene displayed in Figure 2. Notice that the scenes have been shifted over--the appetizer scene (scene 3) is now the active scene, and the text associated with the button is now in the display window.

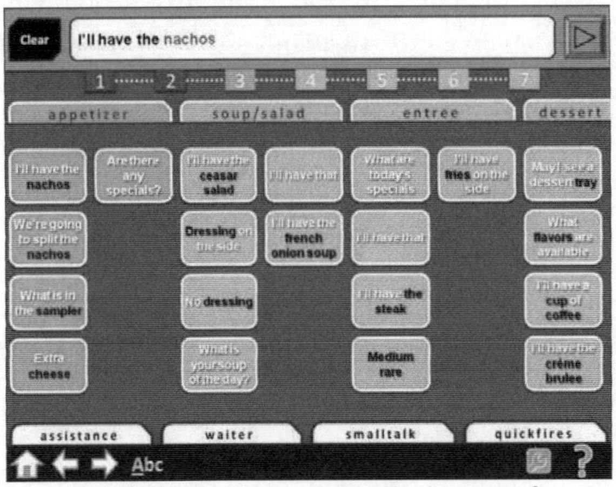

Figure 3: Shifting scenes by selecting text from appetizer scene

Figure 3 illustrates another feature of the system – slot fillers that are specific to a script or scene. Notice that "nachos" is colored differently than the other words in this prestored text. This is an indication that it is a slot-filler and that other options for filling that slot are available. To edit that text, the user clicks on the highlighted word in the display window, and a window such as that in Figure 4 is displayed. The user may then select the filler he/she desires, and it will replace "nachos" in the display.

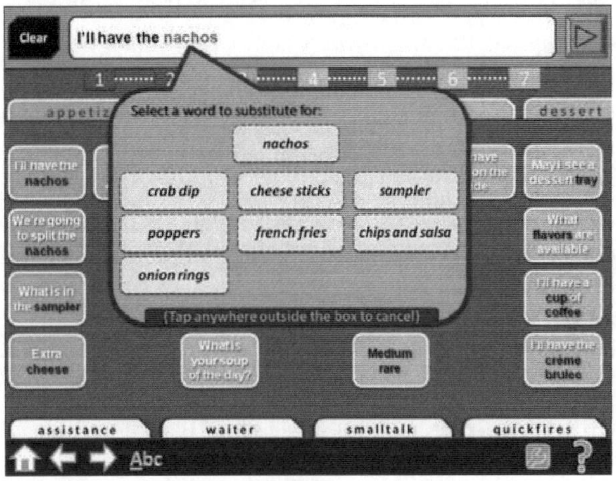

Figure 4: Editing a slot-filler

The system described is currently being implemented. Yet to be integrated is a facility that will enable more extensive editing of the text in the display window and the specifics of easy access to typing via an on-screen keyboard (for instances where the user wishes to type an utterance from scratch rather than using a prestored utterance).

5 Planned Evaluation

Two separate comparative efficacy evaluations will be conducted to test both the efficiency and effectiveness (Schlosser, 1999) of the prototype system in contrast to a differently organized prestored text system. In each evaluation, efficiency will involve a comparison of the two systems, in a training session, with respect to user learning variables (e.g., which system is learned faster, with less instruction time, fewer errors/trials). Effectiveness will involve a comparison, in a virtual public setting environment with a service provider as the partner, dealing with user behavior changes and satisfaction (e.g., which system results in faster rates of prestored message selection, goal attainment, more satisfaction) and partner attitude and behavior changes (e.g., which system leads to more positive attitudes toward the user, more effective conversational behaviors in meeting user goals).

In the first efficacy evaluation, typically speaking, nondisabled adults will be the participants, eliminating bias due to the fact that they will have had no previous experience using AAC systems. A randomized controlled trial will be employed whereby participants will be assigned to either the prototype system group or the standard system group. Each system will contain the same prestored messages, and the same virtual public setting will be used in each group. Results will be used to refine the training phase and modify the prototype software if necessary. In the second evaluation, a single subject experimental design involving an adapted alternating treatment design will be employed with cognitively intact, literate, adult participants who currently use prestored text systems. Although such a design would expose each participant to each system (i.e., the prototype system and the standard system), carryover effects are eliminated due to counterbalancing the order of the two conditions across participants, ensuring that there are two equivalent and functionally independent instructional sets for the conditions (Schlosser, 1999) (in this case, the instructional sets would involve two virtual public settings and corresponding prestored messages), and counterbalancing the sets between conditions.

6 Related Work

Storing and retrieving full utterances has been the focus of a long tradition of work; Todman et al. (2008) contains a nice overview of some of these systems. The ScripTalker system (Dye et al. 1998a) is closest in theory to our system wit perhaps the biggest difference being the variety of utterances available (and the fact that their prototype seemed more geared toward people with low literacy skills. While the overall architecture did rely on the notion of scripts, the actual utterances stored was one per task the user might want to perform. I.e., the scripts themselves were linguistic in nature. Similar uses were found in other work from that same group, for instance see (Alm et al. 1995) and (Dye et al. 1998). In contrast we target users with higher literacy skills and more variety in the prestored text they might want to have available. The script is used to organize the messages but there are many messages available within a particular scene.

Other work such as the Talk System (Todman & Alm, 1997) is intended for social conversation and the organization is quite different. As its intention is so different, one would expect the stored content to need to be updated very often in order to keep it current. This is in contrast to the relatively enduring nature expected in the types of conversations we envision.

Another notable system is the FrameTalker Project (Higgenbotham & Lesher, 2005) uses a looser notion of communication contexts. Our hypothesis is the structure used there does not impose enough organization over the utterances, especially in the type of situations we envision for use. The Contact system is a system that combines notions from both Talk and the FrameTalker projects.

Finally, Langer & Hickey (1997) describe a whole utterance system that retrieved utterances related to keywords via a keyword search on a large database of utterances. In contrast, our system would provide access to presumably a series of utterances relevant to the current situation.

7 Conclusions

AAC systems that use prestored text have a great deal of potential to speed communication rate and improve attitudes of unfamiliar speaking partners towards AAC users in public goal-oriented situations. In this work we applied empirical evidence summarized in a hierarchy of conversational rule violations (Bedrosian et al. 2000) to identify important principles of successful interaction with AAC text. We then attempted to match appropriate NLP technologies with these principles in order to develop a different viewpoint for an AAC system that used prestored text. Our design is based on schema-theory (Schank & Abelson, 1977) and enforces a structure over the prestored text that will minimize irrelevant text and constrain the rest of the text so as to facilitate remembering what text is stored while minimizing keystrokes needed to select the text.

Acknowledgments

We would like to thank Tim Walsh who is responsible for many of the interface design choices and for implementing the prototype system. This work is supported by NIH grant #5 R01 DC003670-06.

References

Alm, N., Morrison, A., & Arnott, J.L. (1995). A communication system based on scripts, plans, and goals for enabling non-speaking people to conduct telephone conversations. *In Proceedings of the IEEE International Conference on Systems, Man and Cybernetics.*

Alm, N., Neumann, H., & van Balkom, H. (2000). Scripts on an AAC system. In *Proceedings of CSUN 2000*, Northridge, CA.

Bedrosian, J. L., Hoag, L. A., & McCoy, K. F. (2003). Relevance and speed of message delivery trade-offs in augmentative and alternative communication. *Journal of Speech, Language, and Hearing Research, 46*, 800-817.

Beukelman, D. R., & Mirenda, P. (2005). *Augmentative and alternative communication: Supporting children and adults with complex communication needs (3rd ed.)*. Baltimore, MD: Paul H. Brookes Pub. Co.

Dye, R., Alm, N., Arnott, J. L., Murray, I.R., & Harper, G. (1998a). SrtipTalker - An AAC System Incorporating Scripts.In *Proceedings of the TIDE Congress (Technology for Inclusive Design and Equality).*

Dye, R., Alm, N., Arnott, J. L., Harper, G., & Morrison, A. (1998). A script-based AAC system for transactional interaction. *Natural Language Engineering, 4*, 57–71.

Grice, H. P. (1975). Logic and conversation. In P. Cole & J. Morgan (Eds.), *Syntax and semantics: Vol. 3 Speech acts* (pp.41-58). New York: Academic Press.

Higginbotham, D.J. & Lesher, G. (2005). The Frametalker Project: Building an Utterance-Based Communication Device. In Proceedings of CSUN Technology and Persons with Disabilities Conference.

Hoag, L., Bedrosian, J., & McCoy, K. (2007, November). *Effects of maxim violation degree on a hierarchy in AAC.* Poster presented at the American Speech-Language-Hearing Association Convention, Boston, MA.

Hoag, L. A., Bedrosian, J. L., McCoy, K. F., & Johnson, D. (2004). Informativeness and speed of message delivery trade-offs in augmentative and alternative communication. *Journal of Speech, Language, and Hearing Research, 47*, 1270-1285.

Hoag, L. A., Bedrosian, J. L., McCoy, K. F., & Johnson, D. E. (2008). Hierarchy of conversational rule violations involving utterance-based augmentative and alternative communication systems. *Augmentative and Alternative Communication, 24*, 149-161.

Langer, S. & Hickey, M. (1997). Automatic Message Indexing and Full Text Retrieval for a Communication Aid. In *Proceedings of Natural Language Processing For Communication Aids a Workshop Associated with ACL 1997*, Madrid, Spain.

McCoy, K. F., Bedrosian, J. L., Hoag, L. A., & Johnson, D. (2007). Brevity and speed of message delivery trade-offs in augmentative and alternative communication. *Augmentative and Alternative Communication, 23*, 76-88.

Schank, R. C., & Abelson, R. P. (1977). Scripts, plans, goals and understanding: An inquiry into human knowledge structures. Hillsdale, NJ: Erlbaum.

Schlosser, R. W. (1999). Comparative efficacy of interventions in augmentative and alternative communication. *Augmentative and Alternative Communication, 15,* 56-68.

Todman, J. (2000). Rate and quality of conversations using a text-storage AAC system: A training study. *Augmentative and Alternative Communication, 16*, 164-179.

Todman, J., & Alm, N. (1997). TALK Boards for social conversation. *Communication Matters, 11*, 13-15.

Todman, J., Alm, N., Higginbotham, J., & File, P. (2008). Whole utterance approaches in AAC. *Augmentative and Alternative Communication, 24,* 235-254.

Trnka, K., McCaw, J., Yarrington, D., McCoy, K.F. , & Pennington, C. (2009) User interaction with word prediction: The effects of prediction quality. *ACM Transactions on Accessible Computing (TACCESS), 1,*17-34.

Vanderheyden, P. B. (1995). Organization of pre-stored text in alternative and augmentative communication systems: An interactive schema-based approach. Technical Report #AAC9501, Applied Science and Engineering Laboratories, Wilmington, DE.

Vanderheyden, P.B., Demasco, P.W., McCoy, K.F., & Pennington, C.A. (1996). A preliminary study into Schema-based access and organization of reusable text in AAC. In Proceedings of RESNA '96 19th Annual Conference, June.

Wobbrock, J. & Myers, B. (2006). From letters to words: Efficient stroke-based word completion for trackball text entry. In Proceedings of the ACM SIGACCESS Conference on Computers and Accessibility (ASSETS), pp. 2

Scanning methods and language modeling for binary switch typing

Brian Roark[†], Jacques de Villiers[†], Christopher Gibbons[°] and Melanie Fried-Oken[°]
[†]Center for Spoken Language Understanding [°]Child Development & Rehabilitation Center
Oregon Health & Science University
{roark,jacques}@cslu.ogi.edu {gibbons,mfo}@ohsu.edu

Abstract

We present preliminary experiments of a binary-switch, static-grid typing interface making use of varying language model contributions. Our motivation is to quantify the degree to which language models can make the simplest scanning interfaces – such as showing one symbol at a time rather than a scanning a grid – competitive in terms of typing speed. We present a grid scanning method making use of optimal Huffman binary codes, and demonstrate the impact of higher order language models on its performance. We also investigate the scanning methods of highlighting just one cell in a grid at any given time or showing one symbol at a time without a grid, and show that they yield commensurate performance when using higher order n-gram models, mainly due to lower error rate and a lower rate of missed targets.

1 Introduction

Augmentative and Alternative Communication (AAC) is a well-defined subfield of assistive technology, focused on methods that assist individuals for whom conventional spoken or written communication approaches are difficult or impossible. Those who cannot make use of standard keyboards for text entry have a number of alternative text entry methods that permit typing. One of the most common of these alternative text entry methods is the use of a binary switch – triggered by button-press, eye-blink or even through event related potentials (ERP) such as the P300 detected in EEG signals – that allows the individual to make a selection based on some method for scanning through alternatives (Lesher et al., 1998). Typing speed is a challenge, yet critically important for usability. One common approach is row/column scanning on a matrix of characters, symbols or images (a 'spelling grid'), which allows the user of a binary yes/no switch to select the row and column of a target symbol, by simply indicating 'yes' (pressing a button or blinking an eye) when the row or column of the target symbol is highlighted. Figure 1 shows the 6×6 spelling grid used for the P300 Speller (Farwell and Donchin, 1988).

For any given scanning method, the use of a binary switch to select from among a set of options (letter, symbols, or images) amounts to the assignment of binary codes to each symbol. For example, the standard row/column scanning algorithm works by scanning each row until a selection is made, then scanning each column until a selection is made, and returning the symbol at the selected row and column. This can be formalized as follows:

```
for i = 1 to (# of rows) do
    HIGHLIGHTROW(i)
    if YESSWITCH
       for j = 1 to (# of columns) do
           HIGHLIGHTCOLUMN(j)
           if YESSWITCH
              return (i, j)
       return (i, 0)
return (0, 0)
```

where the function YESSWITCH returns *true* if the button is pressed (or whatever switch event counts as a 'yes' response) within the parameterized latency. If the function returns $(0, 0)$ then nothing has been selected, requiring rescanning. If the function returns $(i, 0)$ for $i > 0$, then row i has been selected, but columns must be rescanned. Under this scanning method, the binary code for the letter 'J' in the matrix in Figure 1 is 010001; the letter 'T' is 000101.

The length of the binary code for a symbol is re-

A	B	C	D	E	F
G	H	I	J	K	L
M	N	O	P	Q	R
S	T	U	V	W	X
Y	Z	1	2	3	4
5	6	7	8	9	_

Figure 1: Spelling grid such as that used for the P300 speller (Farwell and Donchin, 1988). '_' denotes space.

Proceedings of the NAACL HLT 2010 Workshop on Speech and Language Processing for Assistive Technologies, pages 28–36,
Los Angeles, California, June 2010.

lated to the time required to type it. In the matrix in Figure 1, the space character is in the bottom right-hand corner, yielding the maximum binary code length for that grid size (12), despite that, in typical written English we would expect the space character to be used about 20% of the time. A more efficient strategy would be to place the space character in the upper left-hand corner of the grid, leading to the much shorter binary code '11'.

Ordering symbols in a fixed grid so that frequent symbols are located in the upper left-hand corner is one method for making use of a statistical model of the language so that likely symbols receive the shortest codes. Such a language model, however, does not take into account what has already been typed, but rather assigns its code identically in all contexts. In this paper we examine alternative fixed-grid scanning methods that do take into account context in the language models used to establish codes, i.e., the codes in these methods vary in different contexts, so that high probability symbols receive the shortest codes and hence require the fewest keystrokes. We show that n-gram language models can provide a large improvement in typing speed.

Before presenting our methods and experimental results, we next provide further background on alternative text entry methods, language modeling, and binary coding based on language models.

2 Preliminaries and background

2.1 Alternative text entry

Of the ways in which AAC typing interfaces differ, perhaps most relevant to the current paper is whether the symbol positions are fixed or can move dynamically, because such dynamic layouts facilitate integration of richer language models. For example, if we re-calculate character probabilities after each typed character, then we could re-arrange the characters in the grid so that the most likely are placed in the upper left-hand corner for row/column scanning. Conventional wisdom, however, is that the cognitive overhead of processing a different grid arrangement after every character would slow down typing more than the speedup due to the improved binary coding (Baletsa et al., 1976; Lesher et al., 1998). The GazeTalk system (Hansen et al., 2003), which presents the user with a 3×4 grid and captures which cell the user's gaze fixates upon, is an instance of a dynamically changing grid. The cell layouts are configurable, but typically one cell contains a set of likely word completions; others are allocated to space and backspace; and around half of the cells are allocated to the most likely single character continuation of the input string, based on language model predictions. Hansen et al. (2003) report that users produced more words per minute with a static keyboard than with the predictive grid interface, illustrating the impact of the cognitive overhead that goes along with this sort of scanning.

The likely word completions in the GazeTalk system illustrates another common way in which language modeling is integrated into AAC typing systems. Much of the language modeling research within the context of AAC has been for word completion/prediction for keystroke reduction (Darragh et al., 1990; Li and Hirst, 2005; Trost et al., 2005; Trnka et al., 2006; Trnka et al., 2007; Wandmacher and Antoine, 2007). The typical scenario for this is allocating a region of the interface to contain a set of suggested words that complete what the user has begun typing. The expectation is to derive a keystroke savings when the user selects one of the alternatives rather than typing the rest of the letters. The cognitive load of monitoring a list of possible completions has made the claim that this speeds typing controversial (Anson et al., 2004); yet some results have shown this to speed typing under certain conditions (Trnka et al., 2007).

One innovative language-model-driven AAC typing interface is Dasher (Ward et al., 2002), which uses language models and arithmetic coding to present alternative letter targets on the screen with size relative to their likelihood given the history. Users can type by continuous motion, such as eye gaze or mouse cursor movement, targeting their cursor at the intended letter and moving the cursor from left-to-right through the interface, while its movements are tracked. This is an extremely effective typing interface alternative to keyboards, provided the user has sufficient motor control to perform the required systematic visual scanning. The most severely impaired users, such as those with locked-in syndrome (LIS), have lost the voluntary motor control sufficient for such an interface.

Relying on extensive visual scanning, such as that required in dynamically reconfiguring spelling grids or Dasher, or requiring complex gestural feedback from the user renders a typing interface difficult or impossible to use for those with the most severe impairments. Indeed, even spelling grids like the P300 speller can be taxing as an interface for users. Recent attempts to use the P300 speller as a typing interface for locked-in individuals with ALS found

```
1  A ← V            ▷ initialize A as symbol set V
2  k ← 1            ▷ initialize bit position k to 1
3  while |A| > 1 do
4        P ← {a ∈ A : a[k] = 1}
5        Q ← {a ∈ A : a[k] = 0}
6        Highlight symbols in P
7        if selected then A ← P
8        else A ← Q
9        k ← k + 1
10 return a ∈ A      ▷ Only 1 element in A
```

Figure 2: Algorithm for binary code symbol selection

that the number of items in the grid caused problems for these patients, because of difficulty orienting attention to specific locations in the spelling grid (Sellers et al., 2003). This is another illustration of the need to reduce the cognitive overhead of such interfaces. Yet the success of classification of ERP in a simpler task for this population indicates that the P300 is a binary response mechanism of utility for this task (Sellers and Donchin, 2006).

Simpler interactions via brain-computer interfaces (BCI) hold much promise for effective text communication. Yet these simple interfaces have yet to take full advantage of language models to ease or speed typing. In this paper we will make use of a static grid, or a single letter linear scanning interface, yet scan in a way that allows for the use of contextual language model probabilities when constructing the binary code for each symbol.

2.2 Binary codes for typing interfaces

Row/column scanning, as outlined in the previous section, is not the only means by which the spelling grid in Figure 1 can be used as a binary response typing interface. Rather than highlighting full rows or full columns, arbitrary subsets of letters could be highlighted, and letter selection again driven by a binary response mechanism. An algorithm to do this is as follows. Assign a unique binary code to each symbol in the symbol set V (letters in this case). For each symbol $a \in V$, there are $|a|$ bits in the code representing the letter. Let $a[k]$ be the kth bit of the code for symbol a. We will assume that no symbol's binary code is a prefix of another symbol's binary code. Given such an assignment of binary codes to the symbol set V, the algorithm in Figure 2 can be used to select the target symbol in a spelling grid.

One key question in this paper is how to produce such a binary code, which is how language models can be included in scanning. Figure 3 shows two different binary trees, which yield different binary codes for six letters in a simple, artificial example.

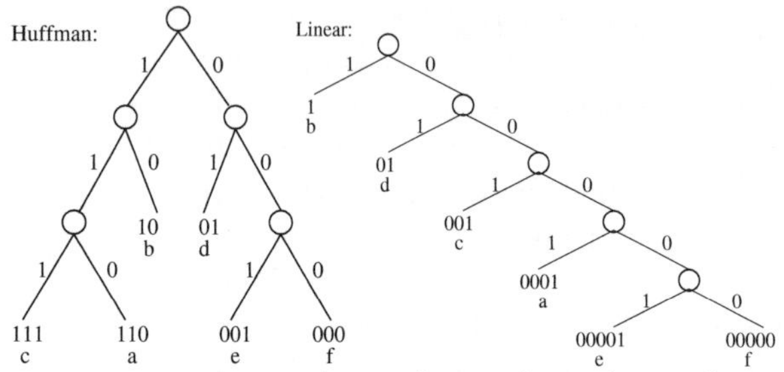

Letter:	a	b	c	d	e	f
Probability:	0.15	0.25	0.18	0.2	0.12	0.1
Huffman bits:	3	2	3	2	3	3
Linear bits:	4	1	3	2	5	5

Figure 3: Two binary trees for encoding letters based on letter probabilities: (1) Huffman coding; and (2) Linear coding via a right-branching tree (right-linear). Expected bits are 2.55 for Huffman and 2.89 for linear coding.

Huffman coding (Huffman, 1952) builds a binary tree that minimizes the expected number of bits according to the provided distribution. There is a linear complexity algorithm for building this tree given a list of items sorted by descending probability.

Another type of binary code, which we will call a linear code, provides a lot of flexibility in the kind of interface that it allows, relative to the other methods mentioned above. In this binary code, each iteration of the WHILE loop in the Figure 2 algorithm would have a set P on line 4 with exactly one member. With such a code, the spelling grid in Figure 1 would highlight exactly one letter at a time for selection. Alternately, symbols could be presented one at a time with no grid, which we call rapid serial visual presentation (RSVP, see Fig.7). Linear coding builds a simple right-linear tree (seen in Figure 3) that preserves the sorted order of the set, putting higher probability symbols closer to the root of the tree, thus obtaining shorter binary codes. Linear coding can never produce codes with fewer expected bits than Huffman coding, though the linear code may reach the minimum under certain conditions.

The simplicity of an interface that presents a single letter at a time may reduce user fatigue, and even make typing feasible for users that cannot maintain focus on a spelling grid. Additionally, single symbol auditory presentation would be possible, for visually impaired individuals, something that is not straightforwardly feasible with the sets of symbols that must be presented when using Huffman codes.

2.3 Language modeling for typing interfaces

The current task is very similar to word prediction work discussed in Section 2.1, except that the prediction interface is the only means by which text is input, rather than a separate window with completions being provided. In principle, the symbols that are being predicted (hence typed) can be from a vocabulary that includes multiple symbol strings such as words. However, a key requirement in a composition-based typing interface is an **open vocabulary** – the user should be able to type any word, whether or not it is in some fixed vocabulary. Included in such a mechanism is the ability to repair: delete symbols and re-type new ones. In contrast, a word prediction component must be accompanied by some additional mechanism in place for typing words not in the vocabulary. The current problem is to use symbol prediction for that core typing interface, and this paper will focus on predicting single ASCII and control characters, rather than multiple character strings. The task is actually very similar to the well known Shannon game (Shannon, 1950), where text is guessed one character at a time.

Character prediction is done in the Dasher and GazeTalk interfaces, as discussed in an earlier section. There is also a letter prediction component to the Sibyl/Sibylle interfaces (Schadle, 2004; Wandmacher et al., 2008), alongside a separate word prediction component. Interestingly, the letter prediction component of Sibylle (Sibyletter) involves a linear scan of the letters, one at a time in order of probability (as determined by a 5-gram character language model), rather than a row/column scanning of the P300 speller. This approach was based on user feedback that the row/column scanning was a much more tiring interface than the linear scan interface (Wandmacher et al., 2008), which is consistent with the results previously discussed on the difficulty of ALS individuals with the P300 speller interface.

Language modeling for a typing interface task of this sort is very different from other common language modeling tasks. This is because, at each symbol in the string, the already typed prefix string is given – there is no ambiguity in the prefix string, modulo subsequent repairs. In contrast, in speech recognition, machine translation, optical character recognition or T9 style text input, the actual prefix string is not known; rather, there is a distribution over possible prefix strings, and a global inference procedure is required to find the best string as a whole. For typing, once the symbol has been produced and not repaired, the model predicting the next symbol is given the true context. This has several important ramifications for language modeling, including the availability of supervised adaptation data and the fact that the models trained with relative frequency estimation are both generative and discriminative. See Roark (2009) for extensive discussion of these issues. Here we will consider n-gram language models of various orders, estimated via smoothed relative frequency estimation (see § 3.1). The principal novelty in the current approach is the principled incorporation of error probabilities into the binary coding approaches, and the experimental demonstration of how linear coding for grids or RSVP interfaces compare to Huffman coding and row/column scanning for grids.

3 Methods

3.1 Character-based language models

For this paper, we use character n-gram models. Carpenter (2005) has an extensive comparison of large scale character-based language models, and we adopt smoothing methods from that paper. It presents a version of Witten-Bell smoothing (Witten and Bell, 1991) with an optimized hyperparameter K, which is shown to be as effective as Kneser-Ney smoothing (Kneser and Ney, 1995) for higher order n-grams. We refer readers to that paper for details on this standard n-gram language modeling approach. For the experimental results presented here, we trained unigram and 8-gram models from the NY Times portion of the English Gigaword corpus.

We performed extensive normalization of this corpus, detailed in Roark (2009). We de-cased the resulting corpus and selected sentences that only included characters that would appear in our 6×6 spelling grid. Those characters are: the 26 letters of the English alphabet, the space character, a delete symbol, comma, period, double and single quote, dash, dollar sign, colon and semi-colon. We used a 42 million character subset of this corpus for training the model. Finally, we appended to this corpus approximately 112 thousand words from the CMU Pronouncing Dictionary (`www.speech.cs.cmu.edu/cgi-bin/cmudict`), which also contained only the symbols from the grid. For hyper-parameter settings, we used a 100k character development set. Our best performing hyper-parameter for the Witten-Bell smoothing was $K = 15$, which is comparable to optimal settings found by Carpenter (2005) for 12-grams.

3.2 Binary codes

Given what has been typed so far, we can use a character n-gram language model to assign probabilities

Figure 4: Row/column scanning interface.

Figure 5: Error in row/column scanning interface.

to all next symbols in the symbol set V. After sorting the set in order of decreasing probability, we can use these probabilities to build binary coding trees for the set. Hence the binary code assigned to each symbol in the symbol set differs depending on what has been typed before. For Huffman coding, we used the algorithm from Perelmouter and Birbaumer (2000) that accounts for any probability of error in following a branch of the tree, and builds the optimal coding tree even when there is non-zero probability of taking a branch in error. Either linear or Huffman codes can be built from the language model probabilities, and can then be used for a typing interface, using the algorithm presented in Figure 2.

3.3 Scanning systems

For these experiments, we developed an interface for controlled testing of typing performance under a range of scanning methods. These include: (i) row/column scanning, both auto scan (button press selects) and step scan (lack of button press selects); (ii) Scanning with a Huffman code, either derived from a unigram language model, or from an 8-gram language model; and (iii) Scanning with a linear code, either on the 6×6 grid, or using RSVP, which shows one symbol at a time. Each trial involved giving subjects a target phrase with instructions to type the phrase exactly as displayed. All errors in typing were required to be corrected by deleting (via ←) the incorrect symbol and re-typing the correct symbol.

Figure 4 shows our typing interface when configured for row/column scanning. At the top of the application window is the target string to be typed by the subject ('we run the risk of failure'). Below that is the buffer displaying what has already been typed ('we run t'). Spaces between words must also be typed – they are represented by the underscore character in the upper left-hand corner of the grid. Spaces are treated like any other symbol in our language model – they must be typed, thus they are predicted along with the other symbols. Figure 5 shows how the display updates when an incorrect character is typed. The errors are highlighted in red, followed by the backarrow symbol to remind users to delete.

If a row has not been selected after a pass over all rows, scanning begins again at the top. After row selection, column scanning commences; if a column is not selected after three passes from left-to-right over the columns, then row scanning re-commences at the following row. Hence, even if a wrong row is selected, the correct symbol can still be typed.

Note that the spelling grid has been sorted in unigram frequency order, so that the most frequent symbols are in the upper left-hand corner. This same grid is used in all grid scanning conditions, and provides language modeling benefit to row/column scanning.

Figure 6 shows our typing interface when configured for what we term Huffman scanning. In this scanning mode, the highlighted subset is dictated by the Huffman code, and is not necessarily contiguous. Not requiring contiguity of highlighted symbols allows the coding to vary with the context, thus allowing use of an n-gram language model. As far as we know, this is the first time that contiguity of highlighting is relaxed in a scanning interface to accommodate Huffman coding. Baljko and Tam (2006) used Huffman coding for a grid scanning interface, but using a unigram model and the grid layout was selected to ensure that highlighted regions would always be contiguous, thus precluding n-gram models.

In our Huffman scanning approach, when the selected set includes just one character, it is typed. As with row/column scanning, when the wrong character is typed, the backarrow symbol must be chosen to delete it. If an error is made in selection that does not result in a typed character – i.e., if the incorrectly selected set has more than one member – then we need some mechanism for allowing the target symbol to still be selected, much as we have a mecha-

Figure 6: Huffman scanning interface.

Figure 7: RSVP scanning interface.

nism in row/column scanning for recovering if the wrong row is selected. Section 3.4 details our novel method for recalculating the binary codes based on an error rate parameter. At no point in typing is any character ruled out from being selected.

The grids shown in Figures 4-6 can be straightforwardly used with linear coding as well, by simply highlighting one cell at a time in descending probability order. Additionally, linear coding can be used with an RSVP interface, shown in Figure 7, which displays one character at a time.

Each interface needs a scan rate, specifying how long to wait for a button press before advancing. The scan rate for each condition was set for each individual during a training/calibration session (see §4.1).

3.4 Errors in Huffman and Linear scanning

In this section we briefly detail how we account for the probability of error in scanning with Huffman and linear codes. The scanning interface takes a parameter p, which is the probability that, when a selection is made, it is correct. Thus $1-p$ is the probability of an error. Recall that if a selection leads to a single symbol, then that symbol is typed. Otherwise, if a selection leads to a set with more than one symbol, then *all* symbol probabilities (even those not in the selected set) are updated based on the error probability and scanning continues. If a non-target (incorrect) symbol is selected, the delete (backarrow) symbol must be chosen to correct the error, after which the typing interface returns to the previous position. Three key questions must be answered in such an approach: (1) how are symbol probabilities updated after a keystroke, to reflect the probability of error? (2) how is the probability of backarrow estimated? and (3) when the typing interface returns to the previous position, where does it pick up the scanning? Here we answer all three questions.

Consider the Huffman coding tree in Figure 3. If the left-branch ('1') is selected by the user, the probability that it was intended is p versus an error with probability $1-p$. If the original probability of a symbol is q, then the updated probability of the symbol is pq if it starts with a '1' and $(1-p)q$ if it starts with a '0'. After updating the scores and re-normalizing over the whole set, we can build a new binary coding tree. The user then selects a branch at the **root** of the new tree. A symbol is finally selected when the user selects a branch leading to a single symbol. The same approach is used with a linear coding tree.

The probability of requiring the delete (backarrow) character can be calculated directly from the probability of keystroke error – in fact, the probability of backarrow is exactly the probability of error $1-p$. To understand why this is the case, consider that a non-target (incorrect) symbol can be chosen according to the approach in the previous paragraph only with a final keystroke error. Any keystroke error that does not select a single symbol does not eliminate the target symbol, it merely re-adjusts the target symbol's probability along with all other symbols. Hence, no matter how many keystrokes have been made, the probability that a selected symbol was not the target symbol is simply the probability that the last keystroke was in error, i.e., $1-p$.

Finally, if backarrow is selected, the previous position is revisited, and the probabilities are reset as though no prior selection had been made.

4 Empirical results

4.1 Subjects and scan rate calibration

We recruited 10 native English speakers between the ages of 24 and 48 years, who had not used our typing interface, are not users of scanning interfaces for typing, and have typical motor function. Each subject participated in two sessions, one for training and calibration of scan rates; and another for testing. We use the phrase set from MacKenzie and Soukoreff (2003) to evaluate typing performance. Of the 500 phrases in that set, 20 were randomly set aside for testing, the other 480 available during training and calibration phases. Five of the 20 evaluation strings were used in this study. We used an Ablenet Jellybean® button as the binary switch. For these trials, to estimate error rates in modeling, we fixed $p = 0.95$, i.e., 5% error rate.

The scan rate for row/column scanning is typically different than for Huffman or linear scanning, since row/column scanning methods allow for anticipation: one can tell from the current highlighting whether the desired row or column will be highlighted next. For the Huffman and linear scanning approaches that we are investigating, that is not the case: any cell can be highlighted (or symbol displayed) at any time, even multiple times in a row. Hence the scan rate for these methods depends more on reaction time than row/column scanning, where anticipation allows for faster rates.

The scan rate also differs between the two row/column scanning approaches (auto scan and step scan), due to the differences in control needed to advance scanning with a button press versus selecting with a button press. We thus ran scan rate calibration under three conditions: row/column step scan; row/column auto scan; and Huffman scanning, using a unigram language model. The Huffman scanning scan rate was then used for all of the Huffman and linear scanning approaches.

Calibration involved two stages for each of the three approaches, and the first stage of all three is completed before running the second stage, thus familiarizing subjects with all interfaces prior to final calibration. The first stage of calibration starts with slow scan rate (1200 ms dwell time), then speeds up the scan rate by reducing dwell time by 200 ms when a target string is successfully typed. Success here means that the string is correctly typed with less than 10% error rate. The subject gets three tries to type a string successfully at a given scan rate, after which they are judged to not be able to complete the task at that rate. In the first stage, this stops the stage for that method and the dwell time is recorded. In the second stage, calibration starts at a dwell time 500 ms higher than where the subject failed in the first stage, and the dwell time decreases by 100 ms increments when target strings are successfully typed. When subjects cannot complete the task at a dwell time, the dwell time then increases at 50 ms increments until they can successfully type a target string.

Table 1 shows the mean (and std) scan rates (dwell time) for each condition. Step scanning generally had a slower scan rate than auto scanning, and Huffman scanning (unsurprisingly) was slowest.

4.2 Testing stage and results

In the testing stage of the protocol, there were six conditions: (1) row/column step scan; (2) row/column auto scan; (3) Huffman scanning with codes derived from the unigram language model; (4) Huffman scanning with codes derived from the 8-gram language model; (5) Linear scanning on the 6×6 spelling grid with codes derived from the 8-gram language model; and (6) RSVP single letter presentation with codes derived from the 8-gram language model. The ordering of the conditions for each subject was randomized. In each condition, instructions were given (identical to instructions during calibration phase), and the subjects typed practice phrases until they successfully reached error rate criterion performance (10% error rate or lower), at which point they were given the test phrases to type.

Recall that the task is to type the stimulus phrase exactly as presented, hence the task is not complete until the phrase has been correctly typed. To avoid non-termination scenarios – e.g., the subject does not recognize that an error has occurred, what the error is, or simply cannot recover from cascading errors – the trial is stopped if the total errors in typing the target phrase reach 20, and the subject is presented with the same target phrase to type again from the beginning, i.e., the example is reset. Only 2 subjects in the experiment had a phrase reset in this way (just one phrase each), both in row/column scanning conditions. Of course, the time and keystrokes spent typing prior to reset are included in the statistics of the condition.

Table 1 shows the mean (and std) of several measures for the 10 subjects. Speed is reported in characters per minute. Bits per character represents the number of keypress and non-keypress (timeout) events that were used to type the symbol. Note that bits per character does not correlate perfectly with speed, since a non-keypress bit due to a timeout takes the full dwell time, while the time for a keypress event may be less than that full time. For any given symbol the bits may involve making an error, followed by deleting the erroneous symbol and retyping the correct symbol. Alternately, the subject may scan pass the target symbol, but still return to type it correctly, resulting in extra keystrokes, i.e., a longer binary code than optimal. In addition to the mean and standard deviation of bits per character, we present the optimal could be achieved with each method. Finally we characterize the errors that are made by subjects by the error rate, which is the num-

Scanning condition		Scan rate (ms) mean (std)	Speed (cpm) mean (std)	Bits per character mean (std)	opt.	Error rate mean (std)	Long code rate mean (std)
row/column	step scan	425 (116)	20.7 (3.6)	8.5 (2.6)	4.5	6.3 (5.1)	29.9 (19.0)
	auto scan	310 (70)	19.1 (2.2)	8.4 (1.2)	4.5	5.4 (2.8)	33.8 (11.5)
Huffman	unigram	475 (68)	12.5 (2.3)	8.4 (1.9)	4.4	4.4 (2.2)	39.2 (13.5)
	8-gram	475 (68)	23.4 (3.7)	4.3 (1.1)	2.6	4.1 (2.2)	19.3 (14.2)
Linear grid	8-gram	475 (68)	23.2 (2.1)	4.2 (0.7)	3.4	2.4 (1.5)	5.0 (4.1)
RSVP	8-gram	475 (68)	20.3 (5.1)	6.1 (2.6)	3.4	7.7 (5.4)	5.2 (4.0)

Table 1: Typing results for 10 users on 5 test strings (total 31 words, 145 characters) under six conditions.

ber of incorrect symbols typed divided by the total symbols typed. The long code rate is the percentage of correctly typed symbols for which a longer than optimal code was used to type the symbol, by making an erroneous selection that does not result in typing the wrong symbol.

We also included a short survey, using a Likert scale for responses, and mean scores are shown in Table 2 for four questions: 1) I was fatigued by the end of the trial; 2) I was stressed by the end of the trial; 3) I liked this trial; and 4) I was frustrated by this trial. The responses showed a consistent preference for Huffman and linear grid conditions with an 8-gram language model over the other conditions.

Survey Question	Row/Column step	auto	Huffman 1-grm	8-grm	Linear grid	RSVP
Fatigued	3.2	2.4	3.6	2.0	2.4	2.8
Stressed	2.7	2.4	2.7	1.5	1.8	2.6
Liked it	2.2	3.3	2.3	4.2	3.8	3.2
Frustrated	3.2	1.7	3.1	1.7	1.7	2.3

Table 2: Mean Likert scores to survey questions (5 = strongly agree; 1 = strongly disagree)

4.3 Discussion of results

While this is a preliminary study of just 10 subjects, several things stand out from the results. First, comparing the three methods using just unigram frequencies to inform scanning (row/column and Huffman unigram), we can see that Huffman unigram scanning is significantly slower than the other two, mainly due to a slower scan rate with no real improvement in bits per character (real or optimal). All three methods have a high rate of longer than optimal codes, leading to nearly double the bits per character that would optimally be required.

Next, with the use of the 8-gram language model in Huffman scanning, both the optimal bits per character and the difference between real and optimal are reduced, leading to nearly double the speed. Interestingly, use of the linear code on the grid leads to fewer bits per character than Huffman scanning, despite nearly 1 bit increase in optimal bits per character, due to a decrease in error rate and a very large decrease in long code rate. We speculate that this is because highlighting a single cell at a time draws the eye to that cell, making visual scanning easier.

Finally, despite using the same model, RSVP is found to be slightly slower than the Huffman 8-gram or Linear grid conditions, though commensurate with the row/column scanning, mainly due to an increase in error rate. Monitoring a single cell, recognizing symbol identity and pressing the switch is apparently somewhat harder than finding the symbol on a grid and waiting for the cell to light up.

5 Summary and future directions

We have presented methods for including language modeling in simple scanning interfaces for typing, and evaluated performance of novice subjects with typical motor control. We found that language modeling can make a very large difference in the usability of the Huffman scanning condition. We also found that, despite losing bits to optimal Huffman coding, linear coding leads to commensurate typing speed versus Huffman coding presumably due to lower cognitive overhead of scanning and thus fewer mistakes. Finally, we found that RSVP was somewhat slower than grid scanning with the same language model and code.

This research is part of a program to make the simplest scanning approaches as efficient as possible, so as to facilitate the use of binary switches for individuals with the most severe impairments, including ERP for locked-in subjects. While our subjects in this study have shown slightly better performance using a grid versus RSVP, these individuals have no problem with visual scanning or fixation on relatively small cells in the grid. It is encouraging that subjects can achieve nearly the same performance with an interface that simply displays an option and requests a yes or a no. We intend to run this study with subjects with impairment, and are incorporating the interfaces with an ERP detection system for use as a brain-computer interface.

Acknowledgments

This research was supported in part by NIH Grant #1R01DC009834-01 and NSF Grant #IIS-0447214. Any opinions, findings, conclusions or recommendations expressed in this publication are those of the authors and do not necessarily reflect the views of the NSF or NIH.

References

D. Anson, P. Moist, M. Przywars, H. Wells, H. Saylor, and H. Maxime. 2004. The effects of word completion and word prediction on typing rates using on-screen keyboards. *Assistive Technology*, 18(2):146–154.

G. Baletsa, R. Foulds, and W. Crochetiere. 1976. Design parameters of an intelligent communication device. In *Proceedings of the 29th Annual Conference on Engineering in Medicine and Biology*, page 371.

M. Baljko and A. Tam. 2006. Indirect text entry using one or two keys. In *Proceedings of the Eigth International ACM Conference on Assistive Technologies (ASSETS)*, pages 18–25.

B. Carpenter. 2005. Scaling high-order character language models to gigabytes. In *Proceedings of the ACL Workshop on Software*, pages 86–99.

J.J. Darragh, I.H. Witten, and M.L. James. 1990. The reactive keyboard: A predictive typing aid. *Computer*, 23(11):41–49.

L.A. Farwell and E. Donchin. 1988. Talking off the top of your head: toward a mental prosthesis utilizing event-related brain potentials. *Electroenceph Clin. Neurophysiol.*, 70:510–523.

J.P. Hansen, A.S. Johansen, D.W. Hansen, K. Itoh, and S. Mashino. 2003. Language technology in a predictive, restricted on-screen keyboard with ambiguous layout for severely disabled people. In *Proceedings of EACL Workshop on Language Modeling for Text Entry Methods*.

D.A. Huffman. 1952. A method for the construction of minimum redundancy codes. In *Proceedings of the IRE*, volume 40(9), pages 1098–1101.

R. Kneser and H. Ney. 1995. Improved backing-off for m-gram language modeling. In *Proceedings of the IEEE International Conference on Acoustics, Speech, and Signal Processing (ICASSP)*, pages 181–184.

G.W. Lesher, B.J. Moulton, and D.J. Higginbotham. 1998. Techniques for augmenting scanning communication. *Augmentative and Alternative Communication*, 14:81–101.

J. Li and G. Hirst. 2005. Semantic knowledge in word completion. In *Proceedings of the 7th International ACM Conference on Computers and Accessibility*.

I.S. MacKenzie and R.W. Soukoreff. 2003. Phrase sets for evaluating text entry techniques. In *Proceedings of the ACM Conference on Human Factors in Computing Systems (CHI)*, pages 754–755.

J. Perelmouter and N. Birbaumer. 2000. A binary spelling interface with random errors. *IEEE Transactions on Rehabilitation Engineering*, 8(2):227–232.

B. Roark. 2009. Open vocabulary language modeling for binary response typing interfaces. Technical Report #CSLU-09-001, Center for Spoken Language Processing, Oregon Health & Science University. `cslu.ogi.edu/publications/ps/roark09.pdf`.

I. Schadle. 2004. Sibyl: AAC system using NLP techniques. In *Proceedings of the 9th International Conference on Computers Helping People with Special needs (ICCHP)*, pages 1109–1015.

E.W. Sellers and E. Donchin. 2006. A p300-based brain-computer interface: initial tests by als patients. *Clinical Neuropsysiology*, 117:538–548.

E.W. Sellers, G. Schalk, and E. Donchin. 2003. The p300 as a typing tool: tests of brain-computer interface with an als patient. *Psychophysiology*, 40:77.

C.E. Shannon. 1950. Prediction and entropy of printed English. *Bell System Technical Journal*, 30:50–64.

K. Trnka, D. Yarrington, K.F. McCoy, and C. Pennington. 2006. Topic modeling in fringe word prediction for AAC. In *Proceedings of the International Conference on Intelligent User Interfaces*, pages 276–278.

K. Trnka, D. Yarrington, J. McCaw, K.F. McCoy, and C. Pennington. 2007. The effects of word prediction on communication rate for AAC. In *Proceedings of HLT-NAACL; Companion Volume, Short Papers*, pages 173–176.

H. Trost, J. Matiasek, and M. Baroni. 2005. The language component of the FASTY text prediction system. *Applied Artificial Intelligence*, 19(8):743–781.

T. Wandmacher and J.Y. Antoine. 2007. Methods to integrate a language model with semantic information for a word prediction component. In *Proceedings of the Conference on Empirical Methods in Natural Language Processing (EMNLP)*, pages 506–513.

T. Wandmacher, J.Y. Antoine, F. Poirier, and J.P. Departe. 2008. Sibylle, an assistive communication system adapting to the context and its user. *ACM Transactions on Accessible Computing (TACCESS)*, 1(1):6:1–30.

D.J. Ward, A.F. Blackwell, and D.J.C. MacKay. 2002. DASHER – a data entry interface using continuous gestures and language models. *Human-Computer Interaction*, 17(2-3):199–228.

I.H. Witten and T.C. Bell. 1991. The zero-frequency problem: Estimating the probabilities of novel events in adaptive text compression. *IEEE Transactions on Information Theory*, 37(4):1085–1094.

A Platform for Automated Acoustic Analysis for Assistive Technology

Suzanne Boyce
Department of Communication Sciences and Disorders
University of Cincinnati
Cincinnati, Ohio, 45267, USA
boycese@ucmail.uc.edu

Harriet Fell
College of Computer and Information Science
Northeastern University
Boston, Massachusetts, 02115, USA
fell@ccs.neu.edu

Joel MacAuslan
Speech Technology and Applied Research
54 Middlesex Turnpike
Bedford, Massachusetts, , USA
joelm@staranalyticalservices.com

Lorin Wilde
Boston University

Boston, Massachusetts, 02180, USA
wildercom@gmail.com

Abstract

The use of speech production data has been limited by a steep learning curve and the need for laborious hand measurement. We are building a tool set that provides summary statistics for measures designed by clinicians to screen, diagnose or provide training to assistive technology users. This will be achieved by extending an existing shareware software platform with "plug-ins" that perform specific measures and report results to the user. The common underlying basis for this tool set is a Stevens' paradigm of landmarks, points in an utterance around which information about articulatory events can be extracted.

1 Introduction

To date, the use of speech production data has been limited by a steep learning curve and the need for laborious hand measurement. Many speech-related studies result in voluminous acoustic data. Many clinicians who design and use assistive technology would like to incorporate acoustic analysis, but have been discouraged because of these technical challenges. We are in the process of developing a set of tools that considerably streamlines the process of analyzing speech production details.

We are building a tool set to provide summary statistics for measures designed by clinicians to screen, diagnose or provide training to patients. This will be achieved by extending an existing shareware software platform with "plug-ins" that perform specific measures and report results to the user. At present, our goal is to use the existing shareware software tool Wavesurfer (Wavesurfer, 2005). The new modules will be set up to report data from a single audio file, or groups of audio files in a standard table format, for easy input to statistical or other analysis software. For example, the data may be imported into a program that correlates speech data with scalp electrode and medication data.

Our tool will include alternative and independently tested algorithms for clinically relevant measures, as well as guidance as to what the speech data may mean.

The common underlying basis for this tool set is a focused set of landmarks derived from Stevens' Lexical Access from Features (LAFF) paradigm (Stevens, 1992, 2002; Liu, 1995; Slifka et al., 2004). In this approach, landmarks are points in an utterance around which information about articulatory events can be extracted.

Proceedings of the NAACL HLT 2010 Workshop on Speech and Language Processing for Assistive Technologies, pages 37–43,
Los Angeles, California, June 2010.

In what follows, we will describe (1) the theoretical rationale of landmarks, (2) the general utility of landmark processing and several examples of clinically related measures, and (3) our current work on developing tools to make landmark analysis more widely available.

2 Landmarks reflect articulation

Landmark analysis is based on the fact that different sounds produce different patterns of abrupt changes in the acoustic signal simultaneously across wide frequency ranges. For instance, the abrupt increase in amplitude for a broad range of frequencies above 3 kHz can be used to indicate the onset of bursts. Likewise, an abrupt decrease in the same frequency bands can be used to indicate the end of frication. The use of onset and offset data in other frequency bands can be used to indicate sonorancy; i.e., intervals when the oral cavity is relatively unconstricted. Examples based on Liu [1995] are listed below.

g(lottis): marks the onset (+g) or offset (-g) of voicing.

s(yllabicity): marks the onset (+s) or offset (-s) of syllabicity, i.e. onsets and releases of voiced sonorant consonants such as /l/ or /r/, vocal tract closures due to voiced stop consonants such as /b/ or /d/.

b(urst): marks the onset (+b) of the burst of air following stop or affricate consonant release, or the onset of frication noise for fricative consonants. Offsets (-b) mark points where aspiration or frication noise ends abruptly due to a stop closure.

V(owel): marks points of peak amplitude in a sonorant region—that is, a region where voicing is evident [Howitt, 2000].

Although much of the past work using landmark processing has been focused on employing a wide variety of landmarks to recognize the lexical content of speech [Juneja and Espy-Wilson 2003, Slifka, *et al.* 2004], the power of these measures is even more apparent when applied to non-lexical attributes.

3 Applications of Landmark Analysis to Assistive Technology

3.1 Tracking Articulatory Precision

Measuring articulatory precision is important to evaluating efficacy of a treatment or in monitoring disease progression, e.g. in Parkinson's disease.

Given that landmarks reflect articulation, tools based on landmarks may be useful for measuring and monitoring articulatory precision [Boyce *et al.* 2005, 2007]. The technique relies on setting empirically derived thresholds for the detection of abrupt acoustic changes in specified frequency bands. Recall that changes in the acoustic signal occur simultaneously across wide frequency ranges. When the onset of energy does not exceed threshold in a particular frequency band, i.e., not quite abrupt enough to trigger the detection of a landmark, then no landmark may be assigned. However, since different sounds produce different patterns, changes detected in other bands at that point in time are either a) assigned to a different landmark, or b) considered to be extraneous. Thus, small acoustic differences in the way speech is produced can be tracked as different patterns of landmarks.

In addition to requirements that a tool for general clinical use must be fast and robust, it must be able to handle a wide variety of speaking styles, dialects, and voices. By focusing on landmarks that specify syllable structure and broad phoneme classes, distinctive differences between phonemes can be ignored. Therefore, the tool is less likely to break down due to problems recognizing specific vocabulary while remaining sensitive to changes in the acoustic signal that reflect articulatory precision of speech.

3.2 Evaluating phonological complexity

Development of speech in early infancy includes the ability to produce increasingly complex phonological structure. Patterns of syllable structure in speech output can be tracked using landmarks, again without reference to specific phonemes or words. In Fell *et al.* [2002], landmarks were grouped into standard syllable patterns and syllables were grouped into utterances. Statistics based on these patterns were then reported to the clinician for various uses in training, screening or diagnosis. Patterns of syllable complexity were used to compute a "vocalization age." This was used in turn to derive screening rules that clinically distinguish infants who may be at risk for later communication or other developmental problems from typically developing infants.

3.3 Measuring and Evaluating "Clear Speech"

"Clear Speech" is an intelligibility-enhancing style of speech that is used to improve communication outcomes. Listeners with hearing impairment derive significant benefit from being addressed with clearly articulated speech. Speech that is more clearly articulated contains more abrupt acoustic changes. The result is that speech with different levels of intelligibility shows different numbers and combinations of landmarks [Boyce *et al.* 2005, 2007].

3.4 Other Applications

In the UCARE project [1995], Cress reported analyzing 40 hours of pre-existing [2005] videotaped sessions of children with physical or neurological impairments using landmark-based tools.

Fell et al. [2004] reported using landmark analysis to follow the progress of several children with severe speech delays. In this project, 10-minute, inhome audio recordings were processed in real-time on a 2002-era PC laptop.

Wade and Möbius [2007] used automated landmark analysis to study speaking rate effects as a measure of disease progression in Parkinson's disease.

DiCicco and Patel [2008] used automatic landmark analysis on dysarthric speech. This study provides quantitative support for the hypothesis [Deller 1991] that dysarthric speech includes erroneous additional acoustic cues, not only malformed or missing ones.

4 Potential Benefits of Landmark Applications

In a small study, Warner-Czyz and Davis [2010] compared consonant–vowel syllable accuracy in early words of children with normal hearing and children with hearing loss who received cochlear implantation. They found and evaluated, via manual coding, approximately 4000 syllables from 48 hours of recordings. This is a project where automatic landmark analysis might have greatly reduced the effort.

Similarly, in a study on tongue-twisters, Matthew Goldrick (Northwestern University) collected 100 hours of data comprising 20,000 tokens in less than three weeks, but found that it required another 600 hours merely to segment and label the data for further analysis. In personal correspondence about another study on single words, he stated:

> A major 'choke point' for speech production research is the need to manually analyze speech data. Given that many thousands of data points are typically required to gain accurate estimates of probability density functions along phonetic dimensions, hundreds of person-hours are typically required to analyze data from a single simple experiment.... If we could gain access to reliable, highly accurate automated tools, we could change the speed of research by an order of magnitude.

Researchers who currently want to use speech analysis as a tool must accept long periods of hand measurements. This discourages researchers who may be more interested in a particular neurological disease or process than in speech research *per se.* It is notoriously difficult to quantify projects not undertaken, or papers not written, but it is telling that, although each of the studies cited above reported positive results from a study of speech articulation, they exist as relative islands in their respective disciplines. We contend that this situation exists largely because of barriers to entry; that is, we believe that many scientists would like to use speech assessment as part of their research, but elect not to do for lack of a convenient tool. The existence of a convenient tool to detect, measure and track subtle changes in speech articulation would constitute an enabling technology.

5 Tools

5.1 Description

In our own work, we have developed an automatic tool for detecting, counting and analyzing acoustic events in the speech signal that are commonly used by scientists to measure differences in speech articulation.

We are now integrating our system with Wavesurfer for certain researchers (linguists, speech-language pathologists, certain engineering and cognitive-science researchers) with a primary interest in inspecting and interpreting the articulation-related features in the waveforms of a corpus: e.g., the placement of landmarks of each type, patterns of clustering, or identification of non-speech sounds to be excised. (See Figure 1).)

For this version, we are implementing user controls ("widgets") to produce automated measures or types of analyses for speech research such as:

- Voice-onset time, VOT.
- Detection of non-harmonic (and harmonic) voicing.
- Identification and suppression or removal of stray sounds, i.e., non-speech.
- Grouping of landmarks into syllable-like clusters.

(Note that Wavesurfer already provides a general pitch-tracking capability for harmonic voicing.)

The Wavesurfer plug-in will also allow the user to output information about an audio file or a directory of audio files, e.g. all the recordings of a child. This information will be in a tab-delimited text file or a spreadsheet. This will allow the speech scientist

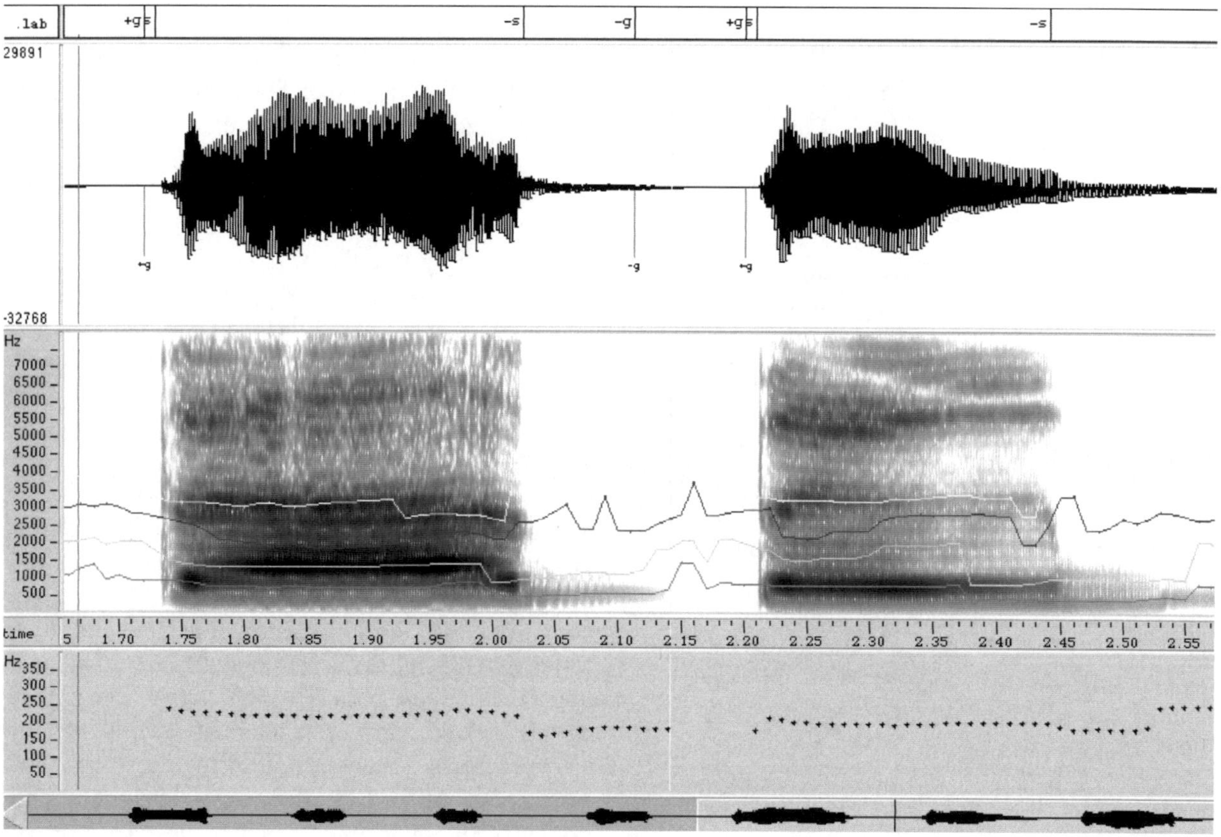

Figure 1: Wavesurfer with landmarks/waveform pane filtered to show only +/-g landmarks, and transcription pane (top) with +/-g and +/-s landmarks

This information will be in a tab-delimited text file or a spreadsheet. This will allow the speech scientist to analyze the output and, for example, to summarize and compare the typically developing children to those diagnosed with autism.

5.2 User Testing

We are currently recruiting potential users to test the system including graduate students and senior researchers in neurosciences and speech-related sciences. So that these users can test the system on a realistic problem, we will provide them with a corpus of annotated, de-identified recordings of children with and without a diagnosis of autism. This will provide context for specific training tasks that we ask of the users and enable them to formulate their own appropriate, if small, research questions that the system can help to answer. We will probe their experiences by logging the questions they have about the system, watching their actions as they attempt to answer the research questions, and asking their opinions of the experience afterward.

6 Requested Features

In an early trial of our Waversurfer plug-in, a user requested the VOT (voice-onset time) measure. In response to this request, we are now adding a VOT-transcription pane to display the automatically computed voice onset times aligned with the waveform, spectrogram, and displayed information. The information in this pane is also automatically saved to a text file that can be analyzed with other software.

This request also led us to include a popup window to show the vowel-space in a recording. Vowel-space measures are conventionally labor-intensive, thus limited to a few instances of specific vowels, and require that the researcher first identify specific instances of these vowels. On the other hand, vocalic landmarks identify the instants where formant frequencies may be reliably estimated, so our tools can quickly and automatically evaluate the full vowel space of a passage. (See Figure 2.)

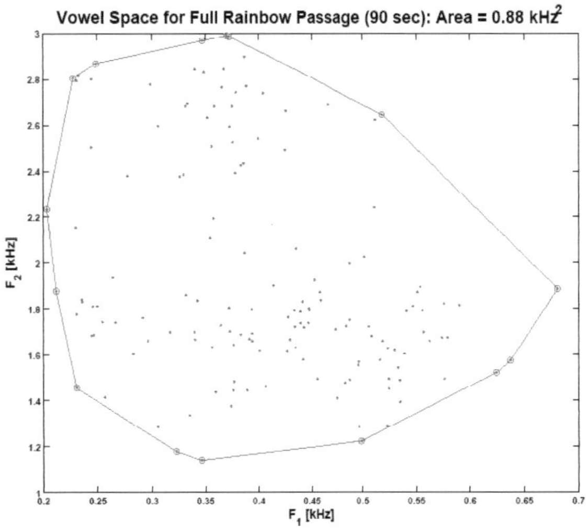

Figure 2: Automatic Vowel-Space Evaluation. Computing the resonant frequencies (formants) at vowel landmarks allows plotting the vowel space, i.e., the scatter of the first two formants against each other. In this case, a female read the complete Rainbow Passage (a standard passage of 3 paragraphs, approx. 90 sec of reading). The system automatically identified all the consonantal and vocalic landmarks, evaluated the formants at ~ 140 stressed vowels, and computed the convex hull ("rubber-band") area, 0.88 kHz^2. Total computation time on a commodity 3 GHz PC was 143 sec (and is directly proportional to the duration of the passage).

7 Challenges for Software development, Challenges for availability

Our algorithms are implemented in MATLAB. Though toolkits that run in MATLAB might be available free, or for a modest price, the MATLAB platform itself is costly, especially for non-academic users. On the other hand, shareware or freeware may have minimal documentation; support that depends entirely on the presence (or absence!) of a knowledgeable user community; and variable standards for testing, correctness, and performance.

A critical hidden cost for any system is the learning curve. For those systems with little documentation and training, this can dwarf the overt costs. Our goal is to make learning easier by creating landmark-processing plug-ins that people can use within software that they already employ.

Such a plan requires a careful balance between the flexibility of a general, extensible system and the simplicity of a small, fixed set of easily documented plug-in capabilities. Our project therefore includes both a small set of simple functions, such as VOT, and software design centered on the needs identified by users from the appropriate research communities. Our design relies on an iterative process of structured interviews and web-based surveys, combined with observations of user experiences with our plug-ins.

This user study extends beyond the matter of functionality and documentation. It also addresses the expectations or requirements for convenient availability, training, and support, and the costs that these imply.

8 Future work

8.1 R – statistical analysis system

We will integrate our software with R (http://www.r-project.org/) for those with a primary interest instead in the derived articulatory-precision information: e.g., syllable production rate, fraction of syllables of a given complexity, or range of vowels.

For this platform, we will implement further user-level functions, with corresponding graphical user interfaces as appropriate, to produce:

- Number of landmarks, optionally excluding those that are automatically detected as noise-related.
- Syllable complexity and statistics of same.
- Utterance complexity.
- Syllable production rate.
- Articulatory precision.
- Vowel space measures.

8.2 Other Platforms

We plan to expand our work to include plugins or packages for integration with a wider (and more powerful) collection of research tools, for example PRAAT, CSL, or even Excel.

8.3 Other Features

We are soliciting input from user communities about the features they would like to see in these tools.

Acknowledgments

This work was funded in part by NIH grant R43 DC010104.

References

Suzanne Boyce, Joel MacAuslan, Ann Bradlow, and Rajka Smiljanič. 2007. Automatic Detection of Differences Between Clear & Conversational Speech, poster presented at *American Speech-Language-Hearing Convention.*

Suzanne Boyce, Ann Bradlow, and Joel MacAuslan. 2005. Landmark analysis of clear and conversational speaking styles, *150th meeting of the Acoustical Society of America.*

Thomas DiCicco and Rupal Patel. 2008. Automatic Landmark Analysis of Dysarthric Speech, *Journal of Medical Speech-Language Pathology*, 16(4):213-219.

Cynthia J. Cress, S. Unrein, A. Weber, S. Krings, H. Fell, J. MacAuslan, and J. Gong. 2005. Vocal Development Patterns in Children at Risk for Being Non-speaking. *ASHA 2005.*

Cynthia J. Cress. 1995. Communicative and symbolic precursors of AAC, Unpublished NIH CIDA Grant: University of Nebraska-Lincoln.

Jack R. Deller, D. Hsu, and Linda J. Ferrier. 1991. On the Use of Hidden Markov Modeling for Recognition of Dysarthric Speech, *Computer Methods and Programs in Biomedicine.* (35)2:125-139.

Harriet J. Fell, Joel MacAuslan, Linda J. Ferrier, Susan G. Worst, and Karen Chenausky. 2002. Vocalization Age as a Clinical Tool. *Procroceedings of the International Conference on Speech and Language Processing.*

Harriet J. Fell, Joel MacAuslan, Cynthia. Cress, Linda J. Ferrier. 2004. visiBabble for Reinforcement of Early Vocalization, *Proceedings of ASSETS 2004.* 161-168.

Wilson Howitt. 2000. *Unpublished Ph.D. dissertation, Massachusetts Institute of Technology.*

Amit Juneja and Carol Espy-Wilson. 2003, Speech Segmentation Using Probabilistic Phonetic Feature Hierarchy and Support Vector Machines. *Proceedings of the International Joint Conference on Neural Networks.*

Sharlene A. Liu. 1995. Landmark Detection for Distinctive Feature-Hyphen Based Speech Recognition, *M.I.T. Doctoral Thesis.*

R, http://www.r-project.org/

Janet Slifka, Kenneth N. Stevens, Sharon Manuel, and Stefanie Shattuck-Hufnagel. 2004. A Landmark-Based Model of Speech Perception: History and Recent Developments. *From Sound to Sense,* 85-90.

Kenneth N. Stevens, 2000. *Acoustic Phonetics*, The MIT Press, Cambridge, Massachusetts.

Kenneth N. Stevens. 2002. Toward a model for lexical access based on acoustic landmarks and distinctive features, *Journal of the Acoustic Society of Am*erica. 111(4):1872-1891.

Kenneth N. Stevens, Sharon Manuel, Stefanie Shattuck-Hufnagel, and Sharlene Liu. 1992. Implementation of a model for lexical access based on features, *Procedings ICSLP (Int. Conf. on Speech & Language Processing)*. 499-502.

Travis Wade, Bernd Möbius. 2007. Speaking rate effects in a landmark-based phonetic exemplar model, *Interspeech 2007*. 402-405.

Wavesurfer.2005. http://www.speech.kth.se/wavesurfer/

An Approach for Anonymous Spelling for Voter Write-Ins Using Speech Interaction

Shaneé Dawkins
Auburn University
3101 Shelby Center for Technology
Auburn University, AL 36849, USA
stw0004@auburn.edu

Juan E. Gilbert
Clemson University
100 McAdams Hall
Clemson, SC 29634, USA
juan@clemson.edu

Abstract

Today, the technology used for voting does not fully address the issues that disabled voters are confronted with during elections. Voters, including those with most disabilities, should be able to vote and verify his or her ballot during elections without the assistance of others. In order for this to happen, a universal design should be incorporated into the development of all voting systems. The research presented here embraces the needs of those who are disabled. The primary objective of this research was to develop a system in which a person, can efficiently, anonymously, and independently write-in a candidate's name during an election. The method presented here uses speech interaction and name prediction to allow voters to privately spell the name of the candidate they intend to write-in. A study was performed to determine the effectiveness and efficiency of the system. The results of the study showed that spelling a name using the predictive method developed is an effective and efficient solution to the aforementioned issues.

1 Introduction*

The 2000 United States Presidential Election will always be remembered for its voting irregularities. The issues with the ballot design during that election led to skepticism of other voting systems and technologies. Not only were there questions regarding the difficulty interpreting the voter's intention, the focus also shifted to the issues surrounding disabled voters. The key issue was that disabled voters needed a way to vote independently and anonymously, while still maintaining system security and efficiency. All voters, including those with most disabilities, should be able to vote and verify his or her ballot during elections privately, without assistance. Today, a properly designed interface is one of the key aspects to running a successful election.

As technology for electronic voting systems continues to develop, there is an increased need for universal design in these systems (VVSG Chapter 3, 2007). A universal design ensures that systems are as usable as possible by as many people as possible regardless of age, ability or situation (Center for Universal Design, 2004). By focusing on the voter and their needs, the design of electronic voting systems will far surpass the ballot designs of the 2000 election.

With the security of voting systems constantly being a major concern, it is often difficult to implement voting technology that incorporates a secure universal design. Some developers today

Proceedings of the NAACL HLT 2010 Workshop on Speech and Language Processing for Assistive Technologies, pages 44–52,
Los Angeles, California, June 2010.

address this issue through the design of their electronic voting systems (Prime III, 2009); however, these electronic voting systems have yet to integrate universal design into the writing-in of a candidate's name.

The objective of this research is to develop a system in which a person, including those with most disabilities, can efficiently, anonymously, and effectively spell a candidate's name through speech interaction. The method presented in this paper is a predictive approach to spelling through speech interaction. This allows voters to quickly and anonymously spell a candidate's name for any position or office during the voting process. The study performed intends to capture and analyze the effectiveness of writing in a candidate's name anonymously through speech. The results of this study could lead to the adaptation of this system in search functions for various other applications.

2 Background

2.1 Election Write-Ins

The method of writing in a candidate's name for a particular United States governing office dates back to the early 19th century (Official Election Site, 2007). Prior to the 1800s, voters would simply call out their choices to a judge and election clerks tallying the votes (Jones, 2003). After the 12th amendment was passed in 1804, paper ballots became the standard method for voting. Voters would bring their own slips of paper as the ballot, on which they wrote candidate's names (History of the Paper Ballot, 2009). Today, a write-in candidate is a candidate whose name does not appear on the ballot. Voters can vote for a write-in candidate by marking the write-in indicator, and writing the candidate's name in space provided on the ballot (Write-in Candidate Requirements, 2010).

2.2 Prime III Electronic Voting System

Prime III is a research prototype electronic voting system. It is a secure, multimodal electronic voting system that delivers the necessary system security, integrity and user satisfaction safeguards in a user-friendly interface that accommodates all people regardless of ability (Prime III, 2009). With Prime III, voters are able to cast their votes through visual interaction and/or through speech interaction. This multimodal approach to electronic voting enables Prime III to incorporate a universal design, which allows nearly all voters to cast their votes independently and privately.

Due to the anonymous nature of voting systems, the candidates that the voter selects must be kept private. Since Prime III integrates speech interaction into the voting process, bystanders may be afforded the opportunity to compromise the privacy of the voter. Bystanders must not be able to hear whom a voter selects for any office, or a voter's decision for any proposition in order to ensure voter – ballot anonymity. Therefore, during the voting process, voters cannot simply say the name of the candidates for which s/he wishes to vote. The speech interface of Prime III implements an interaction in which the voter does not need to explicitly verbalize for which candidate they intend to vote.

The Prime III system uses speech to convey the information on the screen to the voter (e.g. candidates listed for a particular office) through the use of a microphone headset. When an option is presented, the voter chooses the option by speaking, "Vote" into the microphone. If the voter does not wish to choose the current option, they do not say anything and the system moves on to the next prompt. An example dialogue is as follows:

> Prime III: "To vote for the Democratic Party, say vote <beep>"
> Voter: <says nothing>
> Prime III: "To vote for the Republican Party, say vote <beep>"
> Voter: "Vote"

In this example, the voter chose to vote for the Republican Party. Bystanders only hear the voter saying "Vote," instead of a voter's actual choice, which ensures the privacy of the voter and the anonymity of the voter's ballot.

The universal accessibility and anonymous nature of electronic voting highlights the incompleteness in the design of writing in a candidate's name with Prime III. Currently, voters have the ability to write-in a candidate's name in one way: using an onscreen keyboard (Figure 1). When a voter chooses not to vote for a predetermined candidate and to write-in a candidate's name, the keyboard is shown, and the user must use the touchscreen to type the candidate's name. Since this portion of the system is not a multimodal design, the voter must be sighted to write-in a candidate's name.

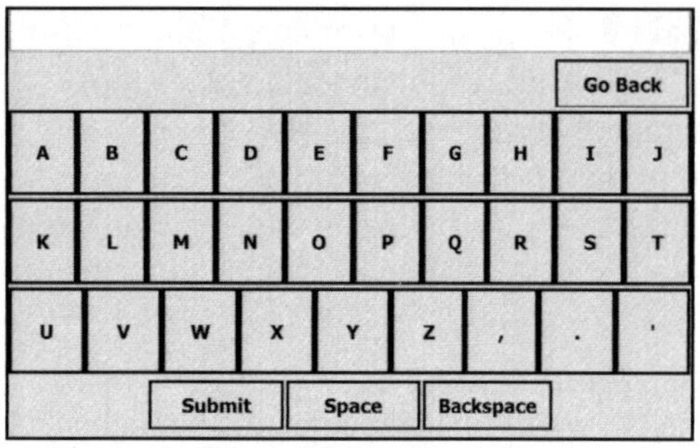

Figure 1. Prime III On-screen Keyboard

2.3 Universal Accessibility in Voting

Help America Vote Act (HAVA) of 2002, was created to prevent the major issues faced in the 2000 United States Presidential Election from happening in future elections (HAVA, 2002). From HAVA, the United States Election Assistance Commission (EAC) was established. One of the goals of the EAC was to adopt Voluntary Voting System Guidelines (VVSG), which expand access for individuals with disabilities to vote privately and independently (VVSG, 2007). The VVSG now addresses the advancement of technology and provides requirements for voting systems to be tested against to ensure functionality, security, and accessibility (VVSG, 2005). Chapter 3 of the 2007 VVSG proposes requirements for the usability and accessibility of electronic voting systems (VVSG Chapter 3, 2007). The VVSG states that all voters must have access to the voting process without discrimination, and that the voting process must be accessible to individuals with disabilities, including non-visual accessibility (VVSG, 2007). It also states that voting systems should be independently accessible to as many voters as possible, which further emphasizes the need for a universal design.

3 Motivation

Currently, there is no solution for writing in a candidate's name that is universally accessible. As stated previously, developing systems with a universal design ensures that the system can be used by anyone, regardless of abilities or disabilities. Prime III, like other electronic voting systems today, simply cannot accommodate a range of voters due to its current write-in system through an on screen keyboard. In order for voters with visual or motor impairments to vote, a voting official must enter the voting booth with him or her to write, or type, the candidate on the ballot for which the voter intends to vote. The lack of multimodality and accessibility in these write-in methods only accommodates sighted voters. This violates the privacy of the voter and the anonymity of the voter's ballot.

The most fitting solution to this problem of voter privacy is to utilize a multimodal voting system that incorporates speech interaction. With the addition of speech, voters, regardless of most physical disabilities, have an option to vote independently. In order to write-in a candidate, a voter could simply speak aloud the name of the person who they intend to write-in. The integration of the speech feature alone enables the system to have a universal design. However, this system is not practical. During election peak times, polling places may have a large voter turnout (Polling Place and Vote Center Management, 2009). With the large number of voters at polling places at any given time, privacy is an enormous issue. In accordance with the Election Assistance Commission (EAC), the voting process must preserve the secrecy of the ballot. The voting process should preclude anyone else from determining the content of a voter's ballot, without the voter's cooperation. If such a determination is made against the wishes of the voter, then his or her privacy has been violated (VVSG Chapter 3, 2007). If a voter is required to explicitly say the name of the candidate for which they intend to write-in, any bystanders within the polling place may be able to hear that name, and know for whom that person voted, thereby violating the voter's privacy and ballot anonymity.

In order to secure voter privacy through speech interaction, voters must communicate with the system using the speech interaction method of Prime III. As explained in section 2.2, this approach allows a voter to make selections throughout the voting process by simply saying, "vote" in response to the system's prompts. Using this method for writing in a candidate's name has its challenges. The system cannot simply prompt names to the voter until the system gets to the name the voter intends to write-in. There are an infinite number of names the voter would have to choose from. For example, it would not be viable for the dialogue to be as follows:

Prime III: "To vote for the Bob Doe, say vote [beep]"
Voter: <says nothing>
Prime III: "To vote for the Bill Doe, say vote [beep]"
Voter: <says nothing>

Prime III: "To vote for the Billy Doe, say vote [beep]"
Voter: <says nothing>

...

If the systems simply made uneducated guesses of the desired name, it would be impossible for the voter to write-in a candidate.

A solution to this problem would be for the voter to spell, rather than say, the desired candidate's name. However, due to voter privacy, the voter cannot simply spell a name aloud. Spelling a write-in candidate's name can only be done privately if the Prime III method of getting input data from the voter, through speech, is applied to the design of the system. Using this method, the system would need to prompt the voter to determine the correct letters to spell the desired candidate's name. This would have to be done for the spelling of the entire name. For example, to spell the name, "Bob," the dialogue would be as follows:

Prime III: "If the first letter of the candidate's name is A, say vote <beep>"
Voter: <says nothing>
Prime III: "If the first letter of the candidate's name is B, say vote <beep>"
Voter: "Vote"
Prime III: "If the second letter of the candidate's name is A, say vote <beep>"
Voter: <says nothing>
Prime III: "If the second letter of the candidate's name is B, say vote <beep>"
Voter: <says nothing>

...

Prime III: "If the second letter of the candidate's name is N, say vote <beep>"
Voter: <says nothing>
Prime III: "If the second letter of the candidate's name is O, say vote <beep>"
Voter: "Vote"

...

Prime III: "If the third letter of the candidate's name is B, say vote <beep>"
Voter: "Vote"

Thus far, this is the best solution. This approach to spelling a candidate's name encompasses voter privacy, integrity, and universal accessibility. However, the above example implements a linear search to spell a write-in candidate's name. For each letter of the candidate's full name, the voter may have to traverse each of the 26 letters of the alphabet. Spelling using this method would take an extremely long time, especially if the letters of the candidate's name were at the end of the alphabet (i.e. "Robert Smith"), or if the candidate's name has several letters (i.e. "Christopher Washington"). Time is a vital factor in voting. Voters want to make their selections and cast their ballots in a reasonable amount of time. This straight linear approach to spell the name of a write-in candidate is long and undesirable, leading to the research presented in this paper. The overall objective of this research is to propose a method to write-in a candidate's name that addresses the issues of time, privacy, and accessibility.

Currently, there is no method to spell a name for writing in a candidate that incorporates a universal design and meets the requirements set forth by the EAC; no system allows an individual with visual or motor impairments to spell a candidate's name privately and securely. In order to solve these major issues, a predictive spelling method was created using speech interaction. The hypothesis is that the predictive spelling method through speech interaction will take less time to spell a candidate's name than the aforementioned linear approach.

4 Design

4.1 Design Overview

The novel approach for writing in a candidate presented in this paper is implemented with a universal design, is private, and is time effective. The proposed design solution utilizes alphabet clustering and implements name prediction as opposed to the linear search method discussed in the previous section. This solution proves to be more time effective for letter selection, and for overall name selection.

Rather than using linear search to traverse the alphabet, which may take an extensive duration of time to complete, this design breaks down the alphabet into clusters of letters, which are then are presented to the voter. The voter then spells a candidate's name by selecting from these letters and the system performs name prediction similar to the methods used in predictive text technology such as Nuance Communications' XT9 (Nuance, 2009). Like in XT9, the voters spelling with our speech system have the option to select from the suggestions made based on the letters spelled. While XT9 utilizes a dictionary database to predict words that the user may intend to type, this system was developed using a database containing only first and last names that the user may intend to spell.

For each letter of the candidate's name, the clusters are presented to the voter for selection using the method discussed in Chapter Three. The voter begins by making the proper selections to spell the candidate's last name. The system first prompts the voter with the alphabet clusters. Once the voter selects the desired cluster, the system then prompts the voter with the letters contained in that cluster. The voter then chooses a letter, and the system moves on to get the next letter of the desired candidate's name. Following every new letter selection, the first cluster presented for the next letter is a cluster of the three most common letters to follow the letters already chosen.

After the voter selects the first three letters of the candidate's name, the system then suggests three names, one of which the voter may intend to write-in. The names suggested are chosen because they have the highest probability to be written in. If the voter selects one of the names suggested, the process is repeated for the intended candidate's first name, resulting in the chosen candidate's full name being written in for the corresponding office on the ballot. If the voter does not intend to write-in one of the names suggested, s/he continues the process of selecting clusters, then letters, until the correct name is suggested, or the name has been spelled in full (see Table 2 for a full example).

4.2 Cluster Selection

The alphabet is broken down into four clusters of five letters, and one cluster of six letters (Table 1). For the first letter of each of the candidate's names, given name and surname, the voter is prompted to choose from one of the five clusters. For each letter to be spelled after the first letter, there is an additional cluster of three letters presented to the voter. This cluster contains the most common next letters, given the letters the candidate has already chosen. For every letter, with the exception of the first letter, the first cluster presented to the voter is the most common letter cluster. This expedites the selection process since the voter is able to make his or her selection at this point, rather than making a selection from the five standard clusters. If the next letter of the name is *not* in the most common letter cluster, the voter is then prompted to select one of the five standard clusters (Table 1).

Cluster Letters
A, B, C, D, E
F, G, H, I, J
K, L, M, N, O
P, Q, R, S, T
U, V, W, X, Y, Z

Table 1. Standard Letter Clusters

The first of these clusters presented to the voter is chosen at random, with the prompts for the remaining clusters following in alphabetical order, in a round robin fashion. The purpose of this randomization is to secure ballot anonymity by ensuring that bystanders will not be able to piece together for whom the voter voted.

4.3 Letter Selection

Once the voter selects the correct cluster containing the next letter of the desired candidate's name, s/he is prompted to choose amongst those letters. The letters presented by the system are dependent on the cluster the voter selected (see Table 2). If the voter selects the cluster of letters {A,B,C,D,E}, s/he is prompted to choose from those letters within that cluster. If the voter selects the cluster of the most common letters, for example, {R, A, E}, s/he is prompted to choose a letter from that common letter cluster. Once the desired letter is chosen, the system moves on to the set of prompts for the voter to select the next letter of the write-in candidate's name (see Table 2).

4.4 Name Database

This prediction system for writing in a candidate's name is made possible through the use of a local database of names. A local database is utilized due to the ban of wireless devices and Internet connections in voting and tabulating machines according to the Voter Confidence and Increased Accessibility Act of 2009 (Holt, 2009 and VCIAA, 2009).

This database contains the most common names in the United States (Butler, 2005). Taken from the United States census in 2000, each name was given a category and a rank. The different categories of names are surnames, male given names, and female given names. Within these categories, each name was given a rank based on popularity. The names that were used most frequently are ranked at the top of the list, while the names infrequently used are at the bottom of the list. The database used in this design contains a table of the top 1000 ranked surnames from the 2000 US Census. The database also has a table for given names; containing the top 1000 ranked male names, and the top 1000 ranked female names.

4.5 Name Prediction

In order to effectively reduce the amount of time a voter spends to write-in a candidate's name, this system utilizes a name prediction method built on the name database described in the previous section. Essentially, the predictions are suggestions to the voter of names that s/he may potentially spell. The names suggested are pulled from the name database depending on the letters already chosen by the voter. If one of the predicted names is correct, the voter does not need to go through the entire spelling process.

The name suggestions are strictly based on the clusters and letters chosen by the voter. When a voter selects a cluster, the system can suggest the most common (highest ranked) name that has a first initial as one of the letters in the cluster. For example, if the voter is selecting the first letter of the candidate's last name, and chooses the cluster "F, G, H, I, J," the system can suggest "Johnson" to be the candidate's last name. Similarly, when a voter selects a letter, the system can suggest the most common name from the letters selected. Furthermore, if the voter is spelling the candidate's last name, and has already selected the letters "J," and "A," the system can suggest "James" as the candidate's last name.

In a best-case scenario, the first name the system suggests would be the name the voter intended to write-in. However, if that is not the case, each suggested name the voter rejects (says nothing) adds unnecessary interaction cycles to the spelling process. For this reason, a different approach was taken to suggest names. Because most names could be suggested correctly given the first three letters, the system waits to suggest names until the voter selects the first three letters. Once the first three letters have been spelled, the system knows if there is a potential match in the database. If there is no match, the system continues to let the voter spell the name intended.

If there is a name in the database that starts with the letters that the voter already selected, that name is then suggested to the voter. At this time, the system suggests up to three names for the voter to select from. If after these initial three suggestions the system has not suggested the intended candidate's name, the system prompts the voter to continue to spell the candidate's name. From this point on, the system suggests one name after the voter selects a cluster, and one name after the voter selects a letter. If the voter rejects a name, it is never suggested again, so that the intended name has a chance at being suggested. An example of the system dialogue is shown in Table 2.

Interaction Mode	Interaction	Letters Already Selected
System	**Say vote if the first letter of the candidate's last name is A, B, C, D, or E**	--
Voter	*Vote*	--
System	**Say vote if the first letter of the candidate's last name is A**	--
Voter	*<says nothing>*	--
System	**Say vote if the first letter of the candidate's last name is B**	--
Voter	*<says nothing>*	--
System	**Say vote if the third letter of the candidate's last name is C**	--
Voter	*Vote*	C
System	**You have selected the letter C. Say vote to delete this letter.**	C
Voter	*<says nothing>*	C
System	**You have selected C as the candidate's last name. Say vote if you are finished spelling the last name.**	C
Voter	*<says nothing>*	C
System	**You will now select the second letter of the candidate's last name.**	C
System	**The next letters are the most common letters. Say vote if the second letter of the candidate's last name is A, E, or O**	C
Voter	*Vote*	C
System	**Say vote if the second letter of the candidate's last name is A**	C
Voter	*Vote*	CA
...		
System	**You have selected the letter R. Say vote to delete this letter.**	CAR
Voter	*<says nothing>*	CAR
System	**Say vote if the candidate's last name is Carter**	CAR
Voter	*<says nothing>*	CAR
System	**Say vote if the candidate's last name is Carroll**	CAR
Voter	*<says nothing>*	CAR
System	**Say vote if the candidate's last name is Carpenter**	CAR
Voter	*<says nothing>*	CAR
System	**You will now select the fourth letter of the candidate's last name**	CAR
System	**The next letters are the most common letters. Say vote if the third letter of the candidate's last name**	CAR

	is L, P, or S	
Voter	*Vote*	CAR
System	**Say vote if the candidate's last name is Carlson**	CAR
Voter	*<says nothing>*	CAR
System	**Say vote if the third letter of the candidate's last name is L**	CAR
Voter	*Vote*	CARL
System	**Say vote if the candidate's last name is Carlisle**	CARL
Voter	*Vote*	**CARLISLE**

Table 2. Example Dialogue for Spelling Last Name, "Carlisle"

5 Experiment and Evaluation

The primary objective of this study was to observe and analyze how people interact with the predictive write-in system through speech. The goal of the study is to determine the time it takes a voter to use the write-in system developed. It is expected that the predictive system will perform significantly faster when spelling a name than the linear system. Additionally, it is expected that the participants in the study will be able to use the system effectively, meaning they will be able to spell their intended names.

5.1 Experimental Method

The participants were directed to fill out a pre-questionnaire to obtain their demographic information and prior usage with computing. Once the pre-questionnaire was completed, a scenario was given, introducing them to the write-in voting process, and to encourage them to treat the study as if it were an actual election. The students then recorded in writing the name they intended to spell, which could be any first and last name of their choosing, with the exception of their own to keep the results anonymous. It was explained to the student that the speech from the system would be coming from the speakers for observational purposes, and that the headset was strictly for the use of the microphone. Data collected during the experiment included the name each participant chose to write-in and the times taken to spell that name.

5.2 Evaluation

A total of 40 participants participated in this study, of which more than 80 percent were undergraduates, Caucasians, and males. Presented in this section are calculated best-case comparisons between the predictive write-in method versus the linear search approach, as well as the experimental results from the study.

Predictive Write-In Results: For the study, participants were required to provide a name to spell so that there was no bias amongst the names spelled. The average length of the full names chosen was 10.43 letters, with a standard deviation of 2.22. The shortest full name was 7 letters in length, and the longest full name was 16 letters in length. Of the 80 first and last names chosen, 71.3% of the names were in the database and suggested to the user. The average time it took for a participant to spell a candidate's full name was 9.52 minutes, with a standard deviation of 3.83. The median time was 8.42 minutes. The average time, for the names given, per letter was 1.09 minutes, with a standard deviation of 45 seconds.

Figure 2 shows a breakdown of times based on the number of letters in the full name spelled. This figure shows the average times taken by participants to spell names of various lengths for the predictive method. Removing the outliers of this chart, the average full name was between 8 and 16 letters, and took an average of 9.23 minutes. These results show that in practice, this system takes much longer than anticipated (see Comparison). Additional observations from the study showed that participant errors were the primary reason that the actual times were much different than what was calculated for the best-case times to spell the same names.

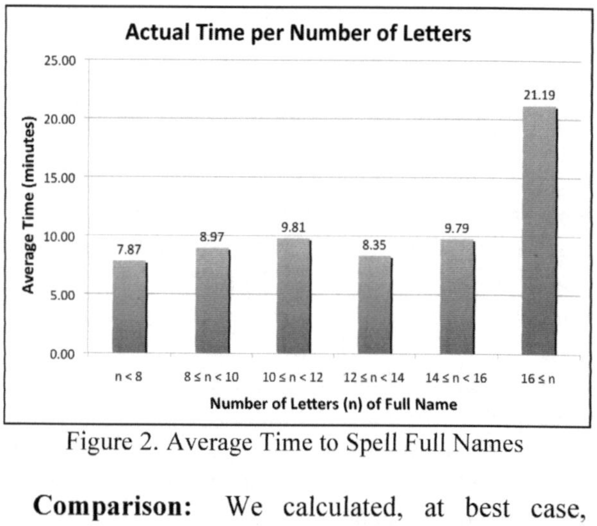

Figure 2. Average Time to Spell Full Names

Comparison: We calculated, at best case, how long it should take someone to spell the names from the study for both systems. In order to determine how long it would take to spell a name, each interaction cycle for the system was broken down and timed. For each method, the sequence of prompts presented to the voter to spell a name is different. The sequences were determined for each system, and compiled for each name spelled. The sequences for the predictive write-in method was constructed under the assumption that the names to be spelled are in the system's name database.

Figure 3 shows the average times taken to spell names of various lengths for the predictive and linear methods. The average time for the full names provided in the study for the calculated linear search method was 15.09 minutes, with a standard deviation of 3.86 (Table 3). The average time to spell the full names for the calculated predictive method was 4.33 minutes, with a standard deviation of 0.17. The median times for the calculated predictive and linear methods were 4.34 and 14.73, respectively. From these results, we can conclude that, on average, the predictive spelling approach is more than three times faster than the linear spelling approach. The predictive spelling method was effective in that 100% of the participants were able to complete the spelling of the intended names.

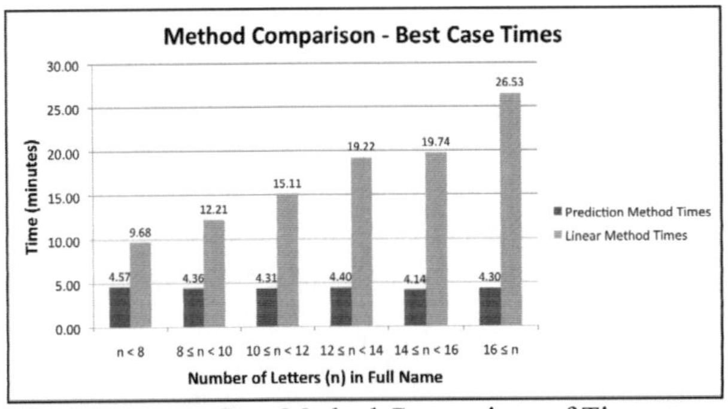

Figure 3. Best-Case Method Comparison of Times to Spell Full Names

	Time to spell full name - Predictive Method (minutes)	Time to spell full name - Linear Method (minutes)
Average	4.33	15.09
Standard Deviation	0.17	3.86
Median	4.34	14.73

Table 3. Calculated Predictive and Linear Method Statistics

6 Conclusion and Future Work

The ultimate goal of electronic voting systems today should be to allow anyone to vote privately and independently using a single design. The EAC provides useful and necessary guidelines to ensure that all eligible citizens have the same access when voting, regardless of a person's disabilities. The primary objective of this research was to embrace these guidelines by developing a system in which a person, regardless of most disabilities, can efficiently, anonymously, and independently write-in a candidate's name during an election. The method designed allows voters to spell a candidate's name discretely through speech interaction, using a predictive approach for efficiency.

The study performed was designed to test the hypothesis, which states that the method designed for predictive spelling through speech interaction will take much less time to spell a candidate's name than the method of linear search. The results of the study suggest that the predictive approach to write-in a candidate's name was more efficient than the linear spelling approach. However, it was determined that, in practice, the participants took longer than calculated to spell a name using the prediction method.

From observing the participants throughout the study, it was considered that the number of errors made during the spelling process might have been the primary reason for the time being so long. Future versions of this system will include increased efficiency for error correction. It may also be beneficial for future studies to include participants of a more diverse demographic, and to collect other metrics for determining efficiency, such as, letters required to spell a name, and number of errors made while spelling and where said errors occurred.

As this method is further developed, it can be adapted by certain search functions. Search applications that utilize a fixed directory will benefit greatly by using the prediction method discussed. This could be especially helpful for people directories, building directories, or telephony systems.

Acknowledgments

This material is based in part upon work supported by the National Science Foundation under Grant Numbers CNS- 0540492 and 0837675. Any opinions, findings, and conclusions or recommendations expressed in this material are those of the author(s) and do not necessarily reflect the views of the National Science Foundation.

References

2007 VVSG Chapter 3: Usability, Accessibility, and Privacy Requirements (2007) [online]. http://www.eac.gov/vvsg/part1/chapter03.php/.

Butler, R., (2005). http://names.mongabay.com/.

Center for Universal Design, N.C. State University (2004). Universal Design Education Online Web Site http://www.udeducation.org/learn/index.asp.

Help America Vote Act. (2002). Public Law 107-252, 107th Congress, United States [online]. http://www.fec.gov/hava/law_ext.txt.

History of the Paper Ballot (2009) [online]. http://www.fairvote.org/righttovote/pballot.pdf.

Jones, D., (2003). A Brief Illustrated History of Voting [online]. http://www.cs.uiowa.edu/~jones/voting/pictures/.

Making Sure Votes Count and Are Counted (2009). http://holt.house.gov/voting.shtml.

Nuance – XT9 Smart Input (2009). http://www.nuance.com/t9/xt9/.

Official Election Site of San Mateo County (2007). http://www.shapethefuture.org/press/2007/090607.asp.

Polling Place and Vote Center Management (2009) [online]. http://www.eac.gov/election/quick-start-management-guides/docs/09-polling-place-and-vote-center-management.pdf/attachment_download/file.

Press Release: 2005 VVSG Adopted (2005). http://www.eac.gov/voting%20systems/docs/eac-adopts-2005-voluntary-voting-system-guidelines.pdf/attachment_download/file.

Prime III: One Machine, One Vote for Everyone. (2009) http://primevotingsystem.org/.

Voluntary Voting System Guidelines Recommendations to the Election Assistance Commission (2007) [online]. http://www.eac.gov/files/vvsg/Final-TGDC-VVSG-08312007.pdf.

Voter Confidence and Increased Accessibility Act of 2009 (2009). Public Law H.R. 2894. [online] http://thomas.loc.gov/cgi-bin/query/z?c111:H.R.2894:.

Write-in Candidate Requirements. Maine 2010 June Primary and November General Election Candidates (2010). [online] http://www.maine.gov/sos/cec/elec/2010/writeincandidateguide.doc.

Using Reinforcement Learning to Create Communication Channel Management Strategies for Diverse Users

Rebecca Lunsford
Center for Spoken Lang. Understanding
Oregon Health & Science University
Beaverton, OR, USA
lunsforr@ohsu.edu

Peter Heeman
Center for Spoken Lang. Understanding
Oregon Health & Science University
Beaverton, OR, USA
heemanp@ohsu.edu

Abstract

Spoken dialogue systems typically do not manage the communication channel, instead using fixed values for such features as the amplitude and speaking rate. Yet, the quality of a dialogue can be compromised if the user has difficulty understanding the system. In this proof-of-concept research, we explore using reinforcement learning (RL) to create policies that manage the communication channel to meet the needs of diverse users. Towards this end, we first formalize a preliminary communication channel model, in which users provide explicit feedback regarding issues with the communication channel, and the system implicitly alters its amplitude to accommodate the user's optimal volume. Second, we explore whether RL is an appropriate tool for creating communication channel management strategies, comparing two different hand-crafted policies to policies trained using both a dialogue-length and a novel *annoyance* cost. The learned policies performed better than hand-crafted policies, with those trained using the annoyance cost learning an equitable tradeoff between users with differing needs and also learning to balance finding a user's optimal amplitude against dialogue-length. These results suggest that RL can be used to create effective communication channel management policies for diverse users.

Index Terms: communication channel, spoken dialogue systems, reinforcement learning, amplitude, diverse users

1 Introduction

Both Spoken Dialog Systems (SDS) and Assistive Technology (AT) tend to have a narrow focus, supporting only a subset of the population. SDS typically aim to support the "average man", ignoring wide variations in potential users' ability to hear and understand the system. AT aims to support people with a recognized disability, but doesn't support those whose impairment is not severe enough to warrant the available devices or services, or those who are unaware or have not acknowledged that they need assistance. However, SDS should be able to meet the needs of users whose abilities fall within, and between, the extremes of severly impaired and perfectly abled.

When aiming to support users with widely differing abilities, the cause of a user's difficulty is less important than adapting the communication channel in a manner that aids understanding. For example, speech that is presented more loudly and slowly can help a hearing-impaired elderly person understand the system, and can also help a person with no hearing loss who is driving in a noisy car. Although one user's difficulty is due to impairment and the other due to an adverse environment, a similar adaptation may be appropriate to both.

During human-human communication, speakers manage the communication channel; implicitly altering their manner of speech to increase the likelihood of being understood while concurrently economizing effort (Lindblom, 1990). In addition to these implicit actions, speakers also make statements referring to breakdowns in the communication chan-

Proceedings of the NAACL HLT 2010 Workshop on Speech and Language Processing for Assistive Technologies, pages 53–61,
Los Angeles, California, June 2010.

nel, explicitly pointing out potential problems or corrections, (e.g. "Could you please speak up?") (Jurafsky et al., 1997).

As for human-computer dialogue, SDS are prone to misrecognition of users' spoken utterances. Much research has focused on developing techniques for overcoming or avoiding system misunderstandings. Yet, as the quality of automatic speech recognition improves and SDS are deployed to diverse populations and in varied environments, systems will need to better attend to possible *human* misunderstandings. Future SDS will need to manage the communication channel, in addition to managing the task, to aid in avoiding these misunderstandings.

Researchers have explored the use of reinforcement learning (RL) to create dialogue policies that balance and optimize measures of task success (e.g., see (Scheffler and Young, 2002; Levin et al., 2000; Henderson et al., 2008; Walker, 2000)). Along these lines, RL is potentially well suited to creating policies for the subtask of managing the communication channel, as it can learn to adapt to the user while continuing the dialogue. In doing so, RL may choose actions that appear costly at the time, but lead to better overall dialogues.

Our long term goal is to learn how to manage the communication channel along with the task, moving away from just "what" to say and also focusing on "how" to say it. For this proof-of-concept, our goals are twofold: 1) to formalize a communication channel model that encompasses diverse users, initially focusing just on explicit user actions and implicit system actions, and 2) to determine whether RL is an appropriate tool for learning an effective communication channel management strategy for diverse users. To explore the above issues, we use a simple communication channel model in which the system needs to determine and maintain an amplitude level that is pleasant and effective for users with differing amplitude preferences and needs. As our goal includes decreasing the amount of potentially annoying utterances (i.e., those in which the system's amplitude setting is in discord with the user's optimal amplitude), we introduce a user-centric cost metric, which we have termed *annoyance cost*. We then compare hand-crafted policies against policies trained using both annoyance and more traditional dialogue-length cost components.

2 Related Work

2.1 How People Manage the Channel

When conversing, speakers implicitly adjust features of their speech (e.g., speaking rate, loudness) to maintain the communication channel. For example, speakers produce Lombard speech when in noisy conditions, produce clear speech to better accommodate a hard of hearing listener, and alter their speech to more closely resemble the interlocutor's (Junqua, 1993; Lindblom, 1990). These changes increase the intelligibility of the speech, thus helping to maintain the communication channel (Payton et al., 1994). Research has also shown that speakers adjust their speaking style when addressing a computer; exhibiting the same speech adaptations seen during human-human communication (Bell et al., 2003; Lunsford et al., 2006).

In addition to altering their speech implicitly, speakers also explicitly point out communication channel problems (Jurafsky et al., 1997). Examples include; requesting a change in speaking rate or amplitude ("Could you please speak up?"), explaining sources of communication channel interference ("Oh, that noise is the coffee grinder."), or asking their interlocutor to repeat an utterance ("What was that?"). These explicit utterances identify some issue with the communication channel that must be remedied before continuing the dialogue. In response, interlocutors will rewind to a previous point in the dialogue and alter their speech to ensure they are understood. This approach, of adapting ones speech in response to a communication problem, occurs even when conversing with a computer (Stent et al., 2008).

Both implicit speech alterations and explicit utterances regarding the communication channel often address issues of amplitude. This is to be expected, as speaking at an appropriate amplitude is critical to maintaining an effective communication channel, with sub-optimal amplitude affecting listeners' understanding and performance (Baldwin and Struckman-Johnson, 2002). In addition, Baldwin (2001) found that audible, but lowered, amplitude can negatively affect both younger and older subjects' reaction time and ability to respond correctly while multitasking, and that elderly listeners are likely to need higher amplitudes than younger listeners to maintain similar performance. Just as low amplitude can be difficult to understand, high amplitude can be annoying, and, in the extreme, cause pain.

2.2 How Systems Manage the Channel

Towards improving listener understanding in a potentially noisy environment, Martinson and Brock (2007) take advantage of the mobility and sensory capabilities of a robot. To determine the best course of action, the robot maintains a noise map of the environment, measuring the environmental noise prior to each TTS utterance. The robot then rotates toward the listener, changes location, alters its amplitude, or pauses until the noise abates. A similar technique, useful for remote listeners who may be in a noisy environment or using a noisy communication medium, could analyze the signal-to-noise ratio to ascertain the noise level in the listener's environment. Although these techniques may be useful for adjusting amplitude to compensate for noise in the listener's environment, they do not address speech alterations needed to accommodate users with different hearing abilities or preferences.

Given the need to adapt to individual users, it seems reasonable that users themselves would simply adjust volume on their local device. However, there are issues with this approach. First, manual adjustment of the volume would prove problematic when the user's hands and eyes are busy, such as when driving a car. Second, during an ongoing dialogue speakers tend to minimize pauses, responding quickly when given the turn (Sacks et al., 1974). Stopping to alter the amplitude could result in longer than natural pauses, which systems often respond to with increasingly lengthy 'timeout' responses (Kotelly, 2003), or repeating the same prompt endlessly (Villing et al., 2008). Third, although we focus on amplitude adaptations in this paper, amplitude is only one aspect of the communication channel. A fully functional communication channel management solution would also incorporate adaptations of features such as speaking rate, pausing, pitch range, emphasis, etc. This extended set of features, because of their number and interaction between them, do not readily lend themselves to listener manipulation.

3 Reinforcement Learning

RL has been used to create dialogue strategies that specify what action to perform in each possible system state so that a minimum dialogue cost is achieved (Walker, 2000; Levin et al., 2000). To accomplish this, RL starts with a policy, namely what action to perform in each state. It then uses this policy, with some exploration, to estimate the cost of getting from each state with each possible action to the final state. As more simulations are run, RL refines its estimates and its current policy. RL will converge to an optimal solution as long as assumptions about costs and state transitions are met. RL is particularly well suited for learning dialogue strategies as it will balance opposing goals (e.g., minimizing excessive confirmations vs. ensuring accurate information).

RL has been applied to a number of dialogue scenarios. For form-filling dialogues, in which the user provides parameters for a database query, researchers have used RL to decide what order to use when prompting for the parameters and to decrease resource costs such as database access (Levin et al., 2000; Scheffler and Young, 2002). System misunderstanding caused by speech recognition errors has also been modeled to determine whether, and how, the system should confirm information (Scheffler and Young, 2002). However, there is no known work on using RL to manage the communication channel so as to avoid *user* misunderstanding.

User Simulation: To train a dialogue strategy using RL, some method must be chosen to emulate realistic user responses to system actions. Training with actual users is generally considered untenable since RL can require millions of runs. As such, researchers create simulated users that mimic the responses of real users. The approach employed to create these users varies between researchers; ranging from simulations that employ only real user data (Henderson et al., 2008), to those that model users with probabilistic simulations based on known realistic user behaviors (Levin et al., 2000). Ai et al. suggest that less realistic user simulations that allow RL to explore more of the dialogue state space may perform as well or better than simulations that statistically recreate realistic user behavior (Ai et al., 2007). For this proof-of-concept work, we employ a hand-crafted user simulation that allows full exploration of the state space.

Costs: Although it is agreed that RL is a viable approach to creating optimal dialogue policies, there remains much debate as to what cost functions result in the most useful policies. Typically, these costs include a measure of efficiency (e.g., number of turns) and a measure of solution quality (e.g., the user successfully completed the transaction) (Scheffler and Young, 2002; Levin et al., 2000). For managing the communication channel, it is unclear how the cost function should be structured. In this work we compare two cost components, a more traditional dialogue-length cost versus a novel annoyance cost, to determine which best supports the creation of useful policies.

4 Communication Channel Model

Based on the literature reviewed in Section 2.1, we devised a preliminary model that captures essential elements of how users manage the communication channel. For now, we only include explicit user actions, in which users directly address issues with the communication channel, as noted by Jurafsky et al. (1997). In addition, the users modeled are both consistent and amenable; they provide feedback every time the system's utterances are too loud or too soft, and abandon the interaction only when the system persists in presenting utterances outside the user's tolerance (either ten utterances that are too loud or ten that are too soft).

For this work, we wish to create policies that treat all users equitably. That is, we do not want to train polices that give preferential treatment to a subset of users simply because they are more common. To accomplish this, we use a flat rather than normal distribution of users within the simulation, with both the optimal amplitude and the tolerance range randomly generated for each user. To represent users with differing amplitude needs, simulated users are modeled to have an optimal amplitude between 2 and 8, and a tolerance range of 1, 3 or 5. For example, a user may have a optimal amplitude of 4, but be able to tolerate an amplitude between 2 and 6.

When interacting with the computer, the user responds with: (a) the answer to the system's query if the amplitude is within their tolerance range; (b) too soft (TS) if below their range; or (c) too loud (TL) if the amplitude is above their tolerance range. As a simplifying assumption, TS and TL represent any user responses that address communication channel issues related to amplitude. For example, the user response "Pardon me?" would be represented by TS and "There's no need to shout!" by TL. With this user model, the user only responds to the domain task when the system employs an amplitude setting within the user's tolerance range.

For the system, we need to ensure that the system's amplitude range can accommodate any user-tolerable amplitude. For this reason, the system's amplitude can vary between 0 and 10, and is initially set to 5 prior to each dialogue. In addition to performing domain actions, the system specifies the amount the amplitude should change: -2, -1, +0, +1, +2. Each system communication to the user consists of both a domain action and the system's amplitude change. Thus, the system manages the communication channel using only implicit actions. If the user responds with TS or TL, the system will then restate what it just said, perhaps altering the amplitude prior to re-addressing the user.

5 Hand-crafted Policies

To help in determining whether RL is an appropriate tool for learning communication channel management strategies, we designed two hand-crafted policies for comparison. The first handcrafted policy, termed *no-complaints*, finds a tolerable amplitude as quickly as possible, then holds that amplitude for the remainder of the dialogue. As such, this policy only changes the amplitude in response to explicit complaints from the user. Specifically, the policy increases the amplitude by 2 after a TS response, and drops it by 2 after a TL. If altering the amplitude by 2 would cause the system to return to a setting already identified as too soft or too loud, the system uses an amplitude change of 1.

The second policy, termed *find-optimal*, searches for the user's optimal amplitude, then maintains that amplitude for the remainder of the dialogue. For this policy, the system first increases the amplitude by 1 until the user responds with TL (potentially in response to the system's first utterance), then decreases the amplitude by 1 until the user either responds with TS or the optimal amplitude is clearly identified based on the previous feedback. An amplitude change of 2 is used only when both the optimal amplitude is obvious and a change of 2 will bring the amplitude setting to the optimal amplitude.

6 RL and System Encoding

To learn communication channel management policies we use RL with system and user actions specified using Information State Update rules (Henderson et al., 2008). Following Heeman (2007), we encode commonsense preconditions rather than trying to learn them, and only use a subset of the information state for RL.

Domain Task: We use a domain task that requires the user to supply 9 pieces of information, excluding user feedback relating to the communication channel. The system has a deterministic way of selecting its actions, thus no learning is needed for the domain task.

State Variables: For RL, each state is represented by two variables; *AmpHistory* and *Progress*. *AmpHistory* models the user by tracking all previous user feedback. In addition, it tracks the current amplitude setting. The string contains one slot for each potential amplitude setting (0 through 10), with the current setting contained within "[]". Thus, at the beginning of each interaction, the string is "`-----[-]-----`", where "-" represents no known data. Each time the user responds, the string is updated to reflect which amplitude settings are too soft ("<"), too loud (">"), or within the user's tolerance ("O"). When the user responds with TL/TS, the system also updates all settings above/below the current setting. The *Progress* variable is required to satisfy the Markov property needed for RL. This variable counts the number of successful information exchanges (i.e., the user did not respond with TS or TL). As the domain task requires 9 pieces of information, the Progress variable ranged from 1 to 9.

Costs: Our user model only allows up to 10 utterances that are too soft or too loud. If the cutoff is reached, the domain task has not been completed, so a solution quality cost of 100 is incurred. Cutting off dialogues in this way has the additional benefit of preventing a policy from looping forever during testing. During training, to allow the system to better model the cost of choosing the same action repeatedly, we use a longer cutoff of 1000 utterances rather than 10.

In addition to solution quality, two different cost components are utilized. The first, a dialogue-length cost (DC), assigns a cost of 1 for each user utterance. The second, an annoyance cost (AC), assigns a cost calculated as the difference between the system's amplitude setting and the user's optimal amplitude. This difference is multiplied by 3 when the system's amplitude setting is below the user's optimal. This multiplier was chosen based on research that demonstrated increased response times and errors during cognitively challenging tasks when speech was presented below, rather than above, typical conversational levels (Baldwin and Struckman-Johnson, 2002). Thus, only utterances at the optimal amplitude have no cost.

7 Results

With the above system and user models, we trained policies using the two cost functions discussed above, eight with the DC component and eight using the AC component. All used Q-Learning and the ϵ-greedy method to explore the state space with ϵ set at 20% (Sutton and Barto, 1998). Dialogue runs were grouped into epochs of 100; after each epoch, the current dialogue policy was updated. We trained each policy for 60,000 epochs. After certain epochs, we tested the policy on 5000 user tasks.

For our simple domain, the solution quality cost remained 0 after about the 100th epoch, as all policies learned to avoid user abandonment. Because of this, only the dialogue-length cost(DC) and annoyance cost(AC) components are reflected in the following analyses.

7.1 DC-Trained Policies

By 40,000 epochs, all eight DC policies converged to one common optimal policy. Dialogues resulting from the DC policies average 9.76 user utterances long. DC policies start each dialogue using the default amplitude setting of 5. After receiving the initial user response, they aggressively explore the amplitude range. If the initial user response is TL (or

DC			
AmpHistory	System	Amp	User
-----[-]-----	Query$_1$ +0	5	TS
<<<<<[<]-----	Query$_1$ +2	7	Answer
<<<<<<-[0]---	Query$_2$ +0	7	Answer
<<<<<<-[0]---	Query$_3$ +0	7	Answer
<<<<<<-[0]---	Query$_4$ +0	7	Answer
<<<<<<-[0]---	Query$_5$ +0	7	Answer
<<<<<<-[0]---	Query$_6$ +0	7	Answer
...	...	...	...
dialogue length cost = 10			

AC			
AmpHistory	System	Amp	User
-----[-]-----	Query$_1$ +1	6	TS
<<<<<<[<]----	Query$_1$ +1	7	Answer
<<<<<<<[0]---	Query$_2$ +1	8	Answer
<<<<<<<0[0]--	Query$_3$ +1	9	Answer
<<<<<<00[0]-	Query$_4$ +1	10	TL
<<<<<<<000[>]	Query$_4$ -2	8	Answer
<<<<<<<0[0]0>	Query$_5$ +0	8	Answer
...	...	...	...
annoyance cost = 12			

Table 1: Comparison of DC (left) and AC (right) interactions with a user who has an optimal amplitude of 8 and a tolerance range of 3. The policies continue as shown, without changing the amplitude level, until all 9 queries are answered.

TS), they continue by decreasing (or increasing) the amplitude by -2 (or +2) until they find a tolerable volume, in which case they stop. Table 1 illustrates the above noted aspects of the policy. Additionally, if the policy receives user feedback that is contrary to the last feedback (i.e., TS after TL, or TL after TS), the policy backtracks one amplitude setting. In addition, if the current amplitude is near the boundary (3 or 7), the policy will change the volume by -1 or +1 as changing it by -2 or +2 would cause it to move outside users' amplitude range of 2-8. In essence, the DC policies are quite straightforward; aggressively changing the amplitude if the user complains, and assuming the amplitude is correct if the user does not complain.

7.2 AC-Trained Policies

By 55,000 epochs, AC policies converged to one of two optimal solutions, with an average annoyance cost of 7.49. As illustrated in Table 1, the behavior of the AC policies is substantially more complex than the DC policies. First, the AC policies start by increasing the amplitude, delivering the first utterance at a setting of 6 or 7. Second, the policies do not stop exploring after they find a tolerable setting, instead attempting to bracket the user's tolerance range, thus identifying the user's optimal amplitude. Third, AC policies sometimes avoid lowering the amplitude, even when doing so would concretely identify the user's optimal amplitude. By doing so, the policies potentially incur a cost of 1 for all following turns, but avoid incurring a one time cost of 3 or 6. In essence, the AC policies attempt to find the user's optimal amplitude but may stop short as they approach the end of the dialogue, favoring a slightly too high amplitude over one that might be too low.

7.3 Comparing AC- and DC- Trained Policies

The costs for the AC and DC trained policy sets cannot be directly compared as each set used a different cost function. However, we can compare them using each others' cost function.

First, we compare the two sets of policies in terms of average dialogue-length. For example, in Table 1, following a DC policy results in a dialogue-length of 10. However, for the same user, following the AC policy results in a dialogue-length of 11, one utterance longer due to the TL response to Query$_4$.

The average dialogue-length of the DC and AC policies, averaged across users, is shown in the rightmost two columns of Figure 1. As expected, the DC policies perform better in terms of dialogue-length, averaging 9.76 utterances long. However, the AC policies average 10.32 utterances long, only 0.52 utterances longer. This similarity in length is to be expected, as system communication outside the user's tolerance range impedes progress and is costly using either cost component.

We also compared the AC and DC policies' average dialogue-length for users with the same optimal amplitude (i.e., each column shows the average cost across users with tolerance ranges of 1, 3 and 5), as shown in Figure 1. From this figure it is clear that there is little difference in dialogue-length between AC and DC policies for users with the same optimal amplitude. In addition, for both policies, the lengths are similar between users with differing optimal amplitudes.

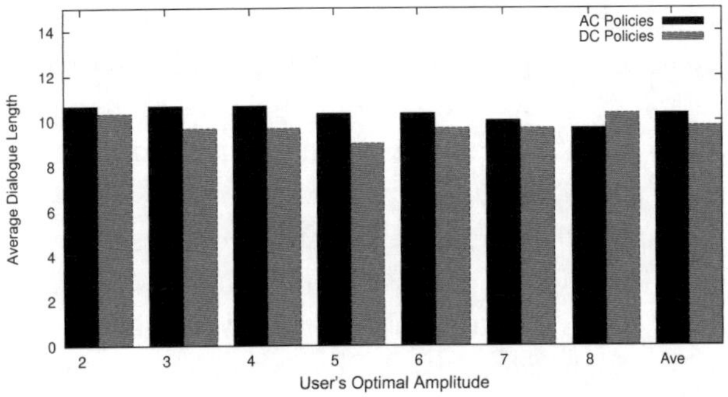

Figure 1: Comparison of the dialogue-length between AC and DC policies for users with differing optimal amplitudes.

Second, we compare the two sets of polices in terms of annoyance costs. For example, in Table 1, following the AC policy results in an annoyance cost of 12. For the same user, following the DC policy results in an annoyance cost of 36; 9 for $Query_1$ as it is three below the user's optimal amplitude, and 3 for each of the following nine utterances as they are all one below optimal.

As shown in the rightmost columns of Figure 2, DC policies average annoyance cost was 13.35, a substantial 78% increase over the average cost of 7.49 for AC policies. Figure 2 also illustrates that the AC and DC policies perform quite differently for users with differing optimal amplitudes. For example, users of the DC policies whose optimal is at (5), or slightly below (4), the system's default setting (5) average lower annoyance costs than those using the AC policies. However, these lowered costs for users in the mid-range is gained at the expense of users whose optimal amplitude is farther afield, especially those users requiring higher amplitude settings. This substantial difference between users with different optimal amplitudes is because, for DC policies, the interaction is often conducted at the very edge of the users' tolerance. In contrast, the AC policies risk more intolerable utterances, but use this information to decrease overall costs by better meeting users' amplitude needs. As such, users of the AC policies can expect the majority of the task to be conducted at, or only one setting above, their optimal amplitude.

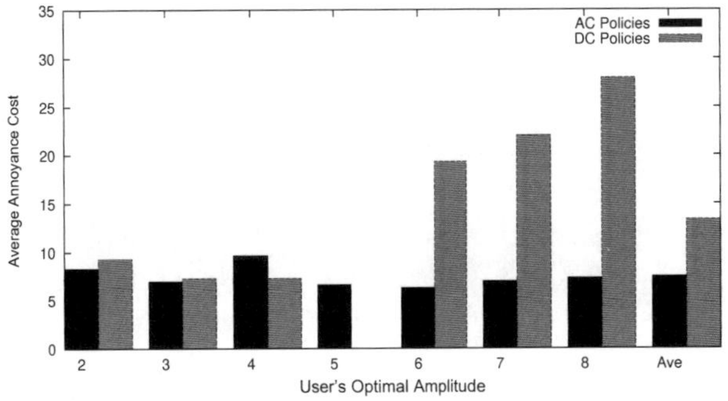

Figure 2: Comparison of the annoyance cost between AC and DC policies for users with differing optimal amplitudes.

7.4 Comparing Hand-crafted and Learned Policies

Each of the two hand-crafted policies were run with each user simulation (i.e., optimal amplitude from 2-8 and tolerance ranges of 1, 3, or 5). In addition, we varied the domain task size, requiring between 4 and 10 pieces of information. DC and AC policies were also trained for these domain task sizes.

As shown in Figure 3, The no-complain policy's annoyance costs ranged from 7.81 for dialogues requiring four pieces of information to 14.67 for those requiring ten pieces. The cost increases linearly with the amount of information required, because the no-complain policy maintains the first amplitude setting found that does not result in a user response of TS or TL. This ensures the amplitude setting is tolerable to the user, but may not be the user's optimal amplitude.

In contrast, the find-optimal policy's annoyance costs initially increase from 9.67 for four pieces of information to 12.24 for seven through ten pieces. The cost does not continue to increase when the amount of information required is greater than seven because, for dialogues long enough to allow the system to concretely identify the user's optimal amplitude, the cost is zero for all subsequent utterances.

Figure 3 also includes the mean annoyance cost for the DC and AC policies. Although one might expect the DC trained policies to resemble the no-complain policy, the learned policy performs slightly better. This difference is because the DC policies learn the range of users' optimal amplitude settings (2-8), and do not move the amplitude below 2 or above 8. In contrast, the no-complain policies

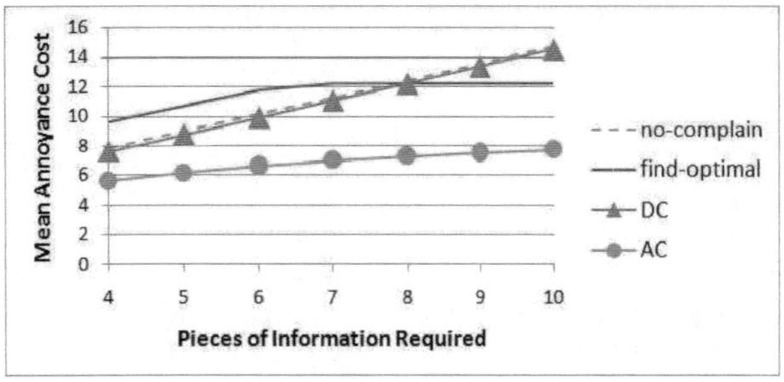

Figure 3: Average user annoyance costs for hand-crafted, DC and AC policies across dialogues requiring differing amounts of information.

behave consistently regardless of the current setting, and thus will incur costs for exploring settings outside the range of users' optimal amplitudes. Similarly, AC policies could be anticipated to closely resemble the find-optimal policy. However, the AC policies average cost is lower than the costs for either hand-crafted policy, regardless of the amount of information required. This difference is, in part, due to differences in behavior at the ends of the users' optimal amplitude range, like the DC policies. However, additional factors include the AC policies' more varied use of amplitude changes and their balancing of the remaining duration of the dialogue against the cost to perform additional exploration, as discussed in subsection 7.2.

8 Discussion and Future Work

The first objective of this work was to create a model of the communication channel that takes into account the abilities and preferences of diverse users. In this model, each user has an optimal amplitude, but will answer a system query delivered within a range around that amplitude, although they find non-preferred, especially too soft, amplitudes annoying. When outside the user's tolerance, the user provides explicit feedback regarding the communication channel breakdown. For the system, the model specifies a composite system action, pairing a domain action with a possible communication channel management action to change the amplitude. By modeling explicit user actions, and implicit system actions, this model captures some essential elements of how people manage the communication channel.

The second objective was to determine whether RL is appropriate for learning communication channel management. As expected, the learned policies found and maintained a tolerable amplitude setting and eliminated user abandonment. We also compared the learned policies with handcrafted solutions, and found that the learned policies performed better. This is primarily due to RL's ability to automatically balance the opposing goals of finding the user's optimal amplitude and minimizing dialogue-length.

An added benefit of RL is that it optimizes the system's behavior for the users on which it is trained. In this work, we purposely used a flat distribution of users, which caused RL to find a policy (especially when using annoyance costs) that does not penalize the outliers, which are usually those with special needs. In fact, we could modify the user distribution, or the simulated users' behavior, and RL would optimize the system's behavior automatically.

In this work, we contrasted dialogue length (DC) against annoyance cost (AC) components. We found that the AC and DC policies share the objective of finding an amplitude setting within the user's tolerance range because both incur stepwise costs for intolerable utterances. But, AC policies further refine this objective by incurring costs for tolerable, but non-optimal, amplitudes as well. AC policies are using information that is not explicitly communicated to the system, but which none-the-less RL can use while learning a policy.

As this was exploratory work, the user model does not yet fully reflect expected user behavior. For example, as the system's amplitude decreases, users may misunderstand the system's query or fail to respond at all. In future work we will use an enhanced user model that includes more natural user behavior. In addition, because we wanted the system to focus on learning a communication channel management strategy, the domain task was fixed. In future work, we will use RL to learn policies that both accomplish a more complex domain task, and model connections between domain tasks and communication channel management. Ultimately, we need to conduct user-testing to measure the efficacy of the communication channel management policies. We feel confident that learned policies trained using a communication channel model which reflects the range of users' abilities and preferences will prove effective for supporting all users.

References

Hua Ai, Joel R. Tetreault, and Diane J. Litman. 2007. Comparing user simulation models for dialog strategy learning. In *NAACL-HLT*, April.

Carryl L. Baldwin and David Struckman-Johnson. 2002. Impact of speech presentation level on cognitive task performance: implications for auditory display design. *Ergonomics*, 45(1):62–74.

Carryl L. Baldwin. 2001. Impact of age-related hearing impairment on cognitive task performance: evidence for improving existing methodologies. In *Human Factors and Ergonomics Society Annual Meeting; Aging*, pages 245–249.

Linda Bell, Joakim Gustafson, and Mattias Heldner. 2003. Prosodic adaptation in humancomputer interaction. In *Proceedings of ICPhS 03*, volume 1, pages 833–836.

Peter Heeman. 2007. Combining reinforcement learning with information-state update rules. In *Proceedings of the Conference of the North American Chapter of the Association for Computational Linguistics*, pages 268–275, Rochester, NY, April.

James Henderson, Oliver Lemon, and Kallirroi Georgila. 2008. Hybrid reinforcement/supervised learning of dialogue policies from fixed data sets. *Comput. Linguist.*, 34(4):487–511.

J. C. Junqua. 1993. The lombard reflex and its role on human listeners and automatic speech recognizers. *The Journal of the Acoustical Society of America*, 93(1):510–524, January.

Dan Jurafsky, Liz Shriberg, and Debra Biasca. 1997. Switchboard: SWBD-DAMSL Coders Manual.

Blade Kotelly. 2003. *The Art and Business of Speech Recognition*. Addison-Wesley, January.

E. Levin, R. Pieraccini, and W. Eckert. 2000. A stochastic model of human-machine interaction for learning dialog strategies. *IEEE Transactions on Speech and Audio Processing*, 8(1):11–23.

Bjorn Lindblom, 1990. *Explaining phonetic variation: A sketch of the H & H theory*, pages 403–439. Kluwer Academic Publishers.

Rebecca Lunsford, Sharon Oviatt, and Alexander M. Arthur. 2006. Toward open-microphone engagement for multiparty interactions. In *Proceedings of the 8th International Conference on Multimodal Interfaces*, pages 273–280, New York, NY, USA. ACM.

Eric Martinson and Derek Brock. 2007. Improving human-robot interaction through adaptation to the auditory scene. In *HRI '07: Proceedings of the ACM/IEEE international conference on Human-robot interaction*, pages 113–120, New York, NY, USA. ACM.

K. L. Payton, R. M. Uchanski, and L. D. Braida. 1994. Intelligibility of conversational and clear speech in noise and reverberation for listeners with normal and impaired hearing. *The Journal of the Acoustical Society of America*, 95(3):1581–1592, March.

Harvey Sacks, Emanuel A. Schlegoff, and Gail Jefferson. 1974. A simplest sytsematic for the organization of turn-taking for conversation. *Language*, 50(4):696–735, December.

K. Scheffler and S. J. Young. 2002. Automatic learning of dialogue strategy using dialogue simulation and reinforcement learning. In *Proceedings of Human Language Technology*, pages 12–18, San Diego CA.

A. Stent, M. Huffman, and S. Brennan. 2008. Adapting speaking after evidence of misrecognition: Local and global hyperarticulation. *Speech Communication*, 50(3):163–178, March.

Richard S. Sutton and Andrew G. Barto. 1998. *Reinforcement Learning: An Introduction*.

Jessica Villing, Cecilia Holtelius, Staffan Larsson, Anders Lindström, Alexander Seward, and Nina Aaberg. 2008. Interruption, resumption and domain switching in in-vehicle dialogue. In *GoTAL '08: Proceedings of the 6th international conference on Advances in Natural Language Processing*, pages 488–499, Berlin, Heidelberg. Springer-Verlag.

Marilyn A. Walker. 2000. An application of reinforcement learning to dialogue strategy selection in a spoken dialogue system for email. *Journal of Aritificial Intelligence Research*, 12:387–416.

A Multimodal Vocabulary for Augmentative and Alternative Communication from Sound/Image Label Datasets

Xiaojuan Ma **Christiane Fellbaum** **Perry R. Cook**
Princeton University
35 Olden St. Princeton, NJ 08544, USA
{xm,fellbaum,prc}@princeton.edu

Abstract

Existing Augmentative and Alternative Communication vocabularies assign multimodal stimuli to words with multiple meanings. The ambiguity hampers the vocabulary effectiveness when used by people with language disabilities. For example, the noun "a missing letter" may refer to a character or a written message, and each corresponds to a different picture. A vocabulary with images and sounds unambiguously linked to words can better eliminate misunderstanding and assist communication for people with language disorders. We explore a new approach of creating such a vocabulary via automatically assigning semantically unambiguous groups of synonyms to sound and image labels. We propose an unsupervised word sense disambiguation (WSD) voting algorithm, which combines different semantic relatedness measures. Our voting algorithm achieved over 80% accuracy with a sound label dataset, which significantly outperforms WSD with individual measures. We also explore the use of human judgments of evocation between members of concept pairs, in the label disambiguation task. Results show that evocation achieves similar performance to most of the existing relatedness measures.

1 Introduction

In natural languages, a word form may refer to different meanings. For instance, the word "fly" means "travel through the air" in context like "fly to New York," while it refers to an insect in the phrase "a fly on the trashcan." Speakers determine the appropriate sense of a polysemous word based on the context. However, people with language disorders and access/retrieval problems, may have great difficulty in understanding words individually or in a context. To overcome such language barriers, visual and auditory representations are introduced to help illustrate concepts (Ma et al., 2009a)(Ma et al., 2010). For example, a person with a language disability can tell the word "fly" refers to "travel through the air" when he sees a plane in the image (rather than an insect); likewise he can distinguish the meaning of "fly" given the plane engine sound vs. the insect buzzing sound. This approach has been employed in Augmentative and Alternative Communication (AAC), in the form of multimodal vocabularies in assistive devices (Steele et al. 1989)(Lingraphica, 2010).

However, current AAC vocabularies assign visual stimuli to words instead of specific meanings, and thus bring in ambiguity when a user with language disability tries to comprehend and communicate a concept. For example, for the word "fly," Lingraphica only has an icon showing a plane and a flock of birds flying. Confusion arises when a sentence like "I want to kill the fly (the insect)" is explained using the airplane/bird icon. Similarly, it will lead to miscommunication if the sound of keys jingling is used to express "a key is missing" when the person intends to refer to a key on the keyboard. People with language impairment are relying on the AAC vocabularies for language access, and any ambiguity may result in communication failure.

To address this problem, we propose building a semantic multimodal AAC vocabulary with visual and auditory representations expressing concepts rather than words (Figure 1), as the backbone of the language assistant system for people with aphasia (Ma et al. 2009b). Our work is exploratory with the following innovations: 1) we target the insufficiency of current assistive vocabularies by resolving ambiguity; 2) we enrich concept inventory and connect concepts through language, environmental sounds, and images (little research has looked into conveying concepts through natural nonspeech sounds); and 3) our vocabulary has a dynamic scalable semantic network structure rather

Proceedings of the NAACL HLT 2010 Workshop on Speech and Language Processing for Assistive Technologies, pages 62–70,
Los Angeles, California, June 2010.

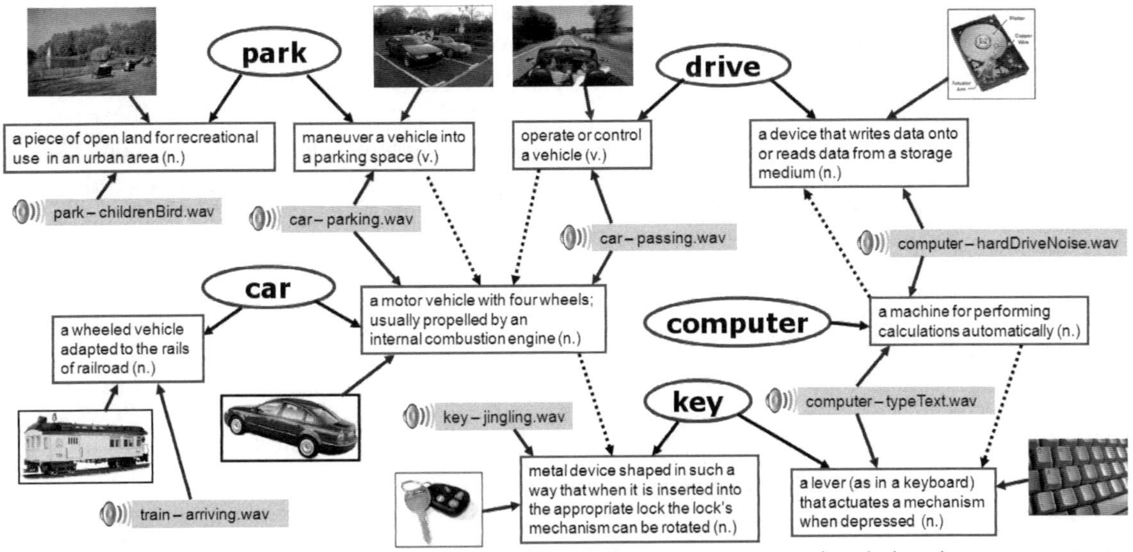

Figure 1. Disambiguated AAC multimedia vocabulary; dash arrows are semantic relations between concepts.

than simply grouping words into categories as conventional assistive devices do.

One intuitive way to build a disambiguated multimodal vocabulary is to manually assign meanings to each word in the existing vocabulary. However, the task is time consuming with poor scalability – no new multimedia representations are generated for concepts that are missing in the vocabulary. ImageNet (Jia et al., 2009) was constructed by people verifying the assignment of web images to given synonym sets (synsets). ImageNet has over nine million images linked to about 15 thousands noun synsets in WordNet (Fellbaum, 1998). Despite the huge human effort, ImageNet, with the goal of creating a computer vision database, does not yet include all the most commonly used words across different parts of speech. It is not yet suitable for a language support application.

We explore a new approach for generating a vocabulary with concept to sound/image associations, that is, conducting word sense disambiguation (WSD) techniques used in Natural Language Processing on sound/image label datasets. For example, the labels "car, drive, fast" for the sound "car – passing.wav" are assigned to synsets "car: a motor vehicle," "drive: operate or control a vehicle," and "fast: quickly or rapidly" via WSD. It means the sound "car – passing.wav" can be used to depict those concepts. This approach is viable because the words in the sound/image labels were shown to evoke one another based on the auditory/visual content, and their meanings can be identified by considering all the tags generated for a given sound or image as a context. With the availability of large sound/image label datasets, the vocabulary created from WSD can be easily expanded.

A variety of WSD methods (e.g. knowledge-based methods (Lesk, 1986), unsupervised methods (Lin, 1997), semi-supervised methods (Hearst, 1991) (Yarowsky, 1995), and supervised methods (Novischi et al., 2007)) were developed and evaluated with corpus data and other text documents like webpages. Compared to the text data that WSD methods work with, labels for sounds and images have unique characteristics. The labels are a bag of words related to the visual/auditory content; there is no syntactic or part of speech information, nor are the words necessarily contextual neighbors. For example, contexts suggest landscape senses for the word pair "bank" and "water", whereas in an image, a person may drink water inside a bank building. Furthermore, few annotated image or sound label datasets are available, making it hard to apply supervised or semi-supervised WSD methods.

To efficiently and effectively create a disambiguated multimodal vocabulary, we need to achieve two goals. First, optimize the accuracy of the WSD algorithm to minimize the work required for manual checking and correction afterwards. Second, construct a semantic network across different parts of speech, and thus explore linking semantic relatedness measures that can capture aspects different from existing ones. In this paper, we target the first goal by proposing an unsupervised sense disambiguation algorithm combining a variety of semantic relatedness measures. We chose an unsupervised method because of the lack of a large manually annotated gold standard. The measure-combined voting algorithm presented here draws advantages from different semantic relatedness measures and has them vote for the best-fitting sense to assign to a label. Evaluation shows that the voting algorithm significantly exceeds WSD with each individual measure.

To approach the second goal, we proposed and tested a semantic relatedness measure called evocation (Boyd-Graber et al., 2006) in disambiguation of sound/image labels. Evocation measures human judgements of relatedness between a directed concepts pair. It provides cross parts of speech evocativeness information which supplements most of the knowledge-based semantic relatedness measures. Evaluation results showed that the performance of WSD with evocation is no worse than most of the relatedness measures that we applied, despite the relatively small size of the current evocation dataset.

2 Dataset: Semantic Labels for Environmental Sounds and Images

Our ultimate goal is to create an AAC vocabulary of associations between environmental sounds and images and groups of synonymous words that are relevant to the content. We are working with two datasets of human labels for multimedia data, SoundNet and the Peekaboom dataset.

2.1 SoundNet Sound Label Dataset

The SoundNet Dataset (Ma, Fellbaum, and Cook, 2009) consists of 327 environmental "soundnails" (5-second audio clips) each with semantic labels collected from participants via a large scale Amazon Mechanical Turk (AMT) study. The soundnails cover a wide range of auditory scenes, from vehicle (e.g. car starting), mechanical tools (e.g. handsaw) and electrical devices (e.g. TV), to natural phenomena (e.g. rain), animals (e.g. a dog barking), and human sounds (e.g. a baby crying). In the AMT study, participants were asked to generate tags for each soundnail labeling its source, possible location, and actions involved in making the sound.

Each soundnail was labeled by over 100 people. The tags were clustered into meaning units that SoundNet refers to as "sense sets." A sense set includes a set of words with similar meanings. For instance, for the soundnail pre-labeled "bag, zipOpen" which is the sound of opening the zipper of a bag, the following sense sets were generated:

(a) "**zipper**" {zipper, zip up, zip, unzip};
(b) "**bag**" {bag, duffle bag, nylon bag, suitcase, luggage, backpack, purse, pack, briefcase};
(c) "**house**" {house, home, building}, and
(d) "**clothes**" {clothes, jacket, coat, pants, jeans, dress, garment}.

The word in **bold** is was judged by SoundNet to be the best representative of the sense set, and other words, possibly belonging to different parts of speech are included in the curly brackets enclosing the sense sets. SoundNet uses sense sets rather than single words because 1) people may use different words to describe the same underlying concept, (e.g. "baby" and "infant;" "rain" as a noun and as a verb); 2) people cannot draw fine distinctions between objects and events that generate similar sounds, and thus may come up with different but related categories (e.g. "plate," "cup," and "bowl" for the dish clinking sound); and 3) people may perceive objects and events that are not explicitly presented in the sound very differently (e.g. "bag" vs. "clothes" for the sound made by a zipper). In this experiment, only sense sets (labels) that were generated by at least 25% of the labelers were used.

In our disambiguation experiment, two kinds of contexts were explored. In the Context 1 scheme, each label is treated separately: all its members plus the representatives of the other sense sets are considered. Take the soundnail "bag, zipOpen" as an example. The context for disambiguating label (a) "**zipper**" {zipper, zip up, zip, unzip} is:

zipper, zip up, zip, unzip, **bag**, **house**, **clothes**.

The context for label (d) "**clothes**" {clothes, jacket, coat, pants, jeans, dress, garment} is:

clothes, jacket, coat, pants, jeans, dress, garment, **zipper**, **bag**, **house**.

In the Context 1 scheme, all **representative** words will be disambiguated multiple times. The final result will be the synset that gets the most votes. In the Context 2 scheme, as for the image dataset described below, all members from each sense set are put together to create the context, and each word is disambiguated only once.

2.2 Peekaboom Image Label Dataset

The ESP Game Dataset (Von Ahn and Dabbish, 2004) contains a large number of web images and human labels produced via an online game. For example, an image of a glass of hard liquor is labeled "full, shot, alcohol, clear, drink, glass, beverage." The Peekaboom Game (Von Ahn et al., 2006) is the successor of the ESP Game. In our experiment, part of the Peekaboom Dataset (3,086 images) was used. For each image, all the labels together form the context for sense disambiguation.

The Peekaboom labels are noisier than the SoundNet labels for several reasons. First, random objects may appear in a picture and thus be included in the labels. For example, an image is labeled "computer, shark" because there is a shark picture on the computer screen. Second, texts in the images are often included in the labels. For example, the word "green" is one of the labels for an image with a street sign "Green St." Third, the Peekaboom labels are not stemmed, which adds another layer of ambiguity. For example, the labels "bridge, building" could refer to a building event or to a built entity. In the experiment, all labels for an image are used in their unstemmed form to construct the context for WSD.

3 Evocation and Other Semantic Relatedness Measures

A set of measures were selected to assess the relatedness between possible senses of words in the sound/image labels. Apart from existing methods, an additional measure, evocation, is introduced.

3.1 Evocation

Evocation (Boyd-Graber et al., 2006) measures concept similarity based on human judgment. It is a directed measure, with evocation(synset A, synset B) defined as how much synset A brings to mind synset B. The evocation dataset has been extended to scores for 100,000 directed synset pairs (Nikolova et al., 2009).

The evocation data were collected independently of WordNet or corpus data. We propose the use of evocation in WSD for image and sound labels for the following reasons. First, the sound and image labels are generated based on human perception of the content and common knowledge. In SoundNet in particular, many of the evoked labels reflected the most obvious objects or events in a sound scene. For example, "bag" and "coat" were evoked from the zipper soundnail. In this case, the evocation score may be a good evaluation of the relatedness between the labels. Second, evocation assesses relatedness of concepts across different parts of speech, which is suitable for identifying image and sound labels containing nouns, verbs, adjectives, adverbs, etc.

This paper is a first attempt to compare the effectiveness of the use of evocation measure in sense disambiguation to the conventional, relatively better tested similarity measures, in the context of assigning synsets to sound/image labels. Considering that the evocation dataset is small in size and susceptible to noise given the method by which it was collected, we have not yet incorporated evocation into the measure-combined voting algorithm described in the Section 4.

3.2 Semantic Relatedness Measures

Nine measures of semantic relatedness[1] between synsets are used in the experiment, both as contributors to the voting algorithm and as baselines for comparison, including:

1) WordNet path based measures.

- "path" – shortest path length between synsets, inversely proportional to the number of nodes on the path.
- "wup" (Wu and Palmer, 1994) – ratio of the depth of the Least Common Subsumer (LCS) to the depths of two synsets in the Wordnet taxonomy.
- "lch" (Leacock and Chodorow, 1998) – considering the length of the shortest path between two synsets to the depth of the WordNet taxonomy.

2) Information and content based measures.

- "res" (Resnik, 1995) – the informational content (IC) of a given corpus of the LCS between two synsets.
- "lin" (Lin, 1997) – the ratio of the IC of the LCS to the IC of the two synsets.
- "jcn" (Jiang and Conrath, 1997) – inversely proportional to the difference between the IC of the two synsets and the IC of the LCS.

[1] "hso" (Hirst and St-Onge, 1998) extensively slows down the WSD process with over five context words, and thus, is not included in the experiment.

3) WordNet definition based measures.

- "lesk" (Banerjee and Pedersen, 2002) – overlaps in the definitions of two synsets.
- "vector" (Patwardhan and Pedersen, 2006) – cosine of the angle between the co-occurrence vector computed from the definitions around the two synsets.
- "vector_pairs" – co-occurrence vectors are computed from definition pairs separately.

The computation of the relatedness scores using measures listed above were carried out by codes from the WordNet::Similarity (Pedersen et al., 2004) and WordNet::SenseRelate projects (Pedersen and Kolhatkar, 2009). In contrast to WordNet::SenseRelated, which employs only one similarity measure in the WSD process, this paper proposes a strategy of having several semantic relatedness measures vote for the best synset for each word. The voting algorithm intends to improve WSD performance by combining conclusions from various measures to eliminate a false result. Since there is no syntax among the words generated for a sound/image, they should all be considered for WSD. Thus, the width of the context window is the total number of words in the context.

4 Label Sense Disambiguation Algorithm

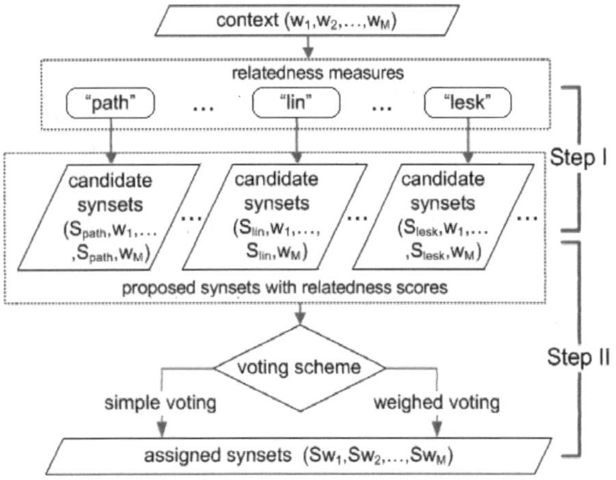

Figure 2. Measure-Combined Voting Algorithm.

Figure 2 shows the overall process of the measure-combined voting algorithm for disambiguating sound/image labels. After the context for WSD is generated, the process is divided into two steps. In Step I, the relatedness scores of each sense of a word based on the context is computed by each measure separately. Step II combines results from all measures and generates the disambiguated synsets for all words in the sound/image labels. Evocation did not participate in Step II.

4.1 Step I: Generate Candidate Synsets Based on Individual Measures

Given the context of M words (w_1, …, w_M), and K relatedness measures (k = 1, …, K), the task is to assign each word w_j (j = 1, …, M) to the synset $s_{x,wj}$ that is the most appropriate within the context. Here, the word w_j has N_j synsets, denoted as $s_{n,wj}$ (n = 1, …, N_j). Step I is to calculate the relatedness score for each synset of each word in the context.

$$score_k(s_{i,w_j}) = \sum_{m=1,\dots,M}^{m\neq j} \max_{n=1,\dots,N_m}(measure_k(s_{i,w_j}, s_{n,w_m}))$$

The evocation score between two sysnets s_a, s_b is the maximum of the directed evocation ratings.

$$score_{evocation}(s_a, s_b) = \max(evocation(s_a, s_b), evocation(s_b, s_a))$$

$$score_{evocation}(s_{i,w_j}) = \sum_{m=1,\dots,M}^{m\neq j} \max_{n=1,\dots,N_m}(score_{evocation}(s_{i,w_j}, s_{n,w_m}))$$

The synset that evocation assigns to word j is the one with the highest score.

$$s_{w_j} = s_{x,w_j}, if\ score_{evocation}(s_{x,w_j}) = \max_{i=1,\dots,N_j}(score_{evocation}(s_{i,w_j}))$$

4.2 Step II: Vote for the Best Candidate

Three voting schemes were tested, including unweighted simple votes, weighted votes among top candidates, and weighted votes among all synsets.

1) Unweighted Simple Votes

Synset $s_{n,wj}$ of word w_j gets a vote from relatedness measure k if its $score_k$ is the maximum among all the synsets for w_j, and it becomes the candidate synset for w_j elected by measure k ($C_{k,wj}$):

$$vote_k(s_{x,w_j}) = \begin{cases} 1, if \quad score_k(s_{x,w_j}) = \max_{i=1,\dots,N_j}(score_k(s_{i,w_j})) \\ 0, else \end{cases}$$

$$candidate_k(s_{w_j}) = s_{x,w_j}, \quad if\ vote_k(s_{x,w_j}) = 1$$

The candidate list for word w_j (candidates(Sw_j)) is the union of all candidate synsets elected by individual relatedness measures.

$$candidates(s_{w_j}) = \underset{k=1,\dots,K}{union}(candidate_k(s_{w_j}))$$

For each candidate in the list, the votes from all measures are calculated. The one receiving the most votes becomes the proposed synset for w_j.

$$voteCount(s_{i,w_j}) = \sum_{k=1}^{K} vote_k(s_{i,w_j})$$

$$s_{w_j} = s_{x,w_j}, if$$

$$voteCount(s_{x,w_j}) = \max_{s_{i,w_j} \in candidates(s_{w_j})} (voteCount(s_{i,w_j}))$$

The evaluation of WSD with evocation and the measure-combined voting algorithm was carried out primarily on the SoundNet label dataset be-

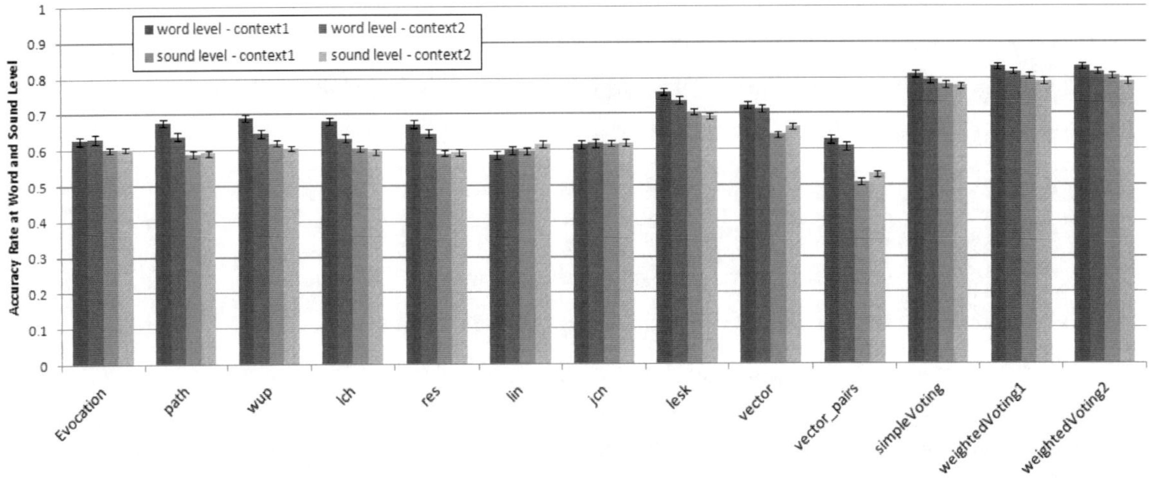

Figure 3. Accuracy rate at word and sound level in comparison among evocation, voting, and nine individual sense similarity measures.

2) Weighted Votes among Top Candidates

The weighted voting scheme avoids a situation where the false results win by a very small margin. The weight under relatedness measure k for $s_{i,wj}$ is calculated as the relative score to the maximum $score_k$ among all synsets for word w_j. It suggests how big of a difference in relatedness score of any given synset is to the highest score among all the possible synsets for the target word.

$$weight_k(s_{x,w_j}) = score_k(s_{x,w_j}) / \max_{i=1,\ldots,N_j} (score_k(s_{i,w_j}))$$

The weighted votes synset $s_{i,wj}$ receives over all measures is the sum of its weight under individual measure. In voting scheme 2, the synset from the candidate list which gets the highest weighted votes becomes the winner.

$$weightedVote(s_{i,w_j}) = \sum_{k=1}^{K} weight_k(s_{i,w_j})$$

$$s_{w_j} = s_{x,w_j}, if$$

$$weightedVote(s_{x,w_j}) = \max_{s_{i,w_j} \in candidates(s_{w_j})} (weightedVote(s_{i,w_j}))$$

3) Weighted Votes among All Synsets

Voting scheme 3 differs from 2 in that the synset from all synsets for word w_j which gets the highest weighted votes is the proposed synset for w_j.

$$s_{w_j} = s_{x,w_j}, if$$

$$weightedVote(s_{x,w_j}) = \max_{i=1,\ldots,N_j} (weightedVote(s_{i,w_j}))$$

5 Evaluation

cause of the availability of ground truth data. SoundNet provides manual annotation for 1,553 different words for 327 soundnails (e.g. the word "road" appears in 41 sounds).

The accuracy rate (precision) was computed for each WSD method. The sound level accuracy of a WSD_k is the average percentage of correct sense assignments over the 327 sounds. The word level accuracy is the mean over 1553 distinctive words. Accuracy rates of different measures at both level accepted the null hypothesis in homogeneity test.

$$\underset{sound-level}{accuracy}(WSD_k) \equiv (\sum_{i=1}^{327} (\%correctness)_i) / 327$$

$$\underset{word-level}{accuracy}(WSD_k) \quad (\sum_{w=1}^{1553} (\%correctness)_w) / 1553$$

Due to the lack of ground truth in the Peekaboom dataset, we only computed the overlap between the WSD result of 3,086 images from the voting algorithm, evocation and each relatedness measures.

5.1 Overall Comparison across WSD methods with Various Relatedness Measures

Figures 3 show the overall comparison among different methods at both sound level and word level. It suggests that the performance of the evocation measure in sense disambiguation is as good as the path-based and context-based measures. The definition-based measures ("lesk" and "vector") are significantly better than other measures if used individually (similar to (Patwardhan et al.2003)).

However, the voting algorithms proposed in this work significantly outperformed each individual measure based on ANOVA results. At sound level, Context 1: ($F(12, 20176) = 102.92$, $p < 0.001$); Context 2: ($F(12, 4238) = 89.42$, $p < 0.001$). At word level, Context 1: ($F(12, 20176) = 68.78$, $p < 0.001$); Context 2: ($F(12, 4238) = 60.72$, $p < 0.001$).

The scheme of composing context (Section 2.1) has significant impact on the accuracy, with Context 1 (taking all members in the related sense set and representatives from the others) outperforming Context 2 (taking all words in all sense sets) at the word level ($F(1, 40352) = 20.19$, $p < 0.001$). The influence of context scheme is not significant at the sound level ($F(1, 8476) = 0.35$, $p = 0.5546$). The interaction between measures and context schemes is not significant, indicating that accuracy differences are similar regardless of context construction.

5.2 Performance of the Voting Algorithm

Figure 4 shows the histogram (distribution) for the accuracy rate at sound and word levels. We see that for the voting algorithm, the accuracy rates are greater than 0.7 for most of the sounds, and greater than 0.9 for majority of the words to disambiguate.

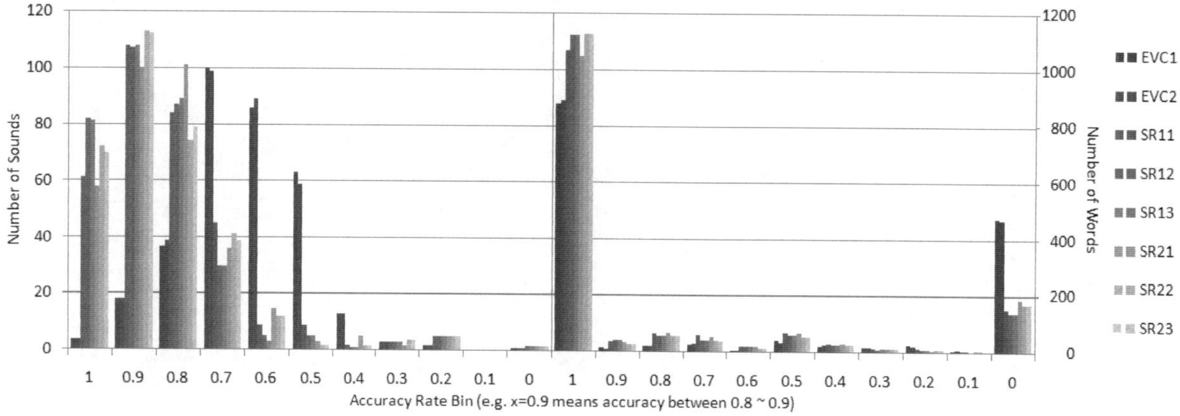

Figure 4. Histogram of accuracy rate at sound (327, left) and word level (1553, right) among different measures, contexts, and voting schemes. EVC1 = Evocation (Context 1); SR11 = Voting (Context 1, voting scheme 1).

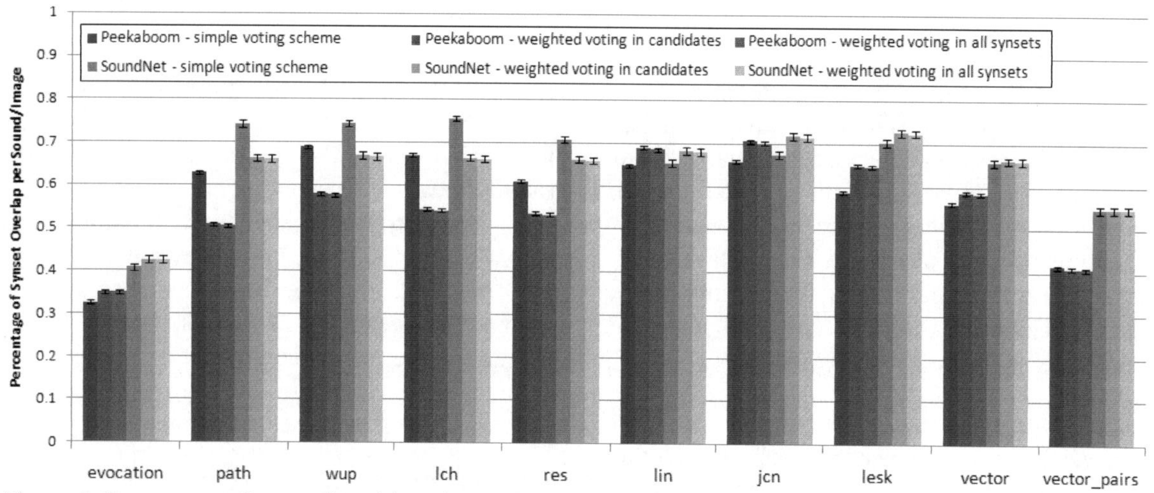

Figure 5. Percentage of sense disambiguation results overlap between voting algorithm, evocation, and individual sense relatedness measures at image (3,086 images) and sound (327 sounds) level.

Figure 5 show the percentage of sense disambiguation results overlapping between voting algorithm and individual relatedness measures. Note that any two methods may come up with different correct results (e.g. "lesk" assigned "chirp" as "a sharp sound" while the voting algorithm assigned "chirp" as "making a sharp sound"). This indicates the change of the contribution of each relatedness measures in different voting schemes. In the simple voting scheme, more disambiguation results came from the "path," "wup," and "lch" (the WordNet path based measures), while the weighted voting scheme took more of the recommendations from "lesk," "lin," and "jcn" (context and definition based measures) into consideration. At the sound level, there is no significant accuracy difference among the three voting schemes, and the influence of the context composition is similar. However, at the word level (Figure 3), the weighted voting schemes significantly outperformed the simple voting scheme ($F(2, 9312) = 5.20$, $p = 0.0055$), and all of them have significantly better accuracy when the context contains mainly members from the same sense set ($F(1, 9312) = 4.79$, $p = 0.0287$).

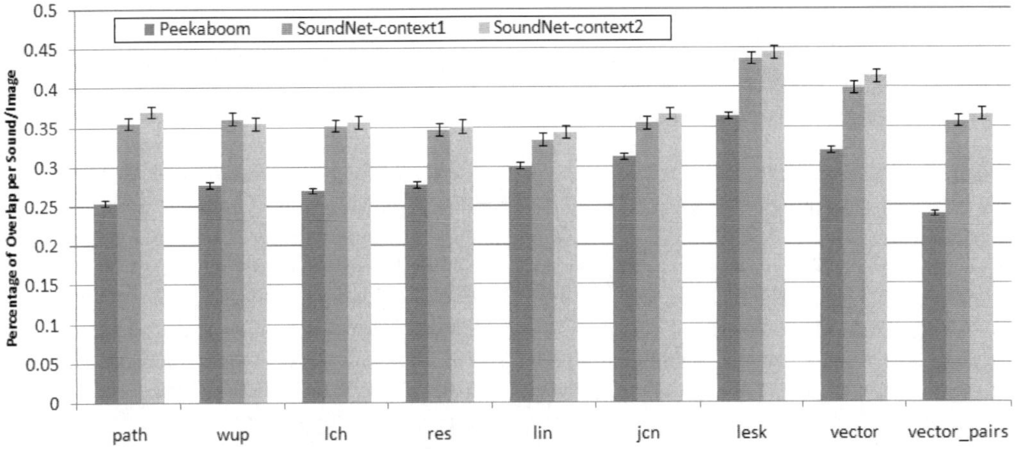

Figure 6. Percentage of WSD results overlap between evocation and various relatedness measures.

5.3 Performance of WSD with Evocation

As shown in Figures 3, the performance of the evocation measure is not significantly different from path-based and some context-based measures at sound level, including "path," "wup," "lch," "res," "lin," and "jcn" (for Context 1, $F(6, 2282) = 2.0582$, $p = 0.0551$; for Context 2, $F(6, 2282) = 1.6679$, $p = 0.1249$); and is significantly better than the vector_pairs measure (for Context 1, $F(1, 652) = 61.37$, $p < 0.001$; for Context 2, $F(1, 652) = 36.47$, $p < 0.001$). At the word level, the performance of the evocation measure is not significantly different from that of measures including "path," "wup," "lch," "res" ($F(4, 7760) = 0.39$, $p = 0.8135$), and "lin," "jcn," and "vector_pairs" ($F(3, 6208) = 1.52$, $p = 0.2077$). Figure 8 (SoundNet) and Figure 9 (Peekaboom) show the percentage of synset assignment overlap between evocation and the other nine relatedness measures. The overlap with "lesk" and "vector" are significantly higher than that with the other measures ($F(8, 5877) = 34.67$, $p < 0.001$). It suggests that evocation as a semantic relatedness measure may be closer to the definition-based measures than path and content based measures.

For the SoundNet dataset, 34% to 44% of evocation WSD results overlap with that of other measures; for the Peekaboom dataset, the overlap is 25% to 35% (Figure 6). Given that evocation performed similarly in accuracy to most of other measures with relatively low overlap in WSD results, evocation may capture different aspects of semantic relatedness from existing measures.

6 Conclusion and Future Work

We explored the construction of a sense disambiguated semantic AAC multimodal vocabulary from sound/image label datasets. Two WSD approaches are introduced to assign specific meanings to environmental sound and image labels, and further create concept-sound/image associations. The measure-combined voting algorithm targets the accuracy of WSD and achieves significantly better performance than each relatedness measure individually. Our second approach applies a new relatedness measure, evocation. Evocation achieves similar performance to most of the existing relatedness measures with sound labels. Results suggest that evocation provides different semantic information from current measures.

Future work includes: 1) expanding the evocation dataset and investigating the potential improvement in its WSD accuracy; 2) incorporating the extended evocation dataset into the voting algorithm; 3) exploring additional information such as image and sound similarity to help with WSD.

Acknowledgments

We thank the Kimberley and Frank H. Moss '71 Princeton SEAS Research Fund for supporting our project.

References

Satanjeev Banerjee and Ted Pedersen. 2002. An Adapted Lesk Algorithm for Word Sense Disambiguation Using WordNet. *Proceedings of the 3rd International Conference on Intelligent Text Processing and Computational Linguistics*.

Jordan Boyd-Graber, Christaine Fellbaum, Daniel Osherson, and Robert Schapire. 2006. Adding Dense, Weighted Connections to WordNet. *Proceedings of the Thirds International WordNet Conference*.

Jia Deng, Wei Dong, Richard Socher, Li -J. Li, Kai Li and Li Fei-Fei. 2009. ImageNet: A Large-Scale Hierarchical Image Database. *Proceedings of the IEEE Computer Vision and Pattern Recognition (CVPR)*.

Christiane Fellbaum, editor. 1998. *WordNet: An Electronic Lexical Database*. MIT Press.

Marti Hearst. 1991. Noun Homograph Disambiguation Using Local Context in Large Text Corpora. *Proc. of the 7th Annual Conference of the University of Waterloo Center for the New OED and Text Research*.

Graeme Hirst and David St. Onge. 1998. Lexical Chains as Representations of Context for the Detection and Correction of Malapropisms. In Christiane Fellbaum, editor, *WordNet: An Electronic Lexical Database*.

Jay Jiang and David Conrath. 1997. Semantic Similarity Based on Corpus Statistics and Lexical Taxonomy. *Proceedings on International Conference on Research in Computational Linguistics*.

Claudia Leacock and Martin Chodorow. 1998. Combining Local Context and WordNet Similarity for Word Sense Identification. In Christiane Fellbaum, editor, *WordNet: An Electronic Lexical Database*.

Michael Lesk. 1986. Automatic Sense Disambiguation Using Machine Readable Dictionaries: How to Tell a Pine Cone from an Ice Cream Cone. *Proceedings of SIGDOC'86*.

Dekang Lin. 1997. Using Syntactic Dependency as a Local Context to Resolve Word Sense Ambiguity. *Proceedings of the 35th Annual Meeting of the Association for Computational Linguistics*, pp. 64-71.

Lingraphica. http://www.aphasia.com/. 2010.

Xiaojuan Ma, Christiane Fellbaum. and Perry Cook. 2010. SoundNet: Investigating a Language Composed of Environmental Sounds. In *Proc. CHI 2010*.

Xiaojuan Ma, Jordan Boy-Graber, Sonya Nikolova, and Perry Cook. 2009a. Speaking Through Pictures: Images vs. Icons. *Proceedings of ASSETS09*.

Xiaojuan Ma, Sonya Nikolova and Perry Cook. 2009b. W2ANE: When Words Are Not Enough - Online Multimedia Language Assistant for People with Aphasia. *Proceedings of ACM Multimedia 2009*.

Sonya Nikolova, Jordan Boyd-Graber, and Christiane Fellbaum. 2009. Collecting Semantic Similarity Ratings to Connect Concepts in Assistive Communication Tools (in press). *Modelling, Learning and Processing of Text-Technological Data Structures, Springer Studies in Computational Intelligence*.

Adrian Novischi, Muirathnam Srikanth, and Andrew Bennett. 2007. Lcc-wsd: System Description for English Coarse Grained All Words Task at SemEval 2007. *Proceedings of the 4th International Workshop on Semantic Evaluations(SemEval-2007)*, pp 223-226.

Siddharth Patwardhan, Satanjeev Benerjee and Ted Pedersen. Using Measures of Semantic Relatedness for Word Sense Disambiguation. 2003. *Proceeding of CICLing2003*, pp. 241-257.

Siddharth Patwardhan and Ted Pedersen Using WordNet Based Context Vectors to Estimate the Semantic Relatedness of Concepts. 2006. *Proceedings of the EACL 2006 Workshop Making Sense of Sense - Bringing Computational Linguistics and Psycholinguistics Together*, pp. 1-8

Ted Pedersen, Siddharth Patwardhan, and Jason Michelizzi. 2004. WorNet::Similarity – Measuring the Relatedness of Concepts. *Proceedings of Human Language Technology Conference of the North American Chapter of the Association for Computational Linguistics Demonstrations*, pp. 38-41.

Ted Pedersen and Varada Kolhatkar. 2009. WordNet::SenseRelate::AllWords - A Broad Coverage Word Sense Tagger that Maximimizes Semantic Relatedness. *Proceedings of Human Language Technology Conference of the North American Chapter of the Association for Computational Linguistics Demonstrations*, pp. 17-20.

Philip Resnik. 1995. Using Information Content to Evaluate Semantic Similarity in a Taxonomy. *Proceedings of the 14th International Joint Conference on Artificial Intelligence*.

Richard Steele, Michael Weinrich, Robert Wertz, Gloria Carlson, and Maria Kleczewska. Computer-based visual communication in aphasia. *Neuropsychologia*. 27(4): pp 409-26. 1989.

Luis von Ahn, Laura Dabbish. 2004. Labeling images with a computer game. *Proceedings of the SIGCHI conference on Human factors in computing systems*, p.319-326.

Luis von Ahn, Ruoran Liu, Manuel Blum. 2006 Peekaboom: a game for locating objects in images. *Proceedings of the SIGCHI conference on Human Factors in computing systems*.

Zhibiao Wu and Martha Palmer. 1994. Verb Semantics and Lexical Selection. *Proc. of ACL*, pp 133-138.

David Yarowsky. 1995. Unsupervised Word Sense Disambiguation Rivaling Supervised Methods. *Proceedings of the 33rd Annual Meeting on Association For Computational Linguistics*.

Workshop on Speech and Language Processing for Assistive Technologies Demo Session

1 "How was School today...?" A Prototype System that Uses Environmental Sensors and NLG to Support Personal Narrative for Children with Complex Communication Needs

Rolf Black, Joseph Reddington, Ehud Reiter, Nava Tintarev and Annalu Waller

We will show an in-situ sensor based prototype that supports personal narrative for children with complex communication needs. We will demonstrate the process from data collection, story generation and editing, to the interactive narration of stories about a child's school day. The challenging environment of a special school for prototype testing will be discussed and improvements of the next generation prototype presented.

2 Interactive SIGHT Demo: Textual Summaries of Simple Bar Charts

Seniz Demir, David Oliver, Edward Schwartz, Stephanie Elzer, Sandra Carberry and Kathleen F. McCoy

Interactive SIGHT is intended to provide people with visual impairments access to the kind of information graphics found in popular media. It works as a browser extension, and is able to generate a summary of a simple bar chart containing its high-level intention as natural language text. The user may request further information about the graphic through a follow-up question facility.

3 Project Jumbo: Transcription as an Assistive Technology for Instant Messaging

Ira R. Forman and Allen K. Wilson

The integration of VoIP into Instant Messaging may be a boon for most of us, but not for those who are deaf and hard of hearing. The IBM Human Ability & Accessibility Center initiated Project Jumbo to address this problem. Our remedy is to add a speech-to-text capability to augment voice services with transcripts. In particular, Project Jumbo augments IBM Lotus Sametime. Project Jumbo, which is transitioning to product status under name IBM AbilityLab Sametime Conference Transcriber, will be demonstrated. The demo consists of a chat between the demonstrator and a remote colleague in which the demonstrator speaks rather than types. A major point of the demo is that interactive communication is a new domain for ASR. This domain differs from dictation in a number of ways; prominent among them is that most speech recognition errors do not need to be corrected.

4 COMUNICA - A Voice Question Answering System for Portuguese

Rodrigo Wilkens, Aline Villavicencio, Leandro Wives, Daniel Muller, Fabio da Silva and Stanley Loh

This is a voice QA system for Brazilian Portuguese that performs speech recognition, text processing, database access and speech synthesis for consulting both structured and unstructured datasets. This system provides multi-modal communication and has the potential to help users with disabilities to access relevant information, and may help to significantly increase digital inclusion.

Proceedings of the NAACL HLT 2010 Workshop on Speech and Language Processing for Assistive Technologies, page 71,
Los Angeles, California, June 2010.

State-Transition Interpolation and MAP Adaptation for HMM-based Dysarthric Speech Recognition

Harsh Vardhan Sharma
Beckman Institute
405 North Mathews Avenue
Urbana, IL 61801, USA
hsharma@illinois.edu

Mark Hasegawa-Johnson
Beckman Institute
405 North Mathews Avenue
Urbana, IL 61801, USA
jhasegaw@illinois.edu

Abstract

This paper describes the results of our experiments in building speaker-adaptive recognizers for talkers with spastic dysarthria. We study two modifications – (a) MAP adaptation of speaker-independent systems trained on normal speech and, (b) using a transition probability matrix that is a linear interpolation between fully ergodic and (exclusively) left-to-right structures, for both speaker-dependent and speaker-adapted systems. The experiments indicate that (1) for speaker-dependent systems, left-to-right HMMs have lower word error rate than transition-interpolated HMMs, (2) adapting all parameters other than transition probabilities results in the highest recognition accuracy compared to adapting any subset of these parameters or adapting all parameters including transition probabilities, (3) performing both transition-interpolation and adaptation gives higher word error rate than performing adaptation alone and, (4) dysarthria severity is not a sufficient indicator of the relative performance of speaker-dependent and speaker-adapted systems.

1 Introduction

After more than two decades of research, speech recognition is a well-established and reliable human-computer interaction technology. The accuracy of the newest generation of large vocabulary speech recognizers, after adaptation to a user without speech pathology, is high enough to provide a useful human-computer interface especially for people who find it difficult to type with a keyboard.

Automatic speech recognition (ASR) systems generally assume that the speech signal is a realisation of some message encoded as a sequence of one or more symbols. To effect the reverse operation of recognising the underlying symbol sequence given a spoken utterance, the continuous speech waveform is first converted to a sequence of equally spaced discrete parameter vectors. The role of the recogniser is to effect a mapping between sequences of speech vectors and the wanted underlying symbol sequences. Most speech recognizers today are based on the *hidden Markov model* (HMM) paradigm: it is assumed that the sequence of observed speech vectors is generated by a Markov model as shown in Fig. 1. A Markov model is a finite state machine which changes state once every time unit and each time t that a state j is entered, a speech vector $\mathbf{o}_t$ is generated from the probability density $b_j(\mathbf{o}_t)$ which

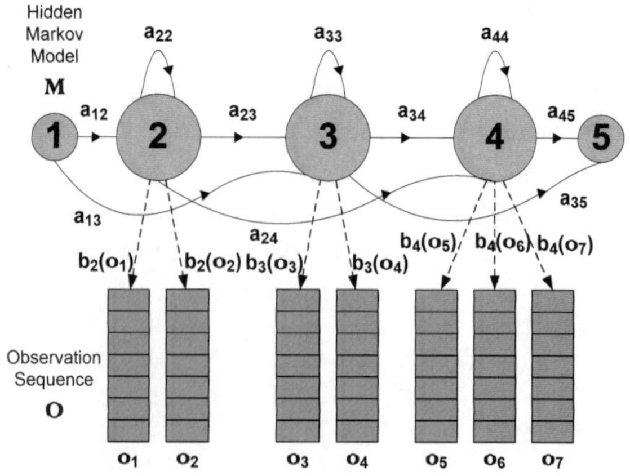

Figure 1: The Markov generation model.

Proceedings of the NAACL HLT 2010 Workshop on Speech and Language Processing for Assistive Technologies, pages 72–79,
Los Angeles, California, June 2010.

is a mixture-Gaussian density for most standard systems. The transition from state i to state j is also probabilistic and is governed by the discrete probability a_{ij}. Fig. 1 shows an example of this process where the five state model moves through the state sequence $X = 1, 2, 2, 3, 3, 4, 4, 4, 5$ in order to generate the sequence $\mathbf{o}_1$ to $\mathbf{o}_7$. The entry and exit states $(1, 5)$ are non-emitting. This is to facilitate the construction of composite models: most systems use HMMs to perform modeling at the phone-level rather than word-level; as such, word-level models are constructed by stringing together phone-level HMMs for the constituent phones.

Fig. 2 shows how HMMs can be used for isolated word recognition. Firstly, an HMM is trained for each vocabulary word using a number of examples of that word – given a set of training examples corresponding to a particular model, the parameters of that model ($\{a_{ij}\}$ and $\{b_j(\mathbf{o}_t)\}$) are determined by a robust and efficient re-estimation procedure. In this example, the vocabulary consists of just three words: "one", "two" and "three". Secondly, to recognise some unknown word, the likelihood (probability) of each model generating that word is calculated and the most likely model identifies the word.

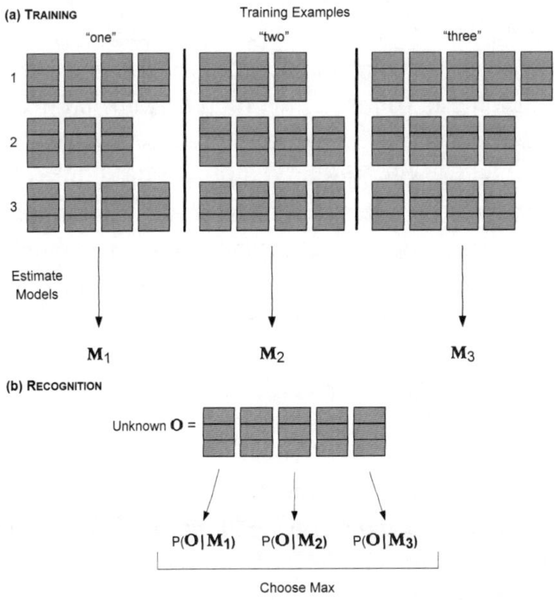

Figure 2: Using HMMs for isolated word recognition.

For creating a speech recognizer for a particular speaker, there are two approaches: one is to create a speaker-dependent (SD) system by utlizing speech of that speaker alone to train the HMMs; the other is to create a speaker-adapted (SA) system by first training the HMMs in a speaker-independent fashion by utlizing speech of several speakers, and then customising the HMMs to the characteristics of the particular speaker by using training examples of their speech to modify the HMM parameters. The parameter values do not get overwritten; they are adjusted using a regularized or constrained machine learning algorithm. Regularization (e.g., using Maximum A Posteriori learning) or constraints (e.g., using linear transformations) allow the SA model to use far more trainable parameters per minute of training data without over-training the system.

Despite the advances in speech technology, their benefits have not been available to people with gross motor impairments mainly because these impairments include a component of *dysarthria* – a group of motor speech disorders resulting from disturbed muscular control of the speech mechanism due to damage of the peripheral or central nervous system. Dysarthria is often a symptom of a gross motor disorder, whose other symptoms usually make it hard to use a keyboard and mouse. Published case studies have shown that some dysarthric users may find it easier to use an ASR system instead of a keyboard (Carlson and Bernstein, 1987; Coleman and Meyers, 1991; Deller et al., 1988; Deller et al., 1991; Fried-Oken, 1985). Polur and Miller studied the development of HMM-based small vocabulary (eight repetitions each of ten digits and fifteen 'command' words in English) SD systems for three male subjects subjectively classified by a trained clinician as moderately dysarthric (Polur and Miller, 2005a; Polur and Miller, 2005b). They found that an ergodic HMM with a slight left-to-right character (called a *transition-interpolated* HMM from hereon) provides higher word recognition accuracy (WRA) than a standard left-to-right HMM, apparently because the transition-interpolated HMM is able to capture outlier events as a backward or nonlinear progress through the intended word. The benefit of using ergodic modeling over left-to-right modeling in distorted speech applications with disruption events, pause events, and limited training data has also been noted earlier by Deller, Hsu and Ferrier (Deller et al., 1991). Section 2.1.2 explains in more detail the difference between these HMM topologies.

Speaking for long periods of time is tiring, especially for a person with dysarthria, therefore it is difficult for a person with dysarthria to train a speaker-dependent ASR. Speaker adaptation then seems a useful method to overcome this obstacle in developing dysarthric speech recognizers. Raghavendra et al. (Raghavendra et al., 2001) have compared recognition accuracies of an SA system and an SD system. They found that the SA system adapted well to the speech of talkers with mild or moderate dysarthria, but the recognition scores were lower than for an unimpaired speaker. The subject with severe dysarthria was able to achieve better performance with the SD system than with the SA system. These findings were also supported by Rudzicz (Rudzicz, 2007) who compared the performance of SD and "SA" systems on the Nemours database (Menendez-Pidal et al., 1996) by varying independently the amount of data for training and the number of Gaussian components used for modeling the output probability distributions. The "SA" technique implemented is not speaker-adaptation in the conventional sense: it uses the parameter values for the speaker-independent system as the starting point to train HMMs for a particular dysarthric speaker. In a training algorithm without regularization or constraint terms, it is possible for a system of this type to over-train, resulting in loss of accuracy on test data from the same speaker, and Rudzicz's results suggest that such over-training may have occurred in some cases. He further concluded that there was not enough data in the database to represent intra-speaker variation.

The study described in this paper investigated the development of medium vocabulary HMM recognizers for dysarthric speech of various degrees of severity with the following aims: (1) to test the performance of SA systems relative to SD systems, for various degrees of dysarthria severity, (2) to test the performance of an SD system employing transition-interpolated HMMs relative to an SD system using strictly left-to-right HMMs, (3) to test the performance of an SA system with transition-interpolated HMMs relative to an SD system having strictly left-to-right HMMs and, (4) to see if the results in the above three cases are essentially a function of the talker's dysarthria severity.

2 Experimental Setup

2.1 Modifications investigated

The following modifications to the HMM structure were studied in our experiments:

2.1.1 Adaptation

All SA systems were developed by adapting a speaker-independent system in a *Maximum A Posteriori* (MAP) manner, as outlined by Gauvain and Lee (Gauvain and Lee, 1991; Gauvain and Lee, 1992). MAP adaptation involves the use of prior knowledge about the model parameter distribution. Hence, if we know what the parameters of the model are likely to be (before observing any adaptation data) using the prior knowledge, we might well be able to make good use of the limited adaptation data, to obtain a decent MAP estimate. For MAP adaptation purposes, the informative priors that are generally used are the speaker independent model parameters (empirical Bayes approach). In (Gauvain and Lee, 1991), they derive expressions of MAP estimates for all HMM parameters except the transition probabilities (Gaussian mixture-component means, diagonal Gaussian mixture-component covariance matrices and, mixture-component weights) and also provide an initialization scheme for the prior density of these parameters. In (Gauvain and Lee, 1992), they derive expressions for MAP estimates of transition probabilities in addition to those for full-covariance Gaussian mixture-component parameters, and provide a MAP variant of the Expectation-Maximization (EM) re-estimation algorithm. All systems developed in our study modeled the observations as mixture of Gaussians with diagonal covariance matrices.

2.1.2 Transition-Interpolation

Fig. 3 illustrates the topologies of strictly left-to-right (LR) and transition-interpolated (TI) HMMs with 3 emitting states. If $\mathbf{A} = \{a_{ij}\}$ be the N $\times$ N transition probability matrix for an N-state HMM, then we have for an LR HMM: for each state i, $0 < a_{ii}\ ,\ a_{i,i+1} < 1$; $a_{ii} + a_{i,i+1} = 1$ and $a_{ij} = 0$ for $j \neq i, i+1$. In other words, each emitting state has only two possible state-transitions: given the current state, the HMM either remains in the same state or moves into the succeeding state; it will not jump over states or go to a preceding state.

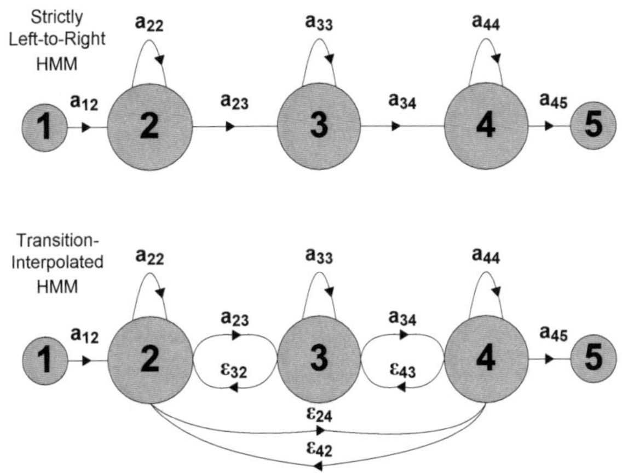

Figure 3: Difference between strictly left-to-right and transition-interpolated HMM topologies.

The TI model is an LR model which has non-zero transition probabilties for jumps and transitions to preceding states from a particular state (for emitting states). These probabilties are however small compared to self-transition and next-state–transition probabilties. A TI HMM is initialized as follows: for each emitting state i, $a_{ij} = \epsilon$ for $j \neq i, i+1$ where $0 < \epsilon << 1$; a_{ii} , $a_{i,i+1} >> \epsilon$ and $\sum_{j=1}^{N} a_{ij} = 1$. After this initialization, the transition probability matrix is re-estimated for speaker-dependent systems using the standard Maximum Likelihood EM algorithm, and for speaker-adapted systems using the MAP variant of the EM algorithm.

2.2 Data used

The experiments described in this paper utilized speech of 7 speakers from the UA-Speech database (Kim et al., 2008). This corpus was constructed with the aim of developing large-vocabulary dysarthric ASR systems which would allow users to enter unlimited text into a computer. All speakers exhibited symptoms of spastic dysarthria, according to an informal evaluation by a certified speech-language pathologist. Each speaker recorded 765 isolated words in 3 blocks of 255 words each; (a) common to all blocks: 10 digits (D), 19 computer commands (C), 26 radio alphabet letters (L), and 100 common words (CW) selected from the Brown corpus of written English; and (b) unique to each block: 100 uncommon words (UW) selected from children's novels digitized by Project Gutenberg. Vocabularies D and CW were primarily composed of monosyllables, C and L of bisyllables, and UW of polysyllabic words. The speakers' speech was affected by dysarthria associated with cerebral palsy. Data acquisition and intelligibility assessment is described in more detail in (Kim et al., 2008). Two hundred distinct words were selected from the recording of the second block: 10 digits, 25 radio alphabet letters, 19 computer commands and, 73 words randomly selected from each of the CW and UW categories. Five naive listeners were recruited for each speaker and were instructed to provide orthographic transcriptions of each word that they thought the speaker said. The percentage of correct responses was then averaged across five listeners to obtain each speakers intelligibility. Table 1 lists the speakers whose speech materials from the UA-Speech database were used, along with their human listener intelligibility ratings. The first letter of the speaker code ('M' or 'F') indicates their gender.

Speaker	Age	Speech Intelligbility (%)
M09	18	high (86%)
M05	21	mid (58%)
M06	18	low (39%)
F02	30	low (29%)
M07	58	low (28%)
F03	51	very low (6%)
M04	>18	very low (2%)

Table 1: Summary of Speaker Information (in decreasing order of human listener intelligibility rating).

For building the "MAP prior" speaker-independent system, the unadapted HMMs were trained on speech from the TIMIT corpus (Garofolo et al., 1993).

2.3 System Configurations

Table 2 lists the characteristics of the various system configurations that were studied: SD stands for speaker-dependent, SA for speaker-adapted; LR implies use of strictly left-to-right HMMs, TI for transition-interpolated HMMs; 'm','v','w','t' respectively denote means, variances, mixture-component weights and transition probabilities. These systems were developed for each of the seven speakers listed in Table 1, and employed word-internal, context-dependent triphone HMMs, with three hidden states and observations modeled as mixture-of-Gaussians. Configuration C00 was developed by Sharma and Hasegawa-Johnson (2009) and is the baseline configuration for the present experiments. For configurations C11 through C15, the speaker-independent systems trained on TIMIT employed left-to-right HMMs. For systems C15, the transition-interpolation was performed after obtaining the speaker-independent TIMIT-trained left-to-right HMMs and before adaptation to the UA-Speech speaker's data: the original non-zero entries in the transition probability matrices were scaled down so that the sum of each row was unity after changing the zero-entries to ϵ. For each speaker, all of blocks 1 and 3 were used as training data (systems C00, C01) or adaptation data (systems C11-C15) and all of block 2 was used for testing. The speaker-independent system was trained on all of TIMIT's training data and was tested on speech of 32 randomly chosen speakers from its test data.

System (Type)	HMM	Parameters adapted
C00 (SD)	LR	—
C01 (SD)	TI	—
C11 (SA)	LR	m
C12 (SA)	LR	m,v
C13 (SA)	LR	m,v,w
C14 (SA)	LR	m,v,w,t
C15 (SA)	TI	m,v,w,t

Table 2: Summary of ASR System Configurations

The features extracted from the speech waveform comprised of 12 Perceptual Linear Prediction coefficients (Hermansky, 1990) for 25 ms Hamming-windowed segments obtained every 10 ms, plus the energy of the windowed segment. 'Velocity' and 'Acceleration' components were also calculated for this 13-dimensional feature, which finally resulted in a 39-dimensional acoustic feature vector.

The measure used for assessing the performance of the developed recognizers is the fraction of task–vocabulary words correctly recognized (in percent), defined in Equation 1.

$$PWC = \frac{\#\ words\ correctly\ recognized}{\#\ words\ attempted} \times 100 \quad (1)$$

For each configuration, the number of Gaussian components in the state-specific observation probability densities was increased (in an iterative manner) in powers of 2, from 1 to 32 components (for C00 and C01) or 64 components (for C11-C15): standard methods for choosing this number (using development test data) could not be employed on account of insufficient data. The results reported in the next section should therefore be interpreted as development test results. In order to avoid overtuning, the number of Gaussian components was constrained to be the same across all speakers. For the speaker-dependent systems (C00 and C01), results are for HMMs with 2 Gaussian components per probability density. For the speaker-adapted systems (C11-C15), results are for HMMs with 32 Gaussian components per probability density: while training the speaker-independent TIMIT system, it was found that the phone recognition accuracy increased monotonically when going from 1 to 32 Gaussian components but decreased when going from 32 to 64 components.

3 Results

Tables 3, 4 list the PWC scores for the various system configurations developed. The speakers are listed in decreasing order of intelligibility rating. The scores for systems C00 are restated here from Sharma and Hasegawa-Johnson (2009) (Table 6, under the column 'T10').

We see that speaker-dependent systems with left-to-right HMMs (C00) have higher recognition accuracy than the speaker-dependent systems with transition-interpolated HMMs (C01), for all speakers except M06. System C11 for a particular speaker, with adaptation of Gaussian means alone performs either better or worse than both systems C00 and C01 for that speaker. System C12 with adaptation of Gaussian means and variances, has better recognition accuracy than both speaker-dependent systems, for all speakers except F02 and M07 (worse than both speaker-dependent systems). System C13 with adaptation of all parameters ex-

	System Configuration			
Speaker	C00	C01	C11	C12
M09	52.04	47.3	57.1	62.1
M05	35.52	33.7	31	39.4
M06	34.01	36.1	38.6	38.5
F02	35.06	32.8	20.8	26.9
M07	43.87	40.7	32	35.9
F03	12.61	11.3	17.4	22.2
M04	2.82	1.7	3.7	4.2

Table 3: PWC scores for each speaker's configurations C00-C12.

	System Configuration			
Speaker	C00	C13	C14	C15
M09	52.04	66.4	65.8	64.2
M05	35.52	45.2	44	38.1
M06	34.01	40.7	40.1	39.2
F02	35.06	30.4	29.7	26.6
M07	43.87	43	41.8	35.9
F03	12.61	27.7	26.2	25.7
M04	2.82	4.2	3.8	3.1

Table 4: PWC scores for each speaker's configurations C00,C13-C15.

cept transition-probabilities has the highest recognition accuracy for all subjects except F02 and M07 (highest among speaker-adapted systems only). System C14 which adapts all parameters including transition probabilities, always performs worse than the corresponding system C13, for all speakers. However, like system C13, it has better recognition accuracy than both speaker-dependent systems for all speakers except F02 and M07. Finally, performing transition-interpolation and adaptation of all parameters (system C15) worsens the performance to below that of the corresponding system C14; additionally, C15 has better recognition accuracy than both speaker-dependent systems whenever the corresponding C13 (and C14) system also performs better than them.

These results are plotted in Fig. 4 along with the human listeners' intelligibility ratings of these speakers (the black circles). For speakers M09 and M05, system C13 with the best overall PWC score is still far from doing as well as human listeners. For

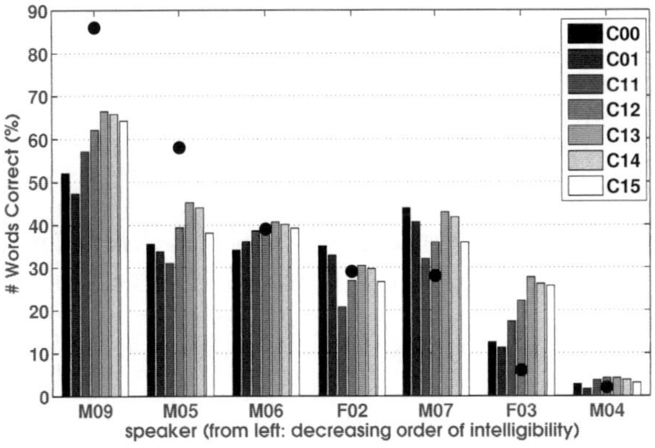

Figure 4: PWC scores for various system configurations (the black circles indicate speakers' human listener intelligibility ratings).

the remaining subjects, it has however been able to do as well or better than human listeners even when it performed worse than the corresponding speaker-dependent systems (C00,C01): in fact, for speaker M06, it does better than human listeners when the speaker-dependent systems don't.

Fig. 5 plots, for all speakers, the percentage difference PWC(x)/PWC(C00)-1 between the PWC of system x ($x \in \{C01 - C15\}$) and the PWC of system C00.

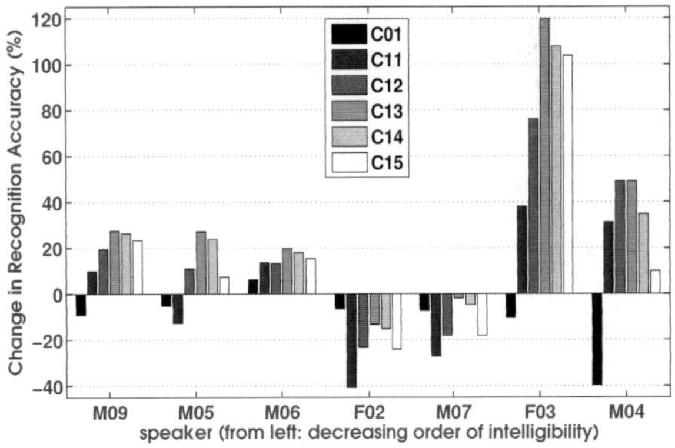

Figure 5: Percentage change in PWC scores for various system configurations relative to configuration C00's PWC score.

For speakers who have an intelligibility rating above 35% or below 25%, the speaker-adapted systems generally do better than their speaker-dependent counterparts. System C01, with transition interpolation, performs worse than system

C00 for all speakers except M06. The surprising result though is that for speakers with highly severe dysarthria (F03 and M04), speaker-adapted systems have substantially better recognition accuracies than their speaker-dependent counterparts, when previous studies have indicated that for such subjects, speaker-dependent systems perform better than speaker-adapted systems.

4 Conclusions

This study investigated adaptation and state-transition interpolation techniques for medium vocabulary HMM-based speech recognition of talkers with spastic dysarthria. It was found that performing transition-interpolation generally worsens recognition performance when compared to left-to-right HMMs. Performing both adaptation and transition-interpolation results in higher recognition accuracy compared to the speaker-dependent system with left-to-right HMMs but adaptation-only systems have still better performance. This implies that state-transitions not accounted for in left-to-right HMMs do not capture (or capture rather poorly) the outlier events that differentiate dysarthric speech from unimpaired speech at the sub-phone level.

The most interesting outcome of our experiments is that for subjects that have very severe dysarthria, speaker-adaptation was able to achieve substantial improvement in recognition accuracy, compared to the speaker-dependent systems. This finding is significant in that it is contrary to the conclusions of previously published studies. The results reported in this paper therefore suggest that the severity of dysarthria as quantified by the subject's intelligibility rating is not a sufficient indicator of the relative performance of speaker-dependent and speaker-adapted systems.

References

Gloria S. Carlson and Jared Bernstein. 1987. Speech Recognition of Impaired Speech. *Proceedings of RESNA 10th Annual Conference on Rehabilitation Technology*, 165–167.

Colette L. Coleman and Lawrence S. Meyers. 1991. Computer Recognition of the Speech of Adults with Cerebral Palsy and Dysarthria. *AAC: Augmentative and Alternative Communication*, 7(1):34–42.

John R. Deller, D. Frank Hsu and Linda J. Ferrier. 1988. Encouraging Results in the Automated Recognition of Cerebral Palsy Speech. *IEEE Transactions on Biomedical Engineering*, 35(3):218–220.

John R. Deller, D. Frank Hsu and Linda J. Ferrier. 1991. On the use of Hidden Markov modelling for Recognition of Dysarthric Speech. *Computer Methods and Programs in Biomedicine*, 35(2):125–139.

Melanie Fried-Oken. 1985. Voice Recognition Device as a Computer Interface for Motor and Speech Impaired People. *Archives of Physical Medicine and Rehabilitation*, 66:678–681.

Jean-luc Gauvain and Chin-hui Lee. 1991. Bayesian Learning of Gaussian Mixture Densities for Hidden Markov Models. *Proceedings of DARPA Speech and Natural Language Workshop*, 272–277.

Jean-luc Gauvain and Chin-hui Lee. 1992. MAP Estimation of Continuous Density HMM: Theory and Applications. *Proceedings of DARPA Speech and Natural Language Workshop*, 185–190.

John S. Garofolo, Lori F. Lamel, William M. Fisher, Jonathan G. Fiscus, David S. Pallett, Nancy L. Dahlgren and Victor Zue. 1993. *TIMIT Acoustic-Phonetic Continuous Speech Corpus*. http://www.ldc.upenn.edu/Catalog/LDC93S1.html.

Hynek Hermansky. 1990. Perceptual Linear Predictive (PLP) Analysis of Speech. *Journal of the Acoustical Society of America*, 87(4):1738–1752.

Heejin Kim, Mark Hasegawa-Johnson, Adrienne Perlman, Jon Gunderson, Thomas Huang, Kenneth Watkin and Simone Frame. 2008. Dysarthric Speech Database for Universal Access Research. *Proceedings of Interspeech, Brisbane, Australia*, 22–26.

Xavier Menendez-Pidal, James B. Polikoff, Shirley M. Peters, Jennie E. Leonzio, H. T. Bunnell. 1996. The Nemours Database of Dysarthric Speech. *Proceedings of the Fourth International Conference on Spoken Language Processing, Philadelphia, PA, USA.*

Prasad D. Polur and Gerald E. Miller. 2005a. Effect of High-Frequency Spectral Components in Computer Recognition of Dysarthric Speech based on a Mel-Cepstral Stochastic Model. *Journal of Rehabilitation Research & Development*, 42(3):363–372.

Prasad D. Polur and Gerald E. Miller. 2005b. Experiments with Fast Fourier Transform, Linear Predictive and Cepstral Coefficients in Dysarthric Speech Recognition Algorithms using Hidden Markov Model. *IEEE Transactions on Neural Systems and Rehabilitation Engineering*, 13(4):558–561.

Parimala Raghavendra, Elisabet Rosengren and Sheri Hunnicutt. 2001. An Investigation of Different Degrees of Dysarthric Speech as Input to Speaker-Adaptive and Speaker-Dependent Recognition Systems. *AAC: Augmentative and Alternative Communication*, 17(4):265–275.

Frank Rudzicz. 2007. Comparing Speaker-Dependent and Speaker-Adaptive Acoustic Models for Recognizing Dysarthric Speech. *Proceedings of ASSETS'07, Tempe, AZ, USA*.

Harsh Vardhan Sharma and Mark Hasegawa-Johnson. 2009. Universal Access: Speech Recognition for Talkers with Spastic Dysarthria. *Proceedings of Interspeech, Brighton, UK*, 1451–1454.

Towards a noisy-channel model of dysarthria in speech recognition

Frank Rudzicz
University of Toronto, Department of Computer Science
Toronto, Ontario, Canada
frank@cs.toronto.edu

Abstract

Modern automatic speech recognition is ineffective at understanding relatively unintelligible speech caused by neuro-motor disabilities collectively called dysarthria. Since dysarthria is primarily an articulatory phenomenon, we are collecting a database of vocal tract measurements during speech of individuals with cerebral palsy. In this paper, we demonstrate that articulatory knowledge can remove ambiguities in the acoustics of dysarthric speakers by reducing entropy relatively by 18.3%, on average. Furthermore, we demonstrate that dysarthric speech is more precisely portrayed as a noisy-channel distortion of an abstract representation of articulatory goals, rather than as a distortion of non-dysarthric speech. We discuss what implications these results have for our ongoing development of speech systems for dysarthric speakers.

1 Introduction

Dysarthria is a set of congenital and traumatic neuro-motor disorders that impair the physical production of speech and affects approximately 0.8% of individuals in North America (Hosom et al., 2003). Causes of dysarthria include cerebral palsy (CP), multiple sclerosis, Parkinson's disease, and amyotrophic lateral sclerosis (ALS). These impairments reduce or remove normal control of the primary vocal articulators but do not affect the abstract production of meaningful, syntactically correct language.

The neurological origins of dysarthria involve damage to the cranial nerves that control the speech articulators (Moore and Dalley, 2005). Spastic dysarthria, for instance, is partially caused by lesions in the facial and hypoglossal nerves, which control the jaw and tongue respectively (Duffy, 2005), resulting in slurred speech and a less differentiable vowel space (Kent and Rosen, 2004). Similarly, damage to the glossopharyngeal nerve can reduce control over vocal fold vibration (i.e., phonation), resulting in guttural or grating raspiness. Inadequate control of the soft palate caused by disruption of the vagus nerve may lead to a disproportionate amount of air released through the nose during speech (i.e., hypernasality).

Unfortunately, traditional automatic speech recognition (ASR) is incompatible with dysarthric speech, often rendering such software inaccessible to those whose neuro-motor disabilities might make other forms of interaction (e.g., keyboards, touch screens) laborious. Traditional representations in ASR such as hidden Markov models (HMMs) trained for speaker independence that achieve 84.8% word-level accuracy for non-dysarthric speakers might achieve less than 4.5% accuracy given severely dysarthric speech on short sentences (Rudzicz, 2007). Our research group is currently developing new ASR models that incorporate empirical knowledge of dysarthric articulation for use in assistive applications (Rudzicz, 2009). Although these models have increased accuracy, the disparity is still high. Our aim is to understand *why* ASR fails for dysarthric speakers by understanding the acoustic and articulatory nature of their speech.

In this paper, we cast the speech-motor interface within the mathematical framework of the noisy-channel model. This is motivated by the charac-

Proceedings of the NAACL HLT 2010 Workshop on Speech and Language Processing for Assistive Technologies, pages 80–88,

terization of dysarthria as a distortion of parallel biological pathways that corrupt motor signals before execution (Kent and Rosen, 2004; Freund et al., 2005), as in the examples cited above. Within this information-theoretic framework, we aim to infer the nature of the motor signal distortions given appropriate measurements of the vocal tract. That is, we ask the following question: Is dysarthric speech a distortion of typical speech, or are they both distortions of some common underlying representation?

2 Dysarthric articulation data

Since the underlying articulatory dynamics of dysarthric speech are intrinsically responsible for complex acoustic irregularities, we are collecting a database of dysarthric articulation. Time-aligned movement and acoustic data are measured using two systems. The first infers 3D positions of surface facial markers given stereo video images. The second uses electromagnetic articulography (EMA), in which the speaker is placed within a cube that produces a low-amplitude electromagnetic field, as shown in figure 1. Tiny sensors within this field allow the inference of articulator positions and velocities to within 1 mm of error (Yunusova et al., 2009).

Figure 1: Electromagnetic articulograph system.

We have so far recorded one male speaker with ALS, five male speakers with CP, four female speakers with CP, and age- and gender-matched controls. Measurement coils are placed as in other studies (e.g., the University of Edinburgh's MOCHA database (Wrench, 1999) and the University of Wisconsin-Madison's x-ray microbeam database (Yunusova et al., 2008)). Specifically, we are interested in the positions of the upper and lower lip (UL and LL), left and right mouth corners (LM and RM), lower incisor (LI), and tongue tip, blade, and dorsum (TT, TB, and TD). Unfortunately, a few of our male CP subjects had a severe gag reflex, and we found it impossible to place more than one coil on the tongue for these few individuals. Therefore, of the tongue positions, only TT is used in this study. All articulatory data are smoothed with third-order median filtering in order to minimize measurement 'jitter'. Figure 2 shows the degree of lip aperture (i.e., the distance between UL and LL) over time for a control and a dysarthric speaker repeating the sequence */ah p iy/*. Here, the dysarthric speech is notably slower and has more excessive movement.

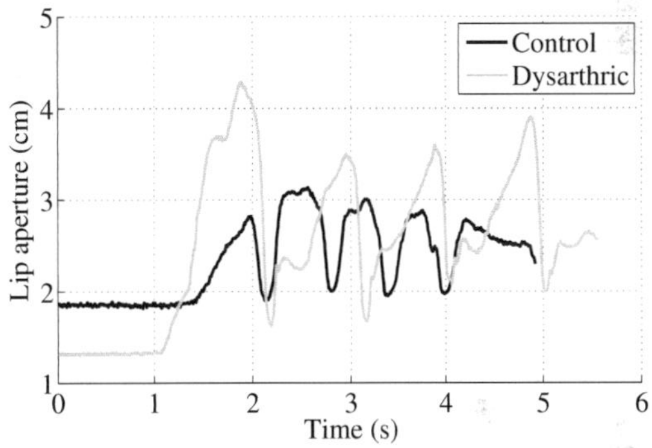

Figure 2: Lip aperture over time for four iterations of */ah p iy/* given a dysarthric and control speaker.

Our dysarthric speech data include random repetitions of phonetically balanced short sentences originally used in the TIMIT database (Zue et al., 1989), as well as pairs of monosyllabic words identified by Kent et al. (1989) as having relevant articulatory contrasts (e.g., *beat* versus *meat* as a stop-nasal contrast). All articulatory data are aligned with associated acoustic data, which are transformed to Mel-frequency cepstral coefficients (MFCCs). Phoneme boundaries and pronunciation errors are being transcribed by a speech-language pathologist to the TIMIT phoneset. Table 1 shows pronunciation errors according to manner of articulation for dysarthric speech. Plosives are mispronounced most often, with substitution errors exclusively caused by errant voicing (e.g. */d/* for */t/*). By comparison, only

5% of corresponding plosives in total are mispronounced in regular speech. Furthermore, the prevalence of deleted affricates in word-final positions, almost all of which are alveolar, does not occur in the corresponding control data.

	SUB (%)			DEL (%)		
	i	m	f	i	m	f
plosives	13.8	18.7	7.1	1.9	1.0	12.1
affricates	0.0	8.3	0.0	0.0	0.0	23.2
fricatives	8.5	3.1	5.3	22.0	5.5	13.2
nasals	0.0	0.0	1.5	0.0	0.0	1.5
glides	0.0	0.7	0.4	11.4	2.5	0.9
vowels	0.9	0.9	0.0	0.0	0.2	0.0

Table 1: Percentage of phoneme substitution (SUB) and deletion (DEL) errors in word-initial (i), word-medial (m), and word-final (f) positions across categories of manner for dysarthric data.

Table 2 shows the relative durations of the five most common vowels and sonorant consonants in our database between dysarthric and control speech. Here, dysarthric speakers are significantly slower than their control counterparts at the 95% confidence interval for */eh/* and at the 99.5% confidence interval for all other phonemes.

Phoneme	duration (μ (σ^2), in ms)		Avg.
	Dysarthric	Control	diff.
/ah/	189.3 (19.2)	120.1 (4.0)	69.2
/ae/	211.6 (16.4)	140.0 (4.4)	71.6
/eh/	160.5 (7.4)	107.3 (2.6)	53.2
/iy/	177.1 (86.7)	105.8 (93.1)	71.3
/er/	220.5 (27.9)	148.6 (59.8)	71.9
/l/	138.5 (8.0)	91.8 (2.4)	46.7
/m/	173.5 (13.4)	94.7 (2.1)	78.8
/n/	168.4 (14.4)	90.9 (2.3)	77.5
/r/	138.8 (8.3)	95.3 (3.4)	43.5
/w/	151.5 (12.0)	84.5 (1.3)	67.0

Table 2: Average lengths (and variances in parentheses) in milliseconds for the five most common vowels and sonorant consonants for dysarthric and control speakers. The last column is the average difference in milliseconds between dysarthric and control subjects.

Processing and annotation of further data from additional dysarthric speakers is ongoing, including measurements of all three tongue positions.

3 Entropy and the noisy-channel model

We wish to measure the degree of statistical disorder in both acoustic and articulatory data for dysarthric and non-dysarthric speakers, as well as the *a posteriori* disorder of one type of data given the other. This quantification will inform us as to the relative merits of incorporating knowledge of articulatory behaviour into ASR systems for dysarthric speakers. Entropy, $H(X)$, is a measure of the degree of uncertainty in a random variable X. When X is discrete, this value is computed with the familiar

$$H(X) = -\sum_{i=1}^{n} p(x_i)\log_b p(x_i),$$

where b is the logarithm base, x_i is a value of X, of which there are n possible, and $p(x_i)$ is its probability. When our observations are continuous, as they are in our acoustic and articulatory database, we must use *differential entropy* defined by

$$H(X) = -\int_X f(X)\log f(X)dX,$$

where $f(X)$ is the probability density function of X. For a number of distributions $f(X)$, the differential entropy has known forms (Lazo and Rathie, 1978). For example, if $f(X)$ is a multivariate normal,

$$\begin{aligned} f_X(x_1,\ldots,x_N) &= \frac{\exp\left(-\frac{1}{2}(x-\mu)^T\Sigma^{-1}(x-\mu)\right)}{(2\pi)^{N/2}|\Sigma|^{1/2}} \\ H(X) &= \tfrac{1}{2}\ln\left((2\pi e)^N|\Sigma|\right), \end{aligned} \quad (1)$$

where μ and Σ are the mean and covariances of the data. However, since we observe that both acoustic and articulatory data follow non-Gaussian distributions, we choose to represent these spaces by mixtures of Gaussians. Huber et al. (2008) have developed an accurate algorithm for estimating differential entropy of Gaussian mixtures based on iteratively merging Gaussians and the approximation

$$\tilde{H}(X) = \sum_{i=1}^{L}\omega_i\left(-\log\omega_i + \tfrac{1}{2}\log((2\pi e)^N|\Sigma_i|\right),$$

where ω_i is the weight of the $i^{th}(1 \leq i \leq L)$ Gaussian and Σ_i is that Gaussian's covariance matrix. This method is used to approximate entropies in the following study, with $L = 32$. Note that while differential entropies *can* be negative and not invariant under change of variables, other properties of entropy are retained (Huber et al., 2008), such as the chain rule for conditional entropy

$$H(Y|X) = H(Y,X) - H(X),$$

which describes the uncertainty in Y given knowledge of X, and the chain rule for mutual information

$$I(Y;X) = H(X) + H(Y) - H(X,Y),$$

which describes the mutual dependence between X and Y. Here, we quantize entropy with the *nat*, which is the natural logarithmic unit, e (≈ 1.44 bits).

3.1 The noisy channel

The noisy-channel theorem states that information passed through a channel with capacity C at a rate $R \leq C$ can be reliably recovered with an arbitrarily low probability of error given an appropriate coding. Here, a message from a finite alphabet is encoded, producing signal $x \in X$. That signal is then distorted by a medium which transmits signal $y \in Y$ according to some distribution $P(Y|X)$. Given that there is some probability that the received signal, y, is corrupted, the message produced by the decoder may differ from the original (Shannon, 1949).

To what extent can we describe the effects of dysarthria within an information-theoretic noisy channel model? We pursue two competing hypotheses within this general framework. The first hypothesis models the assumption that dysarthric speech is a distorted version of typical speech. Here, signal X and Y represent the vocal characteristics of the general and dysarthric populations, respectively, and $P(Y|X)$ models the distortion between them. The second hypothesis models the assumption that *both* dysarthric and typical speech are distorted versions of some common abstraction. Here, Y_d and Y_c represent the vocal characteristics of dysarthric and control speakers, respectively, and X represents a common, underlying mechanism and that $P(Y_d|X)$ and $P(Y_c|X)$ model distortions from that mechanism. These two hypotheses are visualized in figure 3. In each of these cases, signals can be acoustic, articulatory, or some combination thereof.

3.2 Common underlying abstractions

In order to test our hypothesis that both dysarthric and control speakers share a common high-level ab-

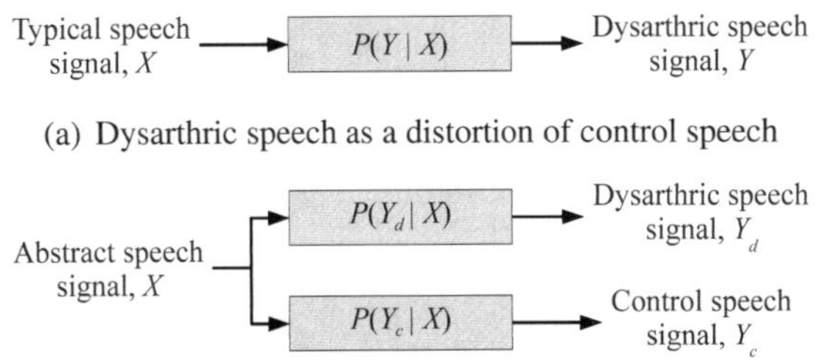

(a) Dysarthric speech as a distortion of control speech

(b) Dysarthric and control speech as distortions of a common abstraction

Figure 3: Sections of noisy channel models that mimic the neuro-motor interface.

straction of the vocal tract that is in both cases distorted during articulation, we incorporate the theory of *task dynamics* (Saltzman and Munhall, 1989). This theory represents the interface between the lexical intentions and vocal tract realizations of speech as a sequence of overlapping *gestures*, which are continuous dynamical systems that describe goal-oriented reconfigurations of the vocal tract, such as bilabial closure during */m/*. Figure 4 shows an example of overlapping gestures for the word *pub*.

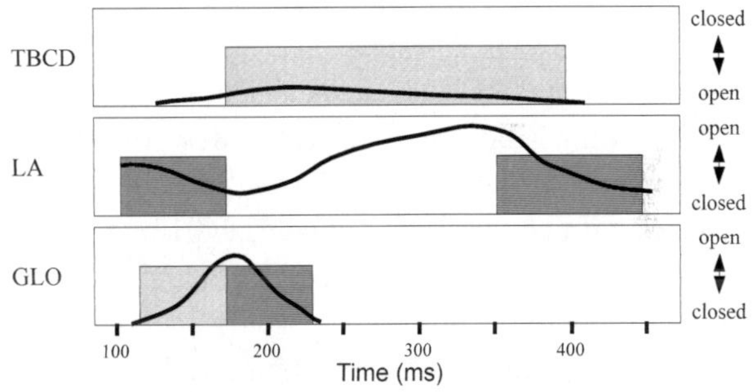

Figure 4: Canonical example *pub* from Saltzman and Munhall (1989) representing overlapping goals for tongue blade constriction degree (TBCD), lip aperture (LA), and glottis (GLO). Boxes represent the present of discretized goals, such as lip closure. Black curves represent the output of the TADA system.

The open-source TADA system (Nam and Goldstein, 2006) estimates the positions of various articulators during speech according to parameters that have been carefully tuned by the authors of TADA according to a generic, speaker-independent representation of the vocal tract (Saltzman and Munhall, 1989). Given a word sequence and a syllable-to-gesture dictionary, TADA produces the continuous tract variable paths that are necessary to produce that sequence. This takes into account various physiological aspects of human speech production, such as interarticulator co-ordination and timing (Nam and Saltzman, 2003).

In this study, we use `TADA` to produce estimates of a global, high-level representation of speech common to both dysarthric and non-dysarthric speakers alike. Given a word sequence uttered by both types of speaker, we produce five continuous curves prescribed by that word sequence in order to match our available EMA data. Those curves are lip aperture and protrusion (LA and LP), tongue tip constriction location and degree (TTCL and TTCD, representing front-back and top-down positions of the tongue tip, respectively), and lower incisor height (LIH). These curves are then compared against actually observed EMA data, as described below.

4 Experiments

First, in section 4.1, we ask whether the incorporation of articulatory data is theoretically useful in reducing uncertainty in dysarthric speech. Second, in section 4.2, we ask which of the two noisy channel models in figure 3 best describe the observed behaviour of dysarthric speech.

Data for this study are collected as described as in section 2. Here, we use data from three dysarthric speakers with cerebral palsy (males M01 and M04, and female F03), as well as their age- and gender-matched counterparts from the general population (males MC01 and MC03, and female FC02). For this study we restrict our analysis to 100 phrases uttered in common by all six speakers.

4.1 Entropy

We measure the differential entropy of acoustics ($H(Ac)$), of articulation ($H(Ar)$), and of acoustics given knowledge of the vocal tract ($H(Ac|Ar)$) in order to obtain theoretical estimates as to the utility of articulatory data. Table 3 shows these quantities across the six speakers in this study. As expected, the acoustics of dysarthric speakers are much more disordered than for non-dysarthric speakers. One unexpected finding is that there is very little difference between speakers in terms of their entropy of articulation. Although dysarthric speakers clearly lack articulatory dexterity, this implies that they nonetheless articulate with a level of consistency similar to their non-dysarthric counterparts[1]. However, the equivocation $H(Ac|Ar)$ is an order of magnitude lower for non-dysarthric speakers. This implies that there is very little ambiguity left in the acoustics of non-dysarthric speakers if we have simultaneous knowledge of the vocal tract, but that quite a bit of ambiguity remains for our dysarthric speakers, despite significant reductions.

	Speaker	$H(Ac)$	$H(Ar)$	$H(Ac\|Ar)$
Dys.	M01	66.37	17.16	50.30
	M04	33.36	11.31	26.25
	F03	42.28	19.33	39.47
	Average	47.34	15.93	38.68
Ctrl.	MC01	24.40	21.49	1.14
	MC03	18.63	18.34	3.93
	FC02	16.12	15.97	3.11
	Average	19.72	18.60	2.73

Table 3: Differential entropy, in nats, across dysarthric and control speakers for acoustic *ac* and articulatory *ar* data.

Table 4 shows the average mutual information between acoustics and articulation for each type of speaker, given knowledge of the phonological manner of articulation. In table 1 we noted a prevalence of pronunciation errors among dysarthric speakers for plosives, but table 4 shows no particularly low congruity between acoustics and articulation for this manner of phoneme. Those pronunciation errors tended to be voicing errors, which would involve the glottis, which is not measured in this study.

Table 4 appears to imply that there is little mutual information between acoustics and articulation in vowels across all speakers. However, this is almost certainly the result of our exclusion of tongue blade and tongue dorsum measurements in order to standardize across speakers who could not manage these sensors. Indeed, the configuration of the entire tongue is known to be useful in discriminating among the vowels (O'Shaughnessy, 2000). An *ad hoc* analysis including all three tongue sensors for speakers F03, MC01, MC03, and FC02 revealed mutual information between acoustics and articula-

[1]This is borne out in the literature (Kent and Rosen, 2004).

Manner	$I(Ac;Ar)$	
	Dys.	Ctrl.
plosives	10.92	16.47
affricates	8.71	9.23
fricatives	9.30	10.94
nasals	13.29	15.10
glides	11.92	12.68
vowels	6.76	7.15

Table 4: Mutual information $I(Ac;Ar)$ of acoustics and articulation for dysarthric and control subjects, across phonological manners of articulation.

tion of 16.81 nats for F03 and 18.73 nats for the control speakers, for vowels. This is compared with mutual information of 11.82 nats for F03 and 13.88 nats for the control speakers across all other manners. The trend seems to be that acoustics are better predicted given more tongue measurements.

In order to better understand these results, we compare the distributions of the vowels in acoustic space across dysarthric and non-dysarthric speech. Vowels in acoustic space are characterized by the steady-state positions of the first two formants (F1 and F2) as determined automatically by applying the pre-emphasized Burg algorithm (Press et al., 1992). We fit Gaussians to the first two formants for each of the vowels in our data, as exemplified in figure 5 and compute the entropy within these distributions. Surprisingly, the entropies of these distributions were relatively consistent across dysarthric (34.6 nats) and non-dysarthric (33.3 nats) speech, with some exceptions (e.g., *iy*). However, vowel spaces overlap considerably more in the dysarthric case signifying that, while speakers with CP can be nearly as acoustically consistent as non-dysarthric speakers, their targets in that space are not as discernible. Some research has shown larger variance among dysarthric vowels relative to our findings (Kain et al., 2007). This may partially be due to our use of natural connected speech as data, rather than restrictive consonant-vowel-consonant non-words.

4.2 Noisy channel

Our task is to determine whether dysarthric speech is best represented as a distorted version of typical speech, or if both dysarthric and typical speech ought to be viewed as distortions of a common ab-

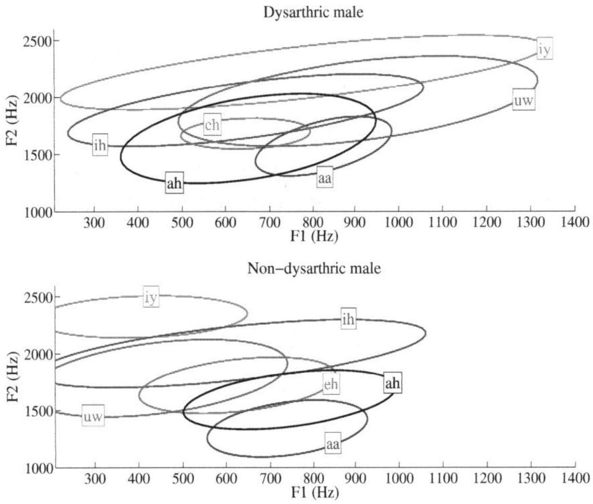

Figure 5: Contours showing first standard deviation in F1 versus F2 space for distributions of six representative vowels in continuous speech for the dysarthric and non-dysarthric male speakers.

stract representation. To explore this question, we design a transformation system that produces the most likely observation in one data space given its counterpart in another and the statistical relationship between the two spaces. This transformation in effect implements the noisy channel itself.

To accomplish this, we learn probability distributions over our EMA data. First, we collect all dysarthric data together and all non-dysarthric data together. We then consider the acoustic (Ac) and articulatory (Ar) subsets of these data. In each case, we train Gaussian mixtures, each with 60 components, over 90% of the data in both dysarthric and non-dysarthric speech. Here, each of the 60 phonemes in the data is represented by one Gaussian component, with the weight of that component determined by the relative proportion of 10 ms frames for that phoneme. Similarly, all training word sequences are passed to TADA, and we train a mixture of Gaussians on its articulatory output.

Across all Gaussian mixtures, we end up with 5 Gaussians tuned to various aspects of each phoneme p: its dysarthric acoustics and articulation ($\mathbf{N}_p^{Ac}(Y_d)$ and $\mathbf{N}_p^{Ar}(Y_d)$), its control acoustics and articulation ($\mathbf{N}_p^{Ac}(Y_d)$ and $\mathbf{N}_p^{Ar}(Y_d)$), and its prescribed articulation from TADA ($\mathbf{N}_p^{Ar}(X)$). Each Gaussian $\mathbf{N}_p^A(B)$ is represented by its mean $\mu_p^{(A,B)}$ and its covariance, $\Sigma_p^{(A,B)}$. Furthermore, we compute the cross-covariance matrix between Gaussians for a given phoneme (e.g., $\Sigma_p^{(Ac,Y_c)\to(Ac,Y_d)}$ is the cross-covariance matrix of the acoustics of the control (Y_c) and dysarthric (Y_d) speech for phoneme p). Given these parameters, we estimate the most likely frame in one domain given its counterpart in another. For example, if we are given a frame of acoustics from a control speaker, we can synthesize the most likely frame of acoustics for a dysarthric speaker, given an application of the noisy channel proposed by Hosom et al. (2003) used to transform dysarthric speech to make it more intelligible. Namely, given a frame of acoustics y_c from a control speaker, we can estimate the acoustics of a dysarthric speaker y_d with:

$$\begin{aligned} f_{Ac}(y_c) =& E(y_d \mid y_c) \\ =& \sum_{i=1}^{P} h_i(y_c) \Big[\mu_i^{(Ac,Y_d)} + \\ & \Sigma_i^{(Ac,Y_c)\to(Ac,Y_d)} \cdot \left(\Sigma_i^{(Ac,Y_c)}\right)^{-1} \cdot \\ & \left(y_c - \mu_i^{(Ac,Y_c)}\right)\Big], \end{aligned} \quad (2)$$

where

$$h_i(y_c) = \frac{\alpha_i N\left(y_c; \mu_i^{(Ac,Y_c)}, \Sigma_i^{(Ac,Y_c)}\right)}{\sum_{j=1}^{P} \alpha_j N\left(y_c; \mu_j^{(Ac,Y_c)}, \Sigma_j^{(Ac,Y_c)}\right)},$$

where α_p is the proportion of the frames of phoneme p in the data. Transforming between different types and sources of data is accomplished merely by substituting in the appropriate Gaussians above.

We now measure how closely the transformed data spaces match their true target spaces. In each case, we transform test utterances (recorded, or synthesized with `TADA`) according to functions learned in training (i.e., we use the remaining 10% of the data for each speaker type). These transformed spaces are then compared against their target space in our data. Table 5 shows the Gaussian mixture phoneme-level Kullback-Leibler divergences given various types of source and target data, weighted by the relative proportions of the phonemes. Each pair of N-dimensional Gaussians ($\mathbf{N}_i$ with mean μ_i and covariance Σ_i) for a given phone and data type is

Type 1	Type 2	KL divergence (10^{-2} nats) Acous.	Artic.
Ctrl.	Dys.	25.36	3.23
Ctrl. → Dys.	Dys.	17.78	2.11
`TADA` → Ctrl.	Ctrl.	N/A	1.69
`TADA` → Dys.	Dys.	N/A	1.84

Table 5: Average weighted phoneme-level Kullback-Leibler divergences.

compared with

$$\begin{aligned} D_{KL}(\mathbf{N}_0 \,||\, \mathbf{N}_1) =& \frac{1}{2}\left(\ln\left(\frac{|\Sigma_1|}{|\Sigma_0|}\right) + \mathrm{trace}(\Sigma_1^{-1}\Sigma_0) \right. \\ & \left. + (\mu_1 - \mu_0)^T \Sigma_1^{-1}(\mu_1 - \mu_0) - N\right). \end{aligned}$$

Our baseline shows that control and dysarthric speakers differ far more in their acoustics than in their articulation. When our control data (both acoustic and articulatory) are transformed to match the dysarthric data, the result is predictably more similar to the latter than if the conversion had not taken place. This corresponds to the noisy channel model of figure 3(a), whereby dysarthric speech is modelled as a distortion of non-dysarthric speech. However, when we model dysarthric and control speech as distortions of a common, abstract representation (i.e., task dynamics) as in figure 3(b), the resulting synthesized articulatory spaces are more similar to their respective observed data than the articulation predicted by the first noisy channel model. Dysarthric articulation predicted by transformations from task-dynamics space differ significantly from those predicted by transformations from control EMA data at the 95% confidence interval.

5 Discussion

This paper demonstrates a few acoustic and articulatory features in speakers with cerebral palsy. First, these speakers are likely to mistakenly voice unvoiced plosives, and to delete fricatives regardless of their word position. We suggest that it might be prudent to modify the vocabularies of ASR systems to account for these expected mispronunciations. Second, dysarthric speakers produce sonorants significantly slower than their non-dysarthric counterparts.

This may present an increase in insertion errors in ASR systems (Rosen and Yampolsky, 2000).

Although not quantified in this paper, we detect that a lack of articulatory control can often lead to observable acoustic consequences. For example, our dysarthric data contain considerable involuntary types of velopharyngeal or glottal noise (often associated with respiration), audible swallowing, and stuttering. We intend to work towards methods of explicitly identifying regions of non-speech noise in our ASR systems for dysarthric speakers.

We have considered the amount of statistical disorder (i.e., entropy) in both acoustic and articulatory data in dysarthric and non-dysarthric speakers. The use of articulatory knowledge reduces the degree of this disorder significantly for dysarthric speakers (18.3%, relatively), though far less than for non-dysarthric speakers (86.2%, relatively). In real-world applications we are not likely to have access to measurements of the vocal tract; however, many approaches exist that estimate the configuration of the vocal tract given only acoustic data (Richmond et al., 2003; Toda et al., 2008), often to an average error of less than 1 mm. The generalizability of such work to new speakers (particularly those with dysarthria) without training is an open research question.

We have argued for noisy channel models of the neuro-motor interface assuming that the pathway of motor command to motor activity is a linear sequence of dynamics. The biological reality is much more complicated. In particular, the pathway of verbal motor commands includes several sources of sensory feedback (Seikel et al., 2005) that modulate control parameters during speech (Gracco, 1995). These senses include exteroceptive stimuli (auditory and tactile), and interoceptive stimuli (particularly proprioception and its kinesthetic sense) (Seikel et al., 2005), the disruption of which can lead to a number of production changes. For instance, Abbs et al. (1976) showed that when conduction in the mandibular branches of the trigeminal nerve is blocked, the resulting speech has considerably more pronunciation errors, although is generally intelligible. Barlow (1989) argues that the redundancy of sensory messages provides the necessary input to the motor *planning* stage, which relates abstract goals to motor activity in the cerebellum. As we continue to develop our articulatory ASR models for dysarthric speakers, one potential avenue for future research involves the incorporation of feedback from the current state of the vocal tract to the motor planning phase. This would be similar, in premise, to the DIVA model (Guenther and Perkell, 2004).

In the past, we have shown that ASR systems that adapt non-dysarthric acoustic models to dysarthric data offer improved word-accuracy rates, but with a clear upper bound approximately 75% below the general population (Rudzicz, 2007). Incorporating articulatory knowledge into such adaptation improved accuracy further, but with accuracy still approximately 60% below the general population (Rudzicz, 2009). In this paper, we have demonstrated that dysarthric articulation can be more accurately represented as a distortion of an underlying model of abstract speech goals than as a distortion of non-dysarthric articulation. These results will guide our continued development of speech systems augmented with articulatory knowledge, particularly the incorporation of task dynamics.

Acknowledgments

This research is funded by Bell University Labs, the Natural Sciences and Engineering Research Council of Canada, and the University of Toronto.

References

James H. Abbs, John W. Folkins, and Murali Sivarajan. 1976. Motor Impairment following Blockade of the Infraorbital Nerve: Implications for the Use of Anesthetization Techniques in Speech Research. *Journal of Speech and Hearing Research*, 19(1):19–35.

H.B. Barlow. 1989. Unsupervised learning. *Neural Computation*, 1(3):295–311.

Joseph R Duffy. 2005. *Motor Speech Disorders: Substrates, Differential Diagnosis, and Management*. Mosby Inc.

Hans-Joachim Freund, Marc Jeannerod, Mark Hallett, and Ramón Leiguarda. 2005. *Higher-order motor disorders: From neuroanatomy and neurobiology to clinical neurology*. Oxford University Press.

Vincent L. Gracco. 1995. Central and peripheral components in the control of speech movements. In Fredericka Bell-Berti and Lawrence J. Raphael, editors, *Introducing Speech: Contempory Issues, for Katherine Safford Harris*, chapter 12, pages 417–431. American Institute of Physics press.

Frank H. Guenther and Joseph S. Perkell. 2004. A neural model of speech production and its application to studies of the role of auditory feedback in speech. In Ben Maassen, Raymond Kent, Herman Peters, Pascal Van Lieshout, and Wouter Hulstijn, editors, *Speech Motor Control in Normal and Disordered Speech*, chapter 4, pages 29–49. Oxford University Press, Oxford.

John-Paul Hosom, Alexander B. Kain, Taniya Mishra, Jan P. H. van Santen, Melanie Fried-Oken, and Janice Staehely. 2003. Intelligibility of modifications to dysarthric speech. In *Proceedings of the IEEE International Conference on Acoustics, Speech, and Signal Processing (ICASSP '03)*, volume 1, pages 924–927, April.

Marco F. Huber, Tim Bailey, Hugh Durrant-Whyte, and Uwe D. Hanebeck. 2008. On entropy approximation for Gaussian mixture random vectors. In *Proceedings of the 2008 IEEE International Conference on In Multisensor Fusion and Integration for Intelligent Systems*, pages 181–188, Seoul, South Korea.

Alexander B. Kain, John-Paul Hosom, Xiaochuan Niu, Jan P.H. van Santen, Melanie Fried-Oken, and Janice Staehely. 2007. Improving the intelligibility of dysarthric speech. *Speech Communication*, 49(9):743–759, September.

Ray D. Kent and Kristin Rosen. 2004. Motor control perspectives on motor speech disorders. In Ben Maassen, Raymond Kent, Herman Peters, Pascal Van Lieshout, and Wouter Hulstijn, editors, *Speech Motor Control in Normal and Disordered Speech*, chapter 12, pages 285–311. Oxford University Press, Oxford.

Ray D. Kent, Gary Weismer, Jane F. Kent, and John C. Rosenbek. 1989. Toward phonetic intelligibility testing in dysarthria. *Journal of Speech and Hearing Disorders*, 54:482–499.

Aida C. G. Verdugo Lazo and Pushpa N. Rathie. 1978. On the entropy of continuous probability distributions. *IEEE Transactions on Information Theory*, 23(1):120–122, January.

Keith L. Moore and Arthur F. Dalley. 2005. *Clinically Oriented Anatomy, Fifth Edition*. Lippincott, Williams and Wilkins.

Hosung Nam and Louis Goldstein. 2006. TADA (TAsk Dynamics Application) manual.

Hosung Nam and Elliot Saltzman. 2003. A competitive, coupled oscillator model of syllable structure. In *Proceedings of the 15th International Congress of Phonetic Sciences (ICPhS 2003)*, pages 2253–2256, Barcelona, Spain.

Douglas O'Shaughnessy. 2000. *Speech Communications – Human and Machine*. IEEE Press, New York, NY, USA.

William H. Press, Saul A. Teukolsky, William T. Vetterling, and Brian P. Flannery. 1992. *Numerical Recipes in C: the art of scientific computing*. Cambridge University Press, second edition.

Korin Richmond, Simon King, and Paul Taylor. 2003. Modelling the uncertainty in recovering articulation from acoustics. *Computer Speech and Language*, 17:153–172.

Kristin Rosen and Sasha Yampolsky. 2000. Automatic speech recognition and a review of its functioning with dysarthric speech. *Augmentative & Alternative Communication*, 16(1):48–60, Jan.

Frank Rudzicz. 2007. Comparing speaker-dependent and speaker-adaptive acoustic models for recognizing dysarthric speech. In *Proceedings of the Ninth International ACM SIGACCESS Conference on Computers and Accessibility*, Tempe, AZ, October.

Frank Rudzicz. 2009. Applying discretized articulatory knowledge to dysarthric speech. In *Proceedings of the 2009 IEEE International Conference on Acoustics, Speech, and Signal Processing (ICASSP09)*, Taipei, Taiwan, April.

Elliot L. Saltzman and Kevin G. Munhall. 1989. A dynamical approach to gestural patterning in speech production. *Ecological Psychology*, 1(4):333–382.

J. Anthony Seikel, Douglas W. King, and David G. Drumright, editors. 2005. *Anatomy & Physiology: for Speech, Language, and Hearing*. Thomson Delmar Learning, third edition.

Claude E. Shannon. 1949. *A Mathematical Theory of Communication*. University of Illinois Press, Urbana, IL.

Tomoki Toda, Alan W. Black, and Keiichi Tokuda. 2008. Statistical mapping between articulatory movements and acoustic spectrum using a Gaussian mixture model. *Speech Communication*, 50(3):215–227, March.

Alan Wrench. 1999. The MOCHA-TIMIT articulatory database, November.

Yana Yunusova, Gary Weismer, John R. Westbury, and Mary J. Lindstrom. 2008. Articulatory movements during vowels in speakers with dysarthria and healthy controls. *Journal of Speech, Language, and Hearing Research*, 51:596–611, June.

Yana Yunusova, Jordan R. Green, and Antje Mefferd. 2009. Accuracy Assessment for AG500, Electromagnetic Articulograph. *Journal of Speech, Language, and Hearing Research*, 52:547–555, April.

Victor Zue, Stephanie Seneff, and James Glass. 1989. Speech Database Development: TIMIT and Beyond. In *Proceedings of ESCA Tutorial and Research Workshop on Speech Input/Output Assessment and Speech Databases (SIOA-1989)*, volume 2, pages 35–40, Noordwijkerhout, The Netherlands.

Collecting a Motion-Capture Corpus of American Sign Language for Data-Driven Generation Research

Pengfei Lu
Department of Computer Science
Graduate Center
City University of New York (CUNY)
365 Fifth Ave, New York, NY 10016
pengfei.lu@qc.cuny.edu

Matt Huenerfauth
Department of Computer Science
Queens College and Graduate Center
City University of New York (CUNY)
65-30 Kissena Blvd, Flushing, NY 11367
matt@cs.qc.cuny.edu

Abstract

American Sign Language (ASL) generation software can improve the accessibility of information and services for deaf individuals with low English literacy. The understandability of current ASL systems is limited; they have been constructed without the benefit of annotated ASL corpora that encode detailed human movement. We discuss how linguistic challenges in ASL generation can be addressed in a data-driven manner, and we describe our current work on collecting a motion-capture corpus. To evaluate the quality of our motion-capture configuration, calibration, and recording protocol, we conducted an evaluation study with native ASL signers.

1 Introduction

American Sign Language (ASL) is the primary means of communication for about one-half million deaf people in the U.S. (Mitchell et al., 2006). ASL has a distinct word-order, syntax, and lexicon from English; it is not a representation of English using the hands. Although reading is part of the curriculum for deaf students, lack of auditory exposure to English during the language-acquisition years of childhood leads to lower literacy for many adults. In fact, the majority of deaf high school graduates in the U.S. have only a fourth-grade (age 10) English reading level (Traxler, 2000).

1.1 Applications of ASL Generation Research

Most technology used by the deaf does not address this literacy issue; many deaf people find it difficult to read the English text on a computer screen or on a television with closed-captioning. Software to present information in the form of animations of ASL could make information and services more accessible to deaf users, by displaying an animated character performing ASL, rather than English text. While writing systems for ASL have been proposed (Newkirk, 1987; Sutton, 1998), none is widely used in the Deaf community. Thus, an ASL generation system cannot produce text output; the system must produce an animation of a human character performing sign language. Coordinating the simultaneous 3D movements of parts of an animated character's body is challenging, and few researchers have attempted to build such systems.

Prior work can be divided into two areas: scripting and generation/translation. Scripting systems allow someone who knows sign language to "word process" an animation by assembling a sequence of signs from a lexicon and adding facial expressions. The eSIGN project created tools for content developers to build sign databases and assemble scripts of signing for web pages (Kennaway et al., 2007). Sign Smith Studio (Vcom3D, 2010) is a commercial tool for scripting ASL (discussed in section 4). Others study generation or machine translation (MT) of sign language (Chiu et al., 2007; Elliot & Glauert, 2008; Fotinea et al., 2008; Huenerfauth, 2006; Karpouzis et al., 2007; Marshall & Safar, 2005; Shionome et al., 2005; Sumihiro et al., 2000; van Zijl & Barker, 2003).

Experimental evaluations of the understandability of state-of-the-art ASL animation systems have shown that native signers often find animations difficult to understand (as measured by compre-

Proceedings of the NAACL HLT 2010 Workshop on Speech and Language Processing for Assistive Technologies, pages 89–97,
Los Angeles, California, June 2010.

hension questions) or unnatural (as measured by subjective evaluation questions) (Huenerfauth et al., 2008). Errors include a lack of smooth inter-sign transitions, lack of grammatically-required facial expressions, and inaccurate sign performances related to morphological inflection of signs.

While current ASL animation systems have limitations, there are several advantages in presenting sign language content in the form of animated virtual human characters, rather than videos:

- Generation or MT software planning ASL sentences cannot just concatenate videos of ASL. Using video clips, it is difficult to produce smooth transitions between signs, subtle motion variations in sign performances, or proper combinations of facial expressions with signs.
- If content must be frequently modified or updated, then a video performance would need to be largely re-recorded for each modification. Whereas, an animation (scripted by a human author) could be further edited or modified.
- Because the face is used to indicate important information in ASL, a human must reveal his or her identity when producing an ASL video. Instead, a virtual human character could perform sentences scripted by a human author.
- For wiki-style applications in which multiple authors are collaborating on information content, ASL videos would be distracting: the person performing each sentence may differ. A virtual human would be more uniform.
- Animations can be appealing to children for use in educational applications.
- Animations allow ASL to be viewed at different angles, at different speeds, or by different virtual humans – depending on the preferences of the user. This can enable education applications in which students learning ASL can practice their ASL comprehension skills.

1.2 ASL is Challenging for NLP Research

Natural Language Processing (NLP) researchers often apply techniques originally designed for one language to another, but research is not commonly ported to sign languages. One reason is that without a written form for ASL, NLP researchers must produce animation and thus address several issues:

- *Timing:* An ASL performance's speed consists of: the speed of individual sign performances, the transitional time between signs, and the insertion of pauses during signing – all of which are based on linguistic factors such as syntactic boundaries, repetition of signs in a discourse, and the part-of-speech of signs (Grosjean et al., 1979). ASL animations whose speed and pausing are incorrect are significantly less understandable to ASL signers (Huenerfauth, 2009).
- *Spatial Reference:* Signers arrange invisible placeholders in the space around their body to represent objects or persons under discussion (Meier, 1990). To perform personal, possessive, or reflexive pronouns that refer to these entities, signers later point to these locations. Signers may not repeat the identity of these entities again; so, their conversational partner must remember where they have been placed. An ASL generator must select which entities should be assigned 3D locations (and where).
- *Inflection:* Many verbs change their motion paths to indicate the 3D location where a spatial reference point has been established for their subject, object, or both (Padden, 1988). Generally, the motion paths of these inflecting verbs change so that their direction goes from the subject to the object (Figure 1); however, their paths are more complex than this. Each verb has a standard motion path that is affected by the subject's and the object's 3D locations. When a verb is inflected in this way, the signer does not need to overtly state the subject/object of a sentence. An ASL generator must produce appropriately inflected verb paths based on the layout of the spatial reference points.

(a.)

(b.)

Figure 1: An ASL inflecting verb "BLAME": (a.) (person on left) blames (person on right), (b.) (person on right) blames (person on left).

- *Coarticulation:* As in speech production, the surrounding signs in a sentence affect finger, hand, and body movements. ASL generators that use overly simple interpolation rules to produce these coarticulation effects yield unnatural and non-fluent ASL animation output.
- *Non-Manuals:* Head-tilt and eye-gaze indicate the 3D location of a verb's subject and object (or other information); facial expressions also indicate negation, questions, topicalization, and other essential syntactic phenomena not conveyed by the hands (Neidle et al., 2000). Animations without proper facial expressions (and proper timing relative to manual signs) cannot convey the proper meaning of ASL sentences in a fluent and understandable manner.
- *Evaluation:* With no standard written form for ASL, string-based metrics cannot be used to evaluate ASL generation output automatically. User-based experiments are necessary, but it is difficult to accurately: screen for *native* signers, prevent English environmental influences (that affect signer's linguistic judgments), and design questions that measure comprehension of ASL animations (Huenerfauth et al., 2008).

1.3 Need for Data-Driven ASL Generation

Due to these challenges, most prior sign language generation or MT projects have been short-lived, producing few example outputs (Zhao et al., 2000; Veale et al., 1998). Further developed systems also have limited coverage; e.g., Marshall and Safar (2005) hand-built translation transfer rules from English to British Sign Language. Huenerfauth (2006) surveys several rule-based systems and discusses how they generally: have limited coverage; often merely concatenate signs; and do not address the *Coarticulation, Spatial Reference, Timing, Non-Manuals,* or *Inflection* issues (section 1.2).

Unfortunately, most prior work is not "data-driven," i.e. not based on statistical modeling of corpora, the dominant successful modern NLP approach. The sign language generation research that has thus far been *the most data-driven* includes:

- Some researchers have used motion-capture (see section 3) to build lexicons of animations of individual signs, e.g. (Cox et al., 2002). However, their focus is recording a single citation form of each sign, not creating annotated corpora of full sentences or discourse. Single-sign recordings do not enable researchers to examine the *Timing, Coarticulation, Spatial Reference, Non-Manuals*, or *Inflection* phenomena (section 1.2), which operate over multiple signs or sentences in an ASL discourse.
- Other researchers have examined how statistical MT techniques could be used to translate from a written language to a sign language. Morrissey and Way (2005) discuss an example-based MT architecture for Irish Sign Language, and Stein et al. (2006) apply simple statistical MT approaches to German Sign Language. Unfortunately, the sign language "corpora" used in these studies consist of transcriptions of the sequence of signs performed, not recordings of actual human performances. A transcription does not capture subtleties in the 3D movements of the hands, facial movements, or speed of an ASL performance. Such information is needed in order to address the *Spatial Reference, Inflection, Coarticulation, Timing*, or *Non-Manuals* issues (section 1.2).
- Seguoat and Braffort (2009) derive models of coarticulation for French Sign Language based on a semi-automated "rotoscoping" annotation of hand location from videos of signing.

1.4 Prior Sign Language Corpora Resources

The reason why most prior ASL generation research has not been data-driven is that sufficiently detailed and annotated sign language corpora are in short supply and are time-consuming to construct. Without a writing system in common use, it is not possible to harvest some naturally arising source of ASL "text"; instead, it is necessary to record the performance of a signer (through video or a motion-capture suit). Human signers must then transcribe and annotate this data by adding time-stamped linguistic details. For ASL (Neidle et al., 2000) and European sign languages (Bungeroth et al., 2006; Crasborn et al., 2004, 2006; Efthimiou & Fotinea, 2007), signers have been videotaped and experts marked time spans when events occur – e.g. the right hand is performing the sign "CAT" during time index 250-300 milliseconds, and the eyebrows are raised during time index 270-300. Such annotation is time-consuming to add; the largest ASL corpus has a few thousand sentences.

In order to learn how to control the movements of an animated virtual human based on a corpus, we need precise hand locations and joint angles of the human signer's body throughout the performance. Asking humans to write down 3D angles and coordinates is time-consuming and inexact; some researchers have used computer vision techniques to model the signers' movements (see survey in (Loeding et al., 2004)). Unfortunately, the complex shape of hands/face, rapid speed, and frequent occlusion of parts of the body during ASL limit the accuracy of vision-based recognition; it is not yet a reliable way to build a 3D model of a signer for a corpus. Motion-capture technology (discussed in section 3) is required for this level of detail.

2 Research Goals & Focus of This Paper

To address the lack of sufficiently detailed and linguistically annotated ASL corpora, we have begun a multi-year project to collect and annotate a motion-capture corpus of ASL (section 3). Digital 3D body movement and handshape data collected from native signers will become a permanent research resource for study by NLP researchers and ASL linguists. This corpus will allow us to create new ASL generation technologies in a data-driven manner by analyzing the subtleties in the motion data and its relationship to the linguistic structure. Specifically, we plan to model where signers tend to place spatial reference points around them in space. We also plan to uncover patterns in the motion paths of inflecting verbs and model how they relate to layout of spatial references points. These models could be used in ASL generation software or could be used to partially automate with work of humans using ASL-scripting systems. To evaluate our ASL models, native signers will be asked to judge ASL animations produced using them. There are several unique aspects of our research:

- We use a novel combination of hand, body, head, and eye motion-tracking technologies and simultaneous video recordings (section 3).
- We collect multi-sentence single-signer ASL discourse, and we annotate novel linguistic information (relevant to spatial reference points).
- We involve ASL signers in the research in several ways: as evaluators of our generation software, as research assistants conducting evaluation studies, and as corpus annotators.

This paper will focus on the first of these aspects of our project. Specifically, section 4 will examine the following research question: *Have we successfully configured and calibrated our motion-capture equipment so that we are recording good-quality data that will be useful for NLP research?*

Since the particular combination of motion-capture equipment we are using is novel and because there have not been prior motion-capture-based ASL corpora projects, section 4 will evaluate whether the data we are collecting is of sufficient quality to drive ASL animations of a virtual human character. In corpus-creation projects for traditional written/spoken languages, researchers typically gather text, audio, or (sometimes) video of human performances. The quality of the gathered recordings is typically easier to verify and evaluate; for motion-capture data collected with a complex configuration of equipment, a more complex experimental design is necessary (section 4).

3 Our Motion-Capture Configuration

The first stage of our research is to accurately and efficiently record 3D motion-capture data from ASL signers. Assuming an ASL signer's pelvis bone is stationary in 3D space, we want to record movement data for the upper body. We are interested in the shapes of each hand; the 3D location of the hands; the 3D orientation of the palms; joint angles for the wrists, elbows, shoulders, clavicle, neck, and waist; and a vector representing the eye-gaze aim. We are using a customized configuration of several commercial motion-capture devices (as shown in Figure 2, worn by a human signer):

- Two Immersion CyberGloves®: The 22 flexible sensor strips sewn into each of these spandex gloves record finger joint angles so that we can record the signer's handshapes. These gloves are ideal for recording ASL because they are flexible and lightweight. Humans viewing a subject wearing the gloves are able to discern ASL fingerspelling and signing.
- Applied Science Labs H6 eye-tracker: This lightweight head-mounted eye-tracker with a near-eye camera records a signer's eye gaze direction. A camera on the headband aims down, and a small clear plastic panel in front of the cheek reflects the image of the subject's eye. When combined with the head tracking information from the IS-900 system below, the H6 identifies a 3D vector of eye-gaze in a room.

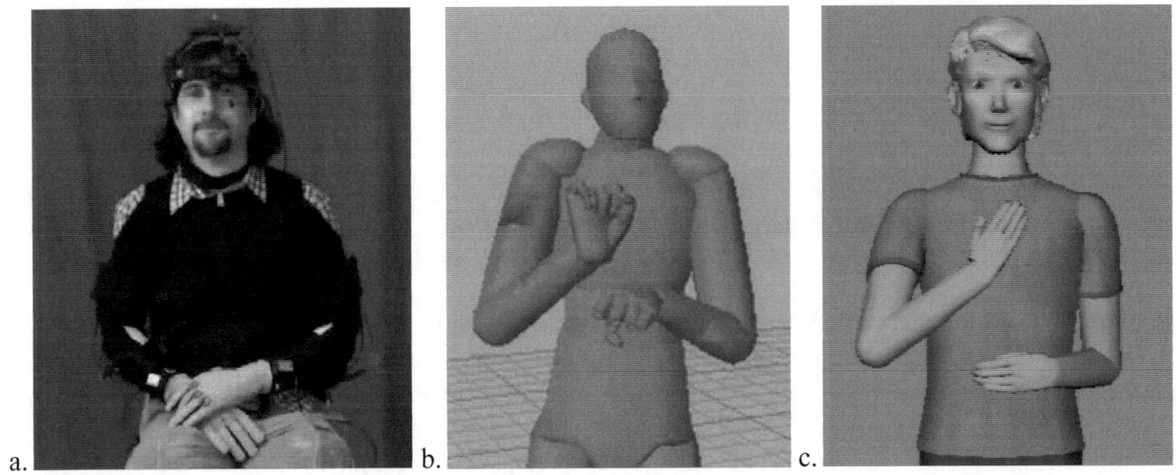

Figure 2: (a) Motion-capture equipment configuration, (b) animation produced from motion-capture data (shown in evaluation study), and (c) animation produced using Sign Smith (shown in evaluation study).

- Intersense IS-900: This acoustical/intertial motion-capture system uses a ceiling-mounted ultrasonic speaker array and a set of directional microphones on a small sensor to record the location and orientation of the signer's head. A sensor sits atop the helmet shown in Figure 2a. IS-900 data is used to compensate for head movement when calculating eye-gaze direction with the Applied Science Labs H6 eye-tracker.
- Animazoo IGS-190: This spandex bodysuit is covered with soft Velcro to which small sensors attach. A sensor placed on each segment of the human's body records inertial and magnetic information. Subjects wearing the suit stand facing north with their arms down at their sides at the beginning of the recording session; given this known starting pose and direction, the system calculates joint angles for the wrists, elbows, shoulders, clavicle, neck, and waist. We do not record leg/foot information in our corpus. Prior to recording data, we photograph subjects standing in a cube-shaped rig of known size; this allows us to identify bone lengths of the human subject, which are needed for the IGS-190 system to accurately calculate joint angles from the sensor data.

Motion-capture recording sessions are videotaped to facilitate later linguistic analysis and annotation. Videotaping the session also facilitates the "clean up" of the motion-capture data in post-processing, during which algorithms are applied to adjust synchronization of different sensors or remove "jitter" or other noise artifacts from the recording. Three digital high-speed video cameras film front view, facial close-up, and side views of the signer – a setup that has been used in video-based ASL-corpora-building projects (Neidle et al., 2000). The front view is similar to Figure 2a (but wider). The facial close-up view is useful when later identifying specific non-manual facial expressions during ASL performances, which are essential to correctly understanding and annotating the collected data. To facilitate synchronizing the three video files during post-processing, a strobe is flashed once at the start of the recording session.

A "blue screen" curtain hangs on the back and side walls of the motion-capture studio. If future computer vision researchers wish to use this corpus to study ASL recognition from video, it is useful to have solid color walls for "chroma key" background removal. Photographic studio lighting with spectra compatible with the eye-tracking system is used to support high-quality video recording.

During data collection, a native ASL signer (called the "prompter") sits directly behind the front-view camera to engage the participant wearing the suit (the "performer") in natural conversation. While the corpus we are collecting consists of unscripted *single-signer* discourse, prior ASL corpora projects have identified the importance of surrounding signers with an ASL-centric environment during data collection (Neidle et al., 2000). English influence in the studio must be minimized to prevent signers from inadvertently code-switching to an English-like form of signing. Thus, it is important that a native signer acts as the prompter, who conversationally suggests topics for the performer to discuss (to be recorded as part of the corpus).

In our first year, we have collected and annotated 58 passages from 6 signers (40 minutes). We prefer to collect multi-sentence passages discussing varied numbers of topics and with few “classifier predicates,” phenomena that aren’t our current research focus. In (Huenerfauth & Lu, 2010), we discuss details of: the genre of discourse we record, our target linguistic phenomena to capture (spatial reference points and inflected verbs), the types of linguistic annotation added to the corpus, and the effectiveness of different “prompts” used to elicit the desired type of spontaneous discourse.

This paper focuses on verifying the quality of the motion-capture data we can record using our current equipment configuration and protocols. We want to measure how well we have compensated for several possible sources of error in recordings:

- If a sensor connection is temporarily lost, then data gaps occur. We have selected equipment that does not require line-of-sight connections and tried to arrange the studio to avoid frequent dropping of any wireless connections.
- We ask subjects to perform a quick head movement and distinctive eye blink pattern at the beginning of the recording session to facilitate “synchronization” of the various motion-capture data streams during post-processing.
- Electronic and physical properties of sensors can lead to “noise” in the data, which we attempt to remove with smoothing algorithms.
- Differences between the bone lengths of the human and the “virtual skeleton” of the animated character being recorded could lead to “retargeting” errors, in which the body poses of the human do not match the recording. We must be careful in the measurement of the bone lengths of the human participant and in the design of the virtual animation skeleton.
- To compensate for differences in how equipment sits on the body on different occasions or on different humans, we must set “calibration” values; e.g., we designed a novel protocol for efficiently and accurately calibrating gloves for ASL signers (Lu & Huenerfauth, 2009).

4 Evaluating Our Collected Motion Data

If a speech synthesis researcher were using a novel microphone technology to record audio performances from human speakers to build a corpus, that researcher would want to experimentally confirm that the audio recordings were of high enough quality for research. Even when perfectly clear audio recordings of human speech are recorded in a corpus, the automatic speech synthesis models trained on this data are not perfect. Degradations in the quality of the corpus would yield even lower quality speech synthesis systems. In the same way, it is essential that we evaluate the quality of the ASL motion-capture data we are collecting.

In an earlier study, we sought to collect motion-data from humans and directly produce animations from them as an “upper baseline” for an experimental study (Huenerfauth, 2006). We were not analyzing the collected data or using it for data-driven generation, we merely wanted the data to directly drive an animation of a virtual human character as a “virtual puppet.” This earlier project used a different configuration of motion-capture equipment, including an earlier version of CyberGloves® and an optical motion-capture system that required line-of-sight connections between infrared emitters on the signer’s body and cameras around the room. Unfortunately, the data collected was so poor that the animations produced from the motion-capture were not an “upper” baseline – in fact, they were barely understandable to native signers. Errors arose from dropped connections, poor calibration, and insufficient removal of data noise.

We have selected different equipment and have designed better protocols for recording high quality ASL data since that earlier study – to compensate for the “noise,” “retargeting,” “synchronization,” and “calibration” issues mentioned in section 3. However, we know that under some recording conditions, the quality of collected motion-capture data is so poor that “virtual puppet” animations synthesized from it are not understandable. We expect that an even higher level of data quality is needed for a motion-capture *corpus*, which will be analyzed and manipulated in order to synthesize novel ASL animations from it. Therefore, we conducted a study (discussed below) to evaluate the quality of our current motion-capture configuration. As in our past study, we use the motion-capture data to directly control the body movements of a virtual human “puppet.” We then ask native ASL signers to evaluate the understandability and naturalness of the resulting animations (and compare them to some baseline animations produced using ASL-animation scripting software).

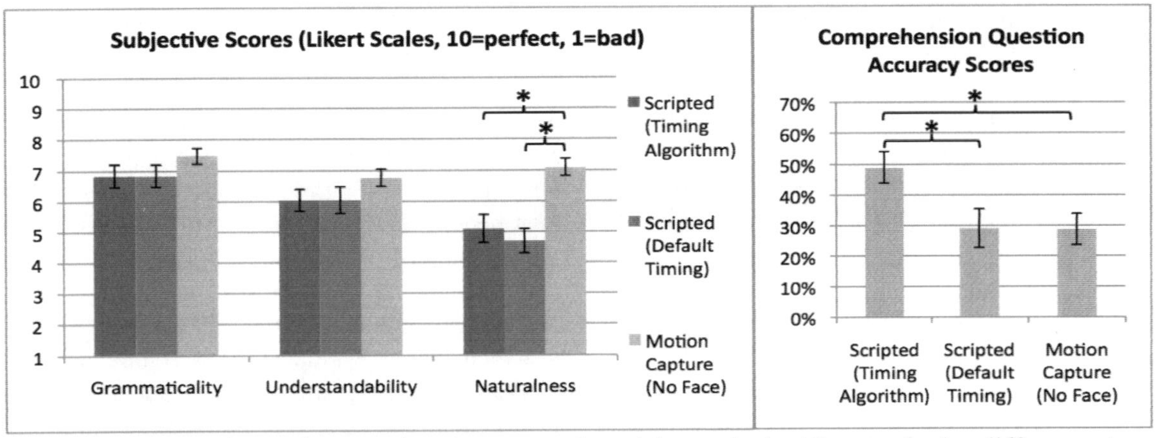

Figure 3: Evaluation and comprehension scores (asterisks mark significant pairwise differences).

In our prior work, a native ASL signer designed a set of ASL stories and corresponding comprehension questions for use in evaluation studies (Huenerfauth, 2009). The stories' average length is approximately 70 signs, and they consist of news stories, encyclopedia articles, and short narratives. We produced animations of each using Sign Smith Studio (SSS), commercial ASL-animation scripting software (Vcom3D, 2010). Signs from SSS's lexicon are placed on a timeline, and linguistically appropriate facial expressions are added. The software synthesizes an animation of a virtual human performing the story (Figure 2c). In earlier work, we designed algorithms for determining sign-speed and pause-insertion in ASL animations based on linguistic features of the sentence. We conducted a study to compare animations with default timing settings (uniform pauses and speed) and animations governed by our timing algorithm – at various speeds. The use of our timing algorithm yielded ASL animations that native signers found more understandable (Huenerfauth, 2009). We are reusing these stories and animations as baselines for comparison in a new evaluation study (below).

While we are collecting *unscripted* passages in our corpus, it is easier to compare the quality of different versions of animations when using a common set of *scripted* stories. Thus, we used the script from 10 of the stories above, and each was performed by a native signer, a 22-year-old male who learned ASL prior to age 2. He wore the full set of motion-capture equipment, and we followed the same calibration process and protocols as we do when recording ASL passages for our corpus. The signer rehearsed and memorized each story; "cue cards" were also available when recording.

Autodesk MotionBuilder software was used to produce a virtual human whose movements were driven by the motion-capture data (see Figure 2b). While our corpus contains *video* of facial expression, our motion-capture equipment does not digitize it; so, the virtual human character has no facial movements. The recorded signer moved at an average speed of 1.12 signs/second, and so for comparison, we selected the version of the scripted ASL animations with the closest speed from our earlier study: 1.2 signs/second. (Since the scripted animations are slightly slower and include linguistic facial expressions, we expected them to receive higher understandability scores than our motion-capture animations.) In our earlier work, we produced two versions of each scripted story: one with default timing and one with our novel timing algorithm. Both versions are used as baselines for comparison in this new study; thus, we compare three versions of the same set of 10 ASL stories.

Using questions designed to screen for native ASL signers developed in prior work (Huenerfauth et al., 2008), we recruited 12 participants to evaluate the ASL animations. A native ASL signer conducted the studies, in which participants viewed an animation and were then asked two types of questions after each: (1) ten-point Likert-scale questions about the ASL animation's grammatical correctness, understandability, and naturalness of movement and (2) multiple-choice comprehension questions about basic facts from the story. The comprehension questions were presented in the form of scripted ASL animations (produced in SSS), and answer choices were presented in the form of clip-art images (so that strong English literacy was not necessary). Identical questions were used to evaluate the motion-capture animations and the scripted animations. Examples of the questions are included in (Huenerfauth, 2009).

Figure 3 displays results of the Likert-scale subjective questions and comprehension-question success scores for the three types of animations evaluated in this study. The scripted animations using our timing algorithm have higher comprehension scores, but the motion-capture animations have higher naturalness scores. All of the other scores for the animations are quite similar. Statistically significant differences are marked with an asterisk ($p<0.05$, Mann-Whitney pairwise comparisons with Bonferroni-corrected p-values). Non-parameteric tests were selected because the Likert-scale responses were not normally distributed.

5 Conclusion and Future Research Goals

The research question addressed by this paper was whether our motion-capture configuration and recording protocols enabled us to collect motion-data of sufficient quality for data-driven ASL generation research. In our study, the evaluation scores of the animations driven by the motion-capture data were similar to those of animations produced using state-of-the-art ASL animation scripting software. This is a promising result, especially considering the slightly faster speed and lack of facial expression information in the motion-capture animations. While this suggests that the data we are collecting is of good quality, the *real* test will be when this corpus is used in future research. If we can build useful ASL-animation generation software based on analysis of this corpus, then we will know that we have sufficient quality of motion-capture data.

5.1 Our Long-Term Research Goal: Making ASL Accessible to More NLP Researchers

It is our goal to produce high-quality broad-coverage ASL generation software, which would benefit many deaf individuals with low English literacy. However, this ambition is too large for any one team; for this technology to become reality, ASL must become a language commonly studied by NLP researchers. For this reason, we seek to build ASL software, models, and experimental techniques to serve as a resource for other NLP researchers. Our goal is to make ASL "accessible" to the NLP community. By developing tools to address some of the modality-specific and spatial aspects of ASL, we can make it easier for other researchers to transfer their new NLP techniques to ASL. The goal is to "normalize" ASL in the eyes of the NLP community. Bridging NLP and ASL research will not only benefit deaf users: ASL will push the limits of current NLP techniques and will thus benefit other work in the field of NLP. Section 1.2 listed six challenges for ASL NLP research; we address several of these in our research:

We have conducted many experimental studies in which signers evaluate the understandability and naturalness of ASL animations (Huenerfauth et al., 2008; Huenerfauth, 2009). To begin to address the *Evaluation* issue (section 1.2), we have published best-practices, survey materials, and experimental protocols for effectively evaluating ASL animation systems through the participation of native signers. We have also published baseline comprehension scores for ASL animations. We will continue to produce such resources in future work.

Our earlier work on timing algorithms for ASL animations (mentioned in section 4) was based on data reported in the linguistics literature (Grosjean et al., 1979). In future work, we want to learn timing models directly from our collected corpus – to further address the *Timing* issue (section 1.2).

To address the issues of *Spatial Reference* and *Inflection* (section 1.2), we plan on analyzing our ASL corpus to build models that can predict where in 3D space signers establish spatial reference points. Further, we will analyze our corpus to analyze how certain ASL verbs are inflected based on the 3D location of their subject and object. We want to build a *parameterized* lexicon of ASL verbs: given a 3D location for subject and object, we want to predict a 3D motion-path for the character's hands for a specific performance of a verb.

While addressing the issues of *Coarticulation* and *Non-Manuals* (section 1.2) are not immediate research priorities, we believe our ASL corpus may also be useful in building computational models of these phenomena for data-driven ASL generation.

Acknowledgments

This material is based upon work supported by the National Science Foundation (Award #0746556), Siemens (Go PLM Academic Grant), and Visage Technologies AB (free academic license for software). Jonathan Lamberton, Wesley Clarke, Kelsey Gallagher, Amanda Krieger, and Aaron Pagan assisted with ASL data collection and experiments.

References

J. Bungeroth, D. Stein, P. Dreuw, M. Zahedi, H. Ney. 2006. A German sign language corpus of the domain weather report. *Proc. LREC 2006 workshop on representation & processing of sign languages.*

Y.H. Chiu, C.H. Wu, H.Y. Su, C.J. Cheng. 2007. Joint optimization of word alignment and epenthesis generation for Chinese to Taiwanese sign synthesis. *IEEE Trans Pattern Anal Mach Intell* 29(1):28-39.

S. Cox, M. Lincoln, J. Tryggvason, M. Nakisa, M. Wells, M. Tutt, S. Abbott. 2002. Tessa, a system to aid communication with deaf people. *Proc. ASSETS.*

O. Crasborn, E. van der Kooij, D. Broeder, H. Brugman. 2004. Sharing sign language corpora online: proposals for transcription and metadata categories. *Proc. LREC 2004 workshop on representation & processing of sign languages*, pp. 20-23.

O. Crasborn, H. Sloetjes, E. Auer, and P. Wittenburg. 2006. Combining video and numeric data in the analysis of sign languages within the ELAN annotation software. *Proc. LREC 2006 workshop on representation & processing of sign languages,* 82-87.

E. Efthimiou, S.E. Fotinea. 2007. GSLC: creation and annotation of a Greek sign language corpus for HCI. *Proc. HCI International.*

R. Elliot, J. Glauert. 2008. Linguistic modeling and language-processing technologies for avatar-based sign language presentation. *Universal Access in the Information Society* 6(4):375-391.

S.E. Fotinea, E. Efthimiou, G. Caridakis, K. Karpouzis. 2008. A knowledge-based sign synthesis architecture. *Univ. Access in Information Society* 6(4):405-418.

F. Grosjean, L. Grosjean, H. Lane. 1979. The patterns of silence: Performance structures in sentence production. *Cognitive Psychology* 11:58-81.

M. Huenerfauth. 2006. Generating American sign language classifier predicates for English-to-ASL machine translation, dissertation, U. of Pennsylvania.

M. Huenerfauth, L. Zhao, E. Gu, J. Allbeck. 2008. Evaluation of American sign language generation by native ASL signers. *ACM Trans Access Comput* 1(1):1-27.

M. Huenerfauth. 2009. A linguistically motivated model for speed and pausing in animations of American sign language. *ACM Trans Access Comput* 2(2):1-31.

M. Huenerfauth, P. Lu. 2010. Annotating spatial reference in a motion-capture corpus of American sign language discourse. *Proc. LREC 2010 workshop on representation & processing of sign languages.*

K. Karpouzis, G. Caridakis, S.E. Fotinea, E. Efthimiou. 2007. Educational resources and implementation of a Greek sign language synthesis architecture. *Computers & Education* 49(1):54-74.

J. Kennaway, J. Glauert, I. Zwitserlood. 2007. Providing signed content on Internet by synthesized animation. *ACM Trans Comput-Hum Interact* 14(3):15.

B. Loeding, S. Sarkar, A. Parashar, A. Karshmer. 2004. Progress in automated computer recognition of sign language, *Proc. ICCHP*, 1079-1087.

P. Lu, M. Huenerfauth. 2009. Accessible motion-capture glove calibration protocol for recording sign language data from deaf subjects. *Proc. ASSETS.*

I. Marshall, E. Safar. 2005. Grammar development for sign language avatar-based synthesis. *Proc. UAHCI.*

R. Meier. 1990. Person deixis in American sign language. In: S. Fischer & P. Siple (eds.), *Theoretical issues in sign language research, vol. 1: Linguistics.* Chicago: University of Chicago Press, 175-190.

R. Mitchell, T. Young, B. Bachleda, M. Karchmer. 2006. How many people use ASL in the United States? *Sign Language Studies* 6(3):306-335.

S. Morrissey, A. Way. 2005. An example-based approach to translating sign language. *Proc. Workshop on Example-Based Machine Translation*, 109-116.

C. Neidle, D. Kegl, D. MacLaughlin, B. Bahan, & R.G. Lee. 2000. *The syntax of ASL: functional categories and hierarchical structure.* Cambridge: MIT Press.

D. Newkirk. 1987. *SignFont Handbook.* San Diego: Emerson and Associates.

C. Padden. 1988. Interaction of morphology & syntax in American sign language. *Outstanding dissertations in linguistics, series IV.* New York: Garland Press.

J. Segouat, A. Braffort. 2009. Toward the study of sign language coarticulation: methodology proposal. *Proc Advances in Comput.-Human Interactions,* 369-374.

T. Shionome, K. Kamata, H. Yamamoto, S. Fischer. 2005. Effects of display size on perception of Japanese sign language---Mobile access in signed language. *Proc. Human-Computer Interaction*, 22-27.

D. Stein, J. Bungeroth, H. Ney. 2006. Morpho-syntax based statistical methods for sign language translation. *Proc. European Association for MT*, 169-177.

K. Sumihiro, S. Yoshihisa, K. Takao. 2000. Synthesis of sign animation with facial expression and its effects on understanding of sign language. *IEIC Technical Report* 100(331):31-36.

V. Sutton. 1998. The Signwriting Literacy Project. In *Impact of Deafness on Cognition AERA Conference.*

C. Traxler. 2000. The Stanford achievement test, ninth edition: national norming and performance standards for deaf and hard-of-hearing students. *J. Deaf Studies and Deaf Education* 5(4):337-348.

L. van Zijl, D. Barker. 2003. South African sign language MT system. *Proc. AFRIGRAPH*, 49-52.

VCom3D. 2010. Sign Smith Studio. http://www.vcom3d.com/signsmith.php

T. Veale, A. Conway, B. Collins. 1998. Challenges of cross-modal translation: English to sign translation in ZARDOZ system. *Machine Translation* 13:81-106.

L. Zhao, K. Kipper, W. Schuler, C. Vogler, N. Badler, M. Palmer. 2000. A machine translation system from English to American sign language. *Proc. AMTA.*

Automated Skimming in Response to Questions for NonVisual Readers

Debra Yarrington
Dept. of Computer and Information Science
University of Delaware
Newark, DE, 19716, USA
yarringt@eecis.udel.edu

Kathleen F. McCoy
Dept. of Computer and Information Science
University of Delaware
Newark, DE, 19716, USA
mccoy@cis.udel.edu

Abstract

This paper presents factors in designing a system for automatically skimming text documents in response to a question. The system will take a potentially complex question and a single document and return a Web page containing links to text related to the question. The goal is that these text areas be those that visual readers would spend the most time on when skimming for the answer to a question. To identify these areas, we had visual readers skim for an answer to a complex question while being tracked by an eye-tracking system. Analysis of these results indicates that text with semantic connections to the question are of interest, but these connections are much looser than can be identified with traditional Question-Answering or Information Retrieval techniques. Instead, we are expanding traditional semantic treatments by using a Web search. The goal of this system is to give non-visual readers information similar to what visual readers get when skimming through a document in response to a question.

1 Introduction

This paper describes semantic considerations in developing a system for giving nonvisual readers information similar to what visual readers glean when skimming through a document in response to a question. Our eventual system will be unique in that it takes both simple and complex questions, will work in an unrestricted domain, will locate answers within a single document, and will return not just an answer to a question, but the information visual skimmers acquire when skimming through a document.

1.1 Goals

Production of our skimming system will require the attainment of three major goals:

1. Achieving an understanding of what information in the document visual skimmers pay attention to when skimming in response to a question
2. Developing Natural Language Processing (NLP) techniques to automatically identify areas of text visual readers focus on as determined in 1.
3. Developing a user interface to be used in conjunction with screen reading software to deliver the visual skimming experience.

In this paper we focus on the first two of these goals. Section 2 will discuss experiments analyzing visual skimmers skimming for answers to questions. Section 3 will discuss developing NLP techniques to replicate the results of Section 2. Section 4 will discuss future work.

1.2 Impetus

The impetus for this system was work done by the author with college students with visual impairments who took significantly longer to complete homework problems than their visually reading counterparts. Students used both ScreenReaders, which read electronic text aloud, and screen magnifiers, which increase the size of text on a screen. While these students were comfortable listening to the screenreader reading at rates of up to 500 words per minute, their experience was quite different from their visual-reading peers. Even after listening to an entire chapter, when they wanted to return to areas of text that contained text relevant to the answer, they had to start listening from the beginning and traverse the document again. Doing

Proceedings of the NAACL HLT 2010 Workshop on Speech and Language Processing for Assistive Technologies, pages 98–106,
Los Angeles, California, June 2010.

homework was a tedious, time-consuming task which placed these students at a serious disadvantage. It is clear that individuals with visual impairments struggle in terms of education. By developing a system that levels the playing field in at least one area, we may make it easier for at least some individuals to succeed.

2 Visual Skimming

If our intention is to convey to nonvisual readers information similar to what visual readers acquire when skimming for answers to questions, we first must determine what information visual readers get when skimming. For our purposes, we were interested in what text readers focused on in connection to a question. While many systems exist that focus on answering simple, fact-based questions, we were more interested in more complex questions in which the answer could not be found using pattern matching and in which the answer would require at least a few sentences, not necessarily contiguous within a document. From an NLP standpoint, locating longer answers with relevant information occuring in more than one place that may or may not have words or word sequences in common with the question poses an interesting and difficult problem. The problem becomes making semantic connections within any domain that are more loosely associated than the synonyms, hypernyms, hyponyms, etc. provided by WordNet (Felbaum, 1998). Indeed, the questions that students had the most difficulty with were more complex in nature. Thus we needed to find out whether visual skimmers were able to locate text in documents relevant to complex questions and, if so, what connections visual skimmers are making in terms of the text they choose to focus on.

2.1 Task Description

To identify how visual readers skim documents to answer questions, we collected 14 questions obtained from students' homework assignments, along with an accompanying document per question from which the answer could be obtained. The questions chosen were on a wide variety of topics and were complex in nature. An example of a typical question is, "According to Piaget, what techniques do children use to adjust to their environment as they grow?" Documents largely consisted of plain text, although each had a title on the first page. They held no images and few subtitles or other areas users might find visually interesting. Twelve of the documents were two pages in length, one was eight pages in length, and one was nine pages long. In each case, the answer to the question was judged by the researchers to be found within a single paragraph in the document.

Forty-three visual reading subjects skimmed for the answer to between 6 – 13 questions. The subjects sat in front of a computer screen to which the Eye Tracker 1750 by Tobii Technologies was installed. The questions and accompanying documents were displayed on the computer screen and, after being calibrated, subjects were tracked as they skimmed for the answer. For the two-page documents, the question appeared at the top of the first page. For the longer documents, the question appeared at the top of each page. Subjects had no time limit for skimming and switched pages by pressing the space bar. When done skimming each document, subjects were asked to select a best answer in multiple choice form (to give them a reason to take the skimming task seriously).

2.2 Results

Results showed that subjects were reliably able to correctly answer the multiple choice question after skimming the document. Of the 510 questions, 423 (about 86%) were answered correctly. The two questions from longer documents were the least likely to be answered correctly (one had 10 correct answers of 21 total answers, and the other had 10 incorrect answers and only one correct answer).

Clearly for the shorter documents, subjects were able to get appropriate information out of the document to successfully answer the question. With that established, we were interested in analyzing the eye tracking data to see if there was a connection between where subjects spent the most time in the document and the question. If there was an understandable connection, the goal then became to automatically replicate those connections and thus automatically locate places in the text where subjects were most likely to spend the most time.

The Tobii Eye Tracking System tracks the path and length of time a subject gazes at a particular point as a subject skims through a document. The system allows us to define Areas of Interest (AOIs) and then track the number of prolonged gaze points

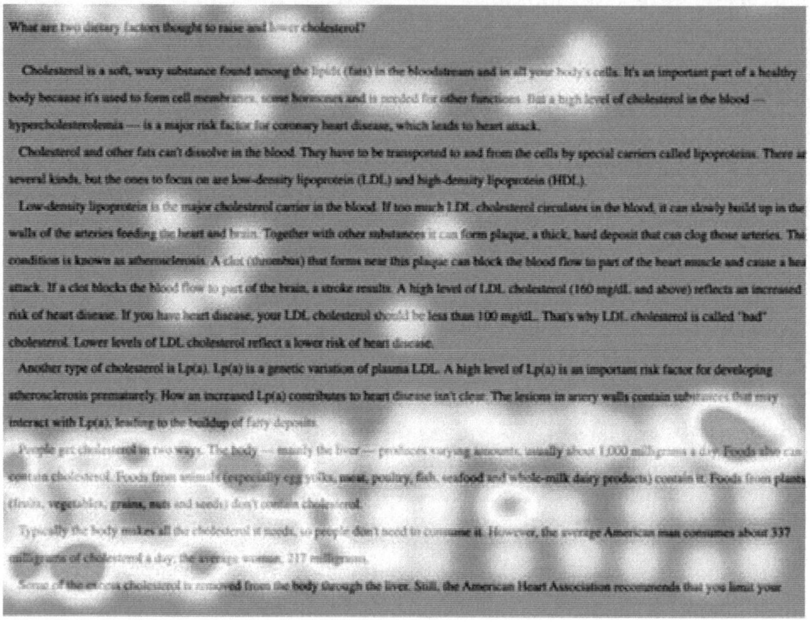

Figure 1. Hot spot image results of skimming for the answer to the question, "What are two dietary factors thought to raise and lower cholesterol?" using the Tobii Eye Tracking System

within those areas of interest. For our analysis, we defined areas of interest as being individual paragraphs. While we purposely chose documents that were predominantly text, each had a title as well. Titles and the few subtitles and lists that occurred in the documents were also defined as separate AOIs. For each skimming activity, the eye tracking system gave us a gaze plot showing the order in which individuals focused on particular areas, and a hot spot image showing the gaze points, with duration indicated with color intensity, that occurred in each AOI (see Figure 1).

In looking at the hot spot images, we found that subjects used three techniques to peruse a document. One technique subjects used was to move their gaze slowly throughout the entire document, indicating that they were most likely reading the document. A second technique used was to move randomly and quickly from top to bottom of the document (described as "fixations distributed in a rough zig-zag down the page" by McLaughlin in reference to speed reading (1969)), without ever focusing on one particular area for a longer period of time. This technique was the least useful to us because it gave very little information A third technique was a combination of the first two, in which the subject's gaze darted quickly and randomly around the page, and then appeared to focus on a particular area for an extended period of time. Figure 1 is a good example of this technique. The data from this group was clearly relevant to our task since their fixation points clearly showed what areas subjects found most interesting while skimming for an answer to a question.

2.3 Analysis of Skimming Data

To determine exactly which AOIs subjects focused on most frequently, we counted the number of gaze points (or focus points) in each AOI (defined as paragraphs, titles, subtitles) across all subjects. In looking at what information individuals focused on while skimming, we found that individuals did focus on the title and subtitles that occurred in the documents. Subjects frequently focused on the first paragraph or paragraphs of a document. There was less of a tendency, but still a trend for focusing on the first paragraph on each page. Interestingly, although a few subjects focused on the first line of each paragraph, this was not a common practice. This is significant because it is a technique available to users of screenreaders, yet it clearly does not give these users the same information that visual skimmers get when skimming through a document.

We also wanted to look at AOIs that did not have physical features that may have attracted attention. Our conjecture was that these AOIs were focused on by subjects because of their semantic relationship to the question. Indeed, we did find evidence of this. Results indicated that subjects did focus on the areas of text containing the answer to the question. As an example, one of the questions used in the study was,

> *"How do people catch the West Nile Virus?"*

The paragraph with the most gaze points for the most subjects was:

> *"In the United States, wild birds, especially crows and jays, are the main reservoir of West Nile virus, but the virus is actually spread by certain species of mosquitoes. Transmission happens when a mosquito bites a bird infected with the West Nile virus and the virus enters the mosquito's bloodstream. It circulates for a few days before settling in the salivary glands. Then the infected mosquito bites an animal or a human and the virus enters the host's bloodstream, where it may cause serious illness. The virus then probably multiplies and moves on to the brain, crossing the blood-brain barrier. Once the virus crosses that barrier and infects the brain or its linings, the brain tissue becomes inflamed and symptoms arise."*

This paragraph contains the answer to the question, yet it has very few words in common with the question. The word it does have in common with the question, 'West Nile Virus', is the topic of the document and occurs fairly frequently throughout the document, and thus cannot account for subjects' focusing on this particular paragraph.

The subjects must have made semantic connections between the question and the answer that cannot be explained by simple word matching or even synonyms, hypernyms and hyponyms. In the above example, the ability of the user to locate the answer hinged on their ability to make a connection between the word 'catch' in the question and its meaning 'to be infected by'. Clearly simple keyword matching won't suffice in this case, yet equally clearly subjects successfully identified this paragraph as being relevant to the question. This suggests that when skimming subjects were able to make the semantic connections necessary to locate question answers, even when the answer was of a very different lexical form than the question.

Other areas of text focused on also appear to have a semantic relationship with the question. For example, with the question,

> *"Why was Monet's work criticized by the public?"*

the second most frequently focused on paragraph was:

> *"In 1874, Manet, Degas, Cezanne, Renoir, Pissarro, Sisley and Monet put together an exhibition, which resulted in a large financial loss for Monet and his friends and marked a return to financial insecurity for Monet. It was only through the help of Manet that Monet was able to remain in Argenteuil. In an attempt to recoup some of his losses, Monet tried to sell some of his paintings at the Hotel Drouot. This, too, was a failure. Despite the financial uncertainty, Monet's paintings never became morose or even all that sombre. Instead, Monet immersed himself in the task of perfecting a style which still had not been accepted by the world at large. Monet's compositions from this time were extremely loosely structured, with color applied in strong, distinct strokes as if no reworking of the pigment had been attempted. This technique was calculated to suggest that the artist had indeed captured a spontaneous impression of nature."*

Of the 30 subjects who skimmed this document, 15 focused on this paragraph, making it the second most focused on AOI in the document, second only to the paragraph that contained the answer (focused on by 21 of the subjects). The above paragraph occurred within the middle of the second page of the document, with no notable physical attributes that would have attracted attention. Upon closer inspection of the paragraph, there are references to "financial loss," "financial insecurity," "losses," "failure," and "financial uncertainty." The paragraph also includes "morose" and "somber" and even "had not been accepted by the world at large." Subjects appeared to be making a connection between the question topic, Monet's work being criticized by the public, and the above terms. Intuitively, we do seem to make this connection. Yet the connection being made is not straightforward and cannot be replicated using the direct semantic connections that are available via WordNet. Indeed, the relationships made are more similar to Hovy and Lin's (1997) Concept Signatures created by clustering words in articles with the same editor-defined classification from the Wall Street Journal. Our system must be able to replicate these connections automatically.

Upon further examination, we found other paragraphs that were focused on by subjects for reasons other than their physical appearance or location, yet their semantic connection to the question was even more tenuous. For instance, when skimming for the answer to the question,

> *"How does marijuana affect the brain?"*

the second most frequently focused on paragraph (second to the paragraph with the answer) was,

> *"The main active chemical in marijuana is THC (delta-9-tetrahydrocannabinol). The protein receptors in the membranes of certain cells bind to THC. Once securely in place, THC kicks off a series of cellular reactions that ultimately lead to the high that users experience when they smoke marijuana."*

While this paragraph does appear to have loose semantic connections with the question, the connections are less obvious than paragraphs that follow it, yet it was this paragraph that subjects chose to focus on. The paragraph is the third to last paragraph on the first page, so its physical location could not explain its attraction to subjects. However, when we looked more closely at the previous paragraphs, we saw that the first paragraph deals with definitions and alternate names for marijuana (with no semantic links to the question), and the second and third paragraph deal with statistics on people who use marijuana (again, with no semantic connection to the question). The fourth paragraph, the one focused on, represents a dramatic semantic shift towards the topic of the question. Intuitively it makes sense that individuals skimming through the document would pay more attention to this paragraph because it seems to represent the start of the area that may contain the answer, not to mention conveying topological information about the layout of the document and general content information as well.

Data collected from these experiments suggest that subjects do make and skim for semantic connections. Subjects not only glean information that directly answers the question, but also on content within the document that is semantically related to the question. While physical attributes of text do attract the attention of skimmers, and thus we must include methods for accessing this data as well, it is clear that in order to create a successful skimming device that conveys information similar to what visual skimmers get when skimming for the answer to a question, we must come up with a method for automatically generating loose semantic connections and then using those semantic connections to locate text skimmers considered relevant within the document.

3 NLP Techniques

In order to automatically generate the semantic connections identified above as being those visual skimmers make, we want to explore Natural Language Processing (NLP) techniques.

3.1 Related Research

Potentially relevant methodologies may be found in Open Domain Question Answering Systems. Open Domain Question Answering Systems involve connecting questions within any domain and potential answers. These systems usually do not rely on external knowledge sources and are limited in the amount of ontological information that can be included in the system. The questions are usually fact-based in form (e.g., "How tall is Mt. Everest?"). These systems take a question and query a potentially large set of documents (e.g., the World Wide Web) to find the answer. A common technique is to determine a question type (e.g., "How many …?" would be classified as 'numerical', whereas "Who was …?" would be classified as 'person', etc.) and then locate answers of the correct type (Abney et al., 2000; Kwok et al., 2001; Srihari and Li, 2000; Galea, 2003). Questions are also frequently reformulated for pattern matching (e.g., "Who was the first American Astronaut in space?" becomes, "The first American Astronaut in space was" (Kwok et al., 2001; Brill et al., 2002)). Many systems submit multiple queries to a document corpus, relying on redundancy of the answer to handle incorrect answers, poorly constructed answers or documents that don't contain the answer (e.g., Brill et al., 2002; Kwok et al.,

2001). For these queries, systems often include synonyms, hypernyms, hyponyms, etc. in the query terms used for document and text retrieval (Hovy et al.,2000; Katz et al., 2005). In an attempt to answer more complex relational queries, Banko et al. (2007) parsed training data into relational tuples for use in classifying text tagged for part of speech, chunked into noun phrases, and then tagged the relations for probability. Soricut and Brill (2006) trained data on FAQ knowledge bases from the World Wide Web, resulting in approximately 1 million question-answer pairs. This system related potential answers to questions using probability models computed using the FAQ knowledge base.

Another area of research that may lend useful techniques for connecting and retrieving relevant text to a question is query-biased text summarization. With many summarization schemes, a good deal of effort has been placed on identifying the main topic or topics of the document. In query biased text summarization, however, the topic is identified a priori, and the task is to locate relevant text within a document or set of documents. In multidocument summarization systems, redundancy may be indicative of relevance, but should be eliminated from the resulting summary. Thus a concern is measuring relevance versus redundancy (Carbonell and Goldstein, 1998; Hovy et al., 2005; Otterbacher et al., 2006). Like Question Answering systems, many summarization systems simply match the query terms, expanded to include synonyms, hypernyms, hyponyms, etc., to text in the document or documents (Varadarajan and Hristidis, 2006; Chali, 2002)

Our system is unique in that it has as its goal not just to answer a question or create a summary, but to return information visual skimmers glean while skimming through a document. Questions posed to the system will range from simple to complex in nature, and the answer must be found within a single document, regardless of the form the answer takes. Questions can be on any topic. With complex questions, it is rarely possible to categorize the type of question (and thus the expected answer type). Intuitively, it appears equally useless to attempt reformulation of the query for pattern matching. This intuition is born out by Soricut and Brill (2006) who stated that in their study reformulating complex questions more often hurt performance than improved it. Answering complex questions within a single document when the answer may not be straightforward in nature poses a challenging problem.

3.2 Baseline Processing

Our baseline system attempted to identify areas of interest by matching against the query in the tradition of Open Domain Question Answering. For our baseline, we used the nonfunction words in each question as our query terms. The terms were weighted with a variant of TF/IDF (Salton and Buckley, 1988) in which terms were weighted by the inverse of the number of paragraphs they occurred in within the document. This weighting scheme was designed to give lower weight to words associated with the document topic and thus conveying less information about relevance to the question. Each query term was matched to text in each paragraph, and paragraphs were ranked for matching using the summation of, for each query term, the number of times it occurred in the paragraph multiplied by its weight.

Results of this baseline ranking were poor. In none of the 14 documents did this method connect the question to the text relevant to the answer. This was expected. This original set of questions was purposely chosen because of the complex relationship between the question and answer text.

Next we expanded the set of query terms to include synonyms, hypernyms, and hyponyms as defined in WordNet (Felbaum, 1998). We included all senses of each word (query term). Irrelevant senses resulted in the inclusion of terms that were no more likely to occur frequently than any other random word, and thus had no effect on the resulting ranking of paragraphs. Again, each of the words in the expanded set of query terms was weighted as described above, and paragraphs were ranked accordingly.

Again, results were poor. Paragraphs ranked highly were no more likely to contain the answer, nor were they likely to be areas focused on by the visual skimmers in our collected skimming data.

Clearly, for complex questions, we need to expand on these basic techniques to replicate the semantic connections individuals make when skimming. As our system must work across a vast array of domains, our system must make these connections "on the fly" without relying on previously defined ontological or other general knowledge. And our system must work quickly: asking individuals to wait long periods of time while the system creates semantic connections and locates appropriate areas of text would defeat the purpose of a system designed to save its users time.

3.3 Semantically-Related Word Clusters

Our solution is to use the World Wide Web to form clusters of topically-related words, with the topic being the question. The cluster of words will be used as query terms and matched to paragraphs as described above for ranking relevant text.

Using the World Wide Web as our corpus has a number of advantages. Because of the vast number of documents that make up the World Wide Web, we can rely on the redundancy that has proved so useful for Question Answering and Text Summarization systems. By creating the word clusters from documents returned from a search using question words, the words that occur most frequently in the related document text will most likely be related in some way to the question words. Even relatively infrequently occurring word correlations can most likely be found in some document existing on the Web, and thus strangely-phrased questions or questions with odd terms will still most likely bring up some documents that can be used to form a cluster. The Web covers virtually all domains. Somewhere on the Web there is almost certainly an answer to questions on even the most obscure topics. Thus questions containing words unique to uncommon domains or questions containing unusual word senses will return documents with appropriate cluster words. Finally, the Web is constantly being updated. Terms that might not have existed even a year ago will now be found on the Web.

Our approach is to use the nonstop words in a question as query terms for a Web search. The search engine we are using is Google (www.google.com). For each search engine query, Google returns an ranked list of URLs it considers relevant, along with a snippet of text it considers most relevant to the query (usually because of words in the snippet that exactly match the query terms). To create the cluster of words related semantically to the question, we are taking the top 50 URLs, going to their correlating Web page, locating the snippet of text within the page, and creating a cluster of words using a 100-word window surrounding the snippet. We are using only nonstop words in the cluster, and weighting the words based on their total number of occurrences in the windows. These word clusters, along with the expanded baseline words, are used to locate and rank paragraphs in our question document.

Our approach is similar in spirit to other researchers using the Web to identify semantic relations. Matsuo et al. (2006) looked at the number of hits of each of two words as a single keyword versus the number of hits using both words as keywords to rate the semantic similarity of two words. Chen et al. (2006) used a similar approach to determine the semantic similarity between two words: with a Web search using word P as the query term, they counted the number of times word Q occurred in the snippet of text returned, and vice versa. Bollegala et al. (2007) determined semantic relationships by extracting lexico-syntactic patterns from the snippets returned from a search on two keywords (e.g.,"'x' is a 'y'") and extracting the relationship of the two words based on the pattern. Sahami and Heilman (2006) used the snippets from a word search to form a set of words weighted using TF/IDF, and then determined the semantic similarity of two keywords by the similarity of two word sets returned in those snippets.

Preliminary results from our approach have been encouraging. For example, with the question, "How does Marijuana affect the brain?", the expanded set of keywords included, "hippocampus, receptors, THC, memory, neuron". These words were present in both the paragraph containing the answer and the second-most commonly focused on paragraph in our study. While neither our baseline nor our expanded baseline identified either paragraph as an area of interest, the semantically-related word clusters did.

4 Future Work

This system is a work in progress. There are many facets still under development, including a finer analysis of visual skimming data, a refinement of the ranking system for locating areas of interest within a document, and the development of the system's user interface.

4.1 Skimming Data Analysis

For our initial analysis, we focused on the length of time users spent gazing at text areas. In future analysis, we will look at the order of the gaze points to determine exactly where the subjects first gazed before choosing to focus on a particular area. This may give us even more information about the type of semantic connection subjects made before choosing to focus on a particular area. In addition, in our initial analysis, we defined AOIs to be paragraphs. We may want to look at smaller AOIs. For example, with longer paragraphs, the text that actually caught the subject's eye may have occurred only in one portion of the paragraph, yet as the analysis stands now the entire content of the paragraph is considered relevant and thus we are trying to generate semantic relationships between the question and potentially unrelated text. While the system only allows us to define AOIs as rectangular areas (and thus we can't do a sentence-by-sentence analysis), we may wish to define AOIs as small as 2 lines of text to narrow in on exactly where subjects chose to focus.

4.2 Ranking System Refinement

It is worth mentioning that, while a good deal of research has been done on evaluating the goodness of automatically generated text summaries (Mani et al.,2002; Lin and Hovy, 2003; Santos et al., 2004) our system is intended to mimic the actions of skimmers when answering questions, and thus our measure of goodness will be our system's ability to recreate the retrieval of text focused on by our visual skimmers. This gives us a distinct advantage over other systems in measuring goodness, as defining a measure of goodness can prove difficult. In future work, we will be exploring different methods of ranking text such that the system returns results most similar to the results obtained from the visual skimming studies. The system will then be used on other questions and documents and compared to data to be collected of visual skimmers skimming for answers to those questions.

Many variations on the ranking system are possible. These will be explored to find the best matches with our collected visual skimming data. Possibilities include weighting keywords differently according to where they came from (e.g., directly from the question, from the text in retrieved Web pages, from text from a Web page ranked high on the returned URL list or lower, etc.), or considering how a diversity of documents might affect results. For instance, if keywords include 'falcon' and 'hawk' the highest ranking URLs will most likely be related to birds. However, in G.I. Joe, there are two characters, Lieutenant Falcon and General Hawk. To get the less common connection between falcon and hawk and G.I. Joe, one may have to look for diversity in the topics of the returned URLs. Another area to be explored will be the effect of varying the window size surrounding the snippet of text to form the bag of words.

4.3 User Interface

The user interface for our system poses some interesting questions. It is important that the output of the system provide the user with information about (1) document topology, (2) document semantics, and (3) information most relevant to answering the question. At the same time, it is important that using the output be relatively fast. The output of the system is envisioned as a Web page with ranked links at the top pointing to sections of the text likely to be relevant to answering the question.

An important issue that must be explored in depth with potential users of the system is the exact form of the output web page. We need to explore the best method for indicating text areas of interest and the overall topology. The goal is that reading the links simulate what a visual skimmer gets from lightly skimming. The user would actually follow the links that appeared to be "worth reading" in more detail in the same way that skimmers focus in on particular text segments that appear worth reading.

5 Conclusion

This system attempts to correlate NLP techniques for creating semantic connections with the semantic connections individuals make. Using the World Wide Web, we may be able to make those semantic connections across any topic in a reasonable amount of time without any previously defined knowledge. We have ascertained that people can and do make semantic links when skimming for answers to questions, and we are currently exploring the best use of the World Wide Web in replicating those connections. In the long run, we envision a system that is user-friendly to nonvisual and low vision readers that will give them an intelligent way to skim through documents for answers to questions.

References

S. Abney, M. Collins, and A. Singhal. 2000. Answer Extraction. *In Proceedings of ANLP 2000*, 296-301.

M. Banko, M. J. Cafarella, S. Soderland, M. Broadhead, and O. Etzioni. 2007. Open information extraction from the Web. In *Proceedings of the 20th International Joint Conference on Artificial Intelligence*, 2670-2676.

D. Bollegala, Y. Matsuo, and M. Ishizuka. 2007. Measuring semantic similarity between words using Web search engines. In *Proceedings of WWW 2007*. 757-766.

Brill, E., Lin, J., Banko, M., Domais, S. and Ng, A. 2001. Data-Intensive Question Answering. In *Proceedings of the TREC-10 Conference, NIST*, Gaithersburg, MD, 183-189.

J. Carbonell and J. Goldstein. 1998. The use of MMR, diversity-based reranking for reordering documents and producing summaries. In *Proceedings of SIGIR '98*, New York, NY, USA, 335-336.

Y. Chali. 2002. Generic and query-based text summarization using lexical cohesion, In *Proceedings of the Fifteenth Canadian Conference on Artificial Intelligence*, Calgary, May, 293-303.

H. Chen, M. Lin, and Y. Wei. 2006. Novel association measures using web search with double checking. In *Proceedings of the COLING/ACL 2006*. 1009-1016.

C. Felbaum. 1998. *WordNet an Electronic Database*, Boston/Cambridge: MIT Press.

A. Galea.2003. Open-domain Surface-Based Question Answering System. In *Proceedings of the Computer Science Annual Workshop (CSAW)*, University of Malta.

E. H. Hovy, L. Gerber, U. Hermjakob, M. Junk, and C.-Y. Lin. 2000. Question Answering in Webclopedia. In *Proceedings of the TREC-9 Conference*. NIST, Gaithersburg, MD. November 2000. 655-664.

E. Hovy and C.Y. Lin. 1997. Automated Text Summarization in SUMMARIST. In *Proceedings of the Workshop on Intelligent Scalable Text Summarization*, Madrid, Spain, 18-24.

Boris Katz, Gregory Marton, Gary Borchardt, Alexis Brownell, Sue Felshin, Daniel Loreto, Jesse Louis-Rosenberg, Ben Lu, Federico Mora, Stephan Stiller, Ozlem Uzuner, and Angela Wilcox. 2005. External Knowledge Sources for Question Answering *Proceedings of the 14th Annual Text REtrieval Conference (TREC2005)*, November 2005, Gaithersburg, MD.

C. Kwok, O. Etzioni, and D.S. Weld. 2001. Scaling Question Answering to the Web. In *Proceedings of the 10th World Wide Web Conference*, Hong Kong, 150-161.

M. Sahami and T. Heilman. 2006. A Web-based kernel function for measuring the similarity of short text snippets. In *Proceedings of 15th International World Wide Web Conference*. 377-386.

Chin-Yew Lin and E.H. Hovy. 2003. Automatic Evaluation of Summaries Using N-gram Co-occurrence Statistics, In *Proceedings of HLT-NAACL*, 71–78.

I. Mani, G. Klein, D. House, L. Hirschman, T. Firmin, and B. Sundheim. 2002. SUMMAC: a text summarization evaluation, *Natural Language Engineering*, 8 (1):43-68.

Y, Matsuo, T. Sakaki, K. Uchiyama, and M. Ishizuka. 2006. Graph-based word clustering using Web search engine. In *Proceedings of EMNLP 2006*, 542-550.

G. Harry McLaughlin. 1969. Reading at "Impossible" Speeds. *Journal of Reading*, 12(6):449-454,502-510.

Radu Soricut and Eric Brill. 2006. Automatic question answering using the web: Beyond the factoid. *Journal of Information Retrieval - Special Issue on Web Information Retrieval*, 9:191–206.

G. Salton, and C. Buckley. 1988. Term-weighting approaches in automatic text retrieval. *Information Processing & Management*, 24, 5, 513-523.

E. J. Santos, A. A. Mohamed, and Q. Zhao. 2004. "Automatic Evaluation of Summaries Using Document Graphs," Text Summarization Branches Out. *Proceedings of the ACL-04 Workshop*, Barcelona, Spain, 66-73.

R. Srihari and W.A. Li. 2000. Question Answering System Supported by Information Extraction. In *Proceedings of the 1st Meeting of the North American Chapter of the Association for Computational Linguistics (NAACL-00)*, 166-172.

R. Varadarajan and V. Hristidis. 2006. A system for query-specific document summarization, *ACM 15th Conference on Information and Knowledge Management (CIKM)*, Arlington, VA, 622-631.

Author Index